THE DEATH OF CHARACTER

DRAMA AND PERFORMANCE STUDIES

Timothy Wiles, *general editor*

Nora M. Alter. *Vietnam Protest Theatre: Staging the Television War.*
Johannes Birringer. *Theatre, Theory, Postmodernism.*
Katherine H. Burkman and John L. Kundert-Gibbs,
editors. *Pinter at Sixty.*
Ejner J. Jensen. *Shakespeare and the Ends of Comedy.*
Jeffrey D. Mason. *Melodrama and the Myth of America.*
Eugène van Erven. *The Playful Revolution:
Theatre and Liberation in Asia.*

THE DEATH OF CHARACTER

Perspectives on Theater after Modernism

Elinor Fuchs

Indiana University Press

Bloomington and Indianapolis

The paper used in this publication meets the minimum
requirements of American National Standard for Information
Sciences—Permanence of Paper for Printed
Library Materials, ANSI Z39.48-1984.

Manufactured in the United States of America

Library of Congress Cataloging-in-Publication Data

Fuchs, Elinor.
The death of character : perspectives on theater after modernism /
Elinor Fuchs.
p.   cm. — (Drama and performance studies)
Includes index.
ISBN 0–253–33038–6 (cl : alk. paper). — ISBN 0–253–21008–9 (pa :
alk. paper)
1. Experimental theater.   2. Theater—United States—Reviews.
3. Experimental drama—History and criticism.   I. Title.
II. Series.
PN2193.E86F83   1996
792'.022—dc20   95–22915

1 2 3 4 5 01 00 99 98 97 96

To the memory of my daring mother
Lillian Ruth Kessler
1908–1993

and of Reza Abdoh, theatrical visionary
1963–1995

Contents

Acknowledgments

I AM BEHOLDEN to many generous friends, colleagues, and institutions. I thank the Rockefeller Foundation and the Bunting Institute of Radcliffe College for their support and encouragement at an early stage of this project. As drafts of chapters emerged, I have benefited from the readings and comments of Gayle Austin of Georgia State University, Ava Baron and Richard Butsch of Ryder College, Alice Benston, Michael Evenden and James W. Flannery of Emory University, Kathleen Hulley of New York University, James Leverett of the Yale School of Drama, Nina da Vinci Nichols of Rutgers, and Rebecca Schneider in her capacity as editor of *TDR*. I am grateful also to editors Erika Munk, then of the *Village Voice*, and James O'Quinn of *American Theatre*, whose contributions both substantive and stylistic are reflected in the "articles and reviews" section of the book, and to Erika's attention to two draft chapters that appeared under her later editorship of *Theater*. I am indebted as well to Rolf Fjelde for our many happy discussions about Ibsen bibliography, and to Herbert Blau for early guidance and valuable advice.

I have learned much from discussions with artists. Elizabeth LeCompte, Richard Foreman, Ruth Maleczech, and Robert Wilson have illuminated my thinking even where interviews with them are not formally reflected in the text. Once-mentors and now collegial friends at the Graduate Center of the City University of New York have given generously of their time and knowledge: Daniel C. Gerould, whose understanding of symbolism and successive avant-gardes lies at the root of all my work; Harry Carlson, whose interest in Strindberg deeply informs my own; and Albert Bermel and Marvin Carlson, whose encouragement has meant much to me. My gratitude also to Diane White, producer of the works of Reza Abdoh, for opening her photo archive to me, and to students, long since gone on to other things, who provided research assistance over the years: Ernest Kerns at Harvard; Peter Collins, Daniel Damkoelher, and Wayne Heller at Columbia; and Steven Frank and the indefatigable Melissa Leonard at New York University. I am also grateful to Karla Oeff for her careful reading of the manuscript.

Finally, I thank my two daughters, Claire Oakes Finkelstein and Katherine Eban Finkelstein, college students at the beginning of this project, and now admirable professional women, for their loving support. I thank Dr. John Ryan for his steadiness and affirmation through much of this writing. Above all, I thank David Cole and Susan Letzler Cole, whose passion for ideas often summoned my own into existence. Their steadfast interest and confidence beckoned this book through many stations to completion.

Several chapters have appeared in earlier versions in *Annals of Scholarship, Theater Three, Modern Drama, Performing Arts Journal, Theater,* and *TDR.* Draft chapters appear in *Sacred Theater,* edited by Bettina Knapp and Daniel Gerould, and in *Signs of Change: Premodern-Modern-Postmodern,* edited by Stephen Barker. Permission has been granted by *American Theatre* and the *Village Voice* to reprint articles that originally appeared in their pages.

THE DEATH OF CHARACTER

Introduction

MY THINKING ON theater after modernism originated in the practical context of seeing new work in the theater and writing accounts of it for weekly newspapers in New York City. It clarified as I began to teach students of theater, and deepened as I read "theory." But its abiding approach has been that of a theater critic in search of language in which to describe new forms, forms that have appeared both in actual theaters and in the theatricalized surround of our contemporary public life and discourse.

Its precise beginning came with an experience in the theater in 1979. I was assigned to review a play being presented in a workshop production at the Public Theater. This was *Leave It to Beaver Is Dead*, of interest because the same 26-year-old artist had written and directed it, composed the music, and was performing in the band that appeared in—or instead of—the third act. It was considered a difficult work, and the producer Joseph Papp was sending it up to the press as a trial balloon. If it "flew," a full production might follow. The *New York Times* effectively killed it the next day. My excited review some days later in the *Soho News* came too late to help. The unknowability of the characters, the strangely synthetic language, the truncated structure, the abrupt shift from play to rock concert, and most of all the frightening relativism of the work's projected universe, seemed almost to suggest the outlines of a new culture or a new way of being. The "new culture" was suggested in the layers of the title, which, in the logic of a world twice-removed, stages real mourning for a false image. My evening in this neorealist world without external referent left me in a prolonged uneasiness, as if my basic ontological security had suddenly become a false memory or the latest disposable product. I had fallen into the mental swoon of postmodernism.

For this vertiginous new perspective, at once artistic and broadly cultural, I lacked at the time a name, much less an adequate vocabulary and grammar. The older categories of fantastic, theatricalist, and the "absurd," whose effects realism underwrites through contrast, had little explanatory power. However, browsing in a bookstore the day after seeing this production, I stumbled upon the "Schizo-Culture" issue of the journal *Semiotexte*. Presently I discovered the(then, to me) fiercely difficult *October*. In this way I began to familiarize m yself with a set of related ideas derived from the world of French critical, psychoanalytic, and feminist theory: Lacan's insight into the symbolic construction of subjectivity, Foucault's announcement of the "end of man," Derrida's attack on the "metaphysics of Presence," Roland Barthes's "death of the

Author," Baudrillard's shattering "precession of the simulacra," Deleuze and Guatarri's "schizoanalysis," Lyotard's collapse of the *"grands récits"* of modernism, and the exposures by Cixous, Irigaray, and Kristeva of masculinist philosophical and psychoanalytic constructions, often in the foregoing theoreticians themselves. This poststructuralist theory, in the aggregate, was the chief articulator of the "crisis of representation," by which one field after another, not only literature but law, sociology, anthropology, history, was sent reeling in the past twenty years. At the point at which I began to discover these theoretical "discourses" they were also providing an intellectual framework for the artistic and cultural phenomena that, especially in the United States, were coming to be understood under the heading of postmodernism.

The mental swoon of postmodernism. It is useful to recall the generally shared sense, circa 1980, by those who suddenly "got" it, that Western culture, led by American culture, was moving into a new, dizzying spiral of Marx's "All that is solid melts into air."[1] Those of us in the arts and the academic world saw it there, in the breakdown of formerly distinct styles and disciplines, and in the vanishing boundaries between high and popular culture. In architecture the severe linearity of the International Style was being supplanted by a rampant eclecticism and what Charles Jencks calls the "double coding" of highbrow and vernacular, classical and industrial, to him "the essential definition of Post-Modernism."[2] In dance such traits could show up in the disconcertingly choiceless mixture of ballet and rock dancing in Twyla Tharp's *Deuce Coupe;*[3] in fiction in the "graffiti" doubling of Kathy Acker's *Don Quixote;*[4] and in theater in the freewheeling pastiche that began to replace unified "concept" productions, especially of the plays of Shakespeare. Instead of, for instance, *Hamlet* on a Caribbean island under a dictatorship, a director might now set Shakespeare in many periods simultaneously, each character carrying his own theatrical world on his back. An example of such multiple-track interpretation was JoAnne Akalaitis's 1991 production of the two parts of *Henry IV* at the Public Theater, in which the court was given a historical setting while the tavern group was edged into the contemporary world of rock 'n roll. Her *Cymbeline* was an even more venturesome instance of this method.

In the university, disciplines and methodologies were losing their traditional boundaries. A startling new equality appeared between "primary" and "secondary" literature. The specificity of literature itself was dissolving in a transtextuality that brought historical documents, philosophical tracts, and law cases under scrutiny in humanities departments, alongside poetry and fiction. In politics, Reagan's theatrical ascendancy brought a hitherto unimagined conflation of the imagery of serious governance and entertainment, a development paralleled by the rise of the notorious "infotainment" programs and other media entanglements of the factual and the fictional.

The blurrings of seemingly firm boundaries were for the most part greeted by the press as stylistic bubbles rather than as tremors from a seismic shift. Yet to those of us who had lived within the modern long enough for its governing assumptions to be absorbed as the way of nature itself, the sense of entering a new and newly unstable culture was acute. The new culture did not seem to us fundamentally nostalgic, as the "style" press often knowingly concluded on the basis of eclecticism and pastiche in architecture and design; if anything it rawly exposed our old nostalgias for "progress," "man," the transparency of "truth," and other modern faiths. The issue of truth was perhaps the most troubling as well as the most difficult to describe, as the culture seemed simultaneously to have entered a period of both legitimate and spurious perspectivism. As Debord said in the 1960s, "The true is a moment of the false."[5] In this new culture, whether or not one had read Lyotard, Habermas, and Andreas Huyssen, and years before the global crisis of political authority became manifest, almost every institution—the presidency, Congress, the military, the clergy, law, medicine, the university and its "core curriculum," marriage, the family—seemed to be entering a "legitimation crisis." On this view, the postmodern might have its stylistic attributes, but did not mark a style so much as a cultural condition, perhaps a particularly uncomfortable and sustained transition.

The deeper postmodern analysis of the late 1970s and 1980s searched out the material and ontological roots of this new condition. In retrospect one can see that its great unifying trait was not so much nihilism or even relativism, as postmodernism's most vehement critics have charged, but a theme more subtle (yet also more observed) that could be thought of as "desubstantiation." To Baudrillard, a circulating charade of imagery—a " 'disembodied' semiotic power"—was replacing the concrete use value of commodities produced by physical labor that in Marx underwrote the production cycle.[6] To Fredric Jameson, rational space was disappearing in the new cultural formation, which reflected the "unimaginable decentering of global capital itself. Not even Einsteinian relativity . . . is capable of giving any kind of adequate figuration to this process. . . . "[7]

Nothing "out there," no one "in here." The interior space known as "the subject" was no longer an essence, an in-dwelling human endowment, but flattened into a social construction or marker in language, the unoccupied occupant of the subject position. "Yet today," (Barthes)

> the subject apprehends himself *elsewhere*, and "subjectivity" can return at another place on the spiral: deconstructed, taken apart, shifted without anchorage: why should I not speak of "myself" since this "my" is no longer "the self"?[8]

The debate on subjectivity has been one of the most fraught of the past twenty years, especially in the early 1980s, when feminists were vociferous in pointing out that just as women were beginning to achieve the status of subjects—the power to wield the "I"—male theorists were declaring the position vacant. Craig Owens's groundbreaking 1983 article describing feminism as a postmodern discourse initially met with a cool reception from feminists.[9] By the late 1980s, however, feminists and queer theorists were generally finding poststructuralist theories of subjectivity politically valuable.

Desubstantiation was the theme of a meditative 1985 Pompidou Center exhibition, *Les immatériaux*, designed in part by the philosopher of the postmodern, Jean-François Lyotard. It was intended to convey to the visitor an experience of the invisible—the new world of information technology and subatomic particle physics, and what were presented as corresponding cultural processes such as nonlinearity, flux, multichannel perception, and simulation. The exhibit intentionally had no defined order; different paths might be taken through its many spaces, paths that could be tracked by an electronic card distributed to each patron. Even the show's catalogue, consisting of a series of unnumbered and unattached pages, was without fixed sequence. The press release publicizing the exhibit stressed that the visitor was not to be contained in "linear time," as she is by radio and film, the media of modernism. Interestingly, the show implied a new ascendancy of theater in the postmodern age. Under the heading *"moi au théâtre,"* the catalogue was introduced by a quotation from Beckett's *The Unnamable*, and the largest space at the exhibit was devoted to a *Théâtre du non-corps*, where voices played over a shifting light and hologram performance.[10]

The sense of an emptiness at the heart of matter can be traced in much of the new theater. The Wooster Group performs *Brace-Up!*, their version of *The Three Sisters*. But instead of staging a material representation of characters suffering loss, departure, and exile from a distant center, they convert these experiences into a negative space or absence in the staging of the play itself. Irina, fearful of growing old without experiencing life, is played by a 75-year-old woman in a wheelchair. An invisible centrifugal force seems to glue the actors to the periphery of the playing area. From this position they speak into microphones, sometimes with their backs to the audience while video monitors bring us their faces; often live actors will communicate with absent partners on video monitors.[11]

The central image of playwright Suzan-Lori Parks's *The America Play*, the Great Hole of History, is also an absence, the archeological remains of a theme park in which are buried simulations and imitations, such as a replica of George Washington's wooden teeth and false Abe Lincoln beards. In *2 Samuel 11, etc.*, David Greenspan compresses broken fragments of telephone conversations and luncheon chatter spanning friendships and families over three generations into an act-length speech spoken by a single male figure. The representation of the community that is theater's special province has not been lost, but the community now floats behind the play through multiple absences—of the speakers, of the full sense of their speech, of the locations where such speech might take place. The community has dissolved into the electronic ether.

Des McAnuff's *Leave It to Beaver Is Dead*, actually written in 1974 and first performed in Toronto in 1975, was one of the earlier plays to reflect this sense of groundlessness. Both nostalgically and prophetically, it pointed to a cultural transition whose outward symptoms later became increasingly visible.[12] With only ten performances in New York and an appearance in an anthology published by a fringe California press, this play might be surprised to find itself solemnized as a cultural icon poised between epistemes. Nevertheless, I want to give an account of it here, not least because it illuminates the somewhat delicate approach of this study, which treats theater as a crucial mediating term between the heterogenous fullness of life and the clarifying abstractions of theory.

After his absence as an unsuccessful premed student, during which time he has made one or more suicide attempts, a young man named Dennis returns to his commune in a large American city. In the sixties the commune operated a free drug clinic that survived on government grants. Now it's the seventies, and the group has taken to running a nocturnal profit-making project called "The Show." Their process is deliberately clouded, but it seems they service clients' fantasies with a mind-bending combination of interrogation, mockery, kindness, menace, and seduction, all simulated through games, play, play within play, plays on words. They flirt with danger, simulating "accidents" that they document in photographs.

In the clinic days, Dennis, an advocate of authority, order, and cleanliness, had been the group's undisputed leader. But now the group has been taken over by a powerful woman named Lizzard, who may or may not be Loretta, a drug addict once treated at the former clinic. Lizzard and her two male cohorts, Dennis's old school chums, no longer practice cleanliness and order. The place is a junkyard of props from The Show, a "contemporary laboratory . . . as well as a museum of the Fifties and Sixties complete with hub caps, juke box, malt shop stools, water pipes and traces of glitter."[13] Setting out to "save" Dennis by introducing him to the new ethos, the group counters his increasingly desperate efforts to take control with what we can only assume must be the procedures of The Show. With escalating menace, Lizzard hammers at Dennis's normative values and hierarchic ways of thinking as symptoms of false consciousness. Eventually, Dennis slips across a boundary. He suddenly begs to try out the new ideas on a feckless client who wanders in off the street. Dennis is exhilarated, but there is trouble, danger, a struggle in the bathroom, blood, the client collapses, Dennis staggers out, and . . . blackout. There are murmurs of "It's all right, it's all right," the mantra left over from the drug clinic days.[14]

The audience is expecting a third act, in part to find out what happened (Was anyone hurt? Will we see, or have we seen, The Show?), and also because we have been told that a band called "Terry and the Afghans" will be arriving at midnight. Instead, conventional expectations of clarification and reconciliation are frustrated. Returning from a second intermission, we become audience to an act-length rock concert. Is this final show part of The Show in the play, or just a show after the play? The characters, or the performers—we don't know which "frame" we are in—sing, play, and dance along with the musicians. The lyrics stir a mood of impending apocalypse, one song repeating over and over, "Save the children! Save the children!"[15]

I have said that postmodernism may prove to be a painful transition between systems of value, and *Leave It to Beaver Is Dead* is nothing if not a play about transition. Its returning hero finds a new world where public values have dematerialized into private fantasies, just as the "Love Striparama All Nude Show" now occupies the site of an old-time neighborhood tavern. In the new world people's real names are dismissed as "strictly conceptual," as one character shrugs. In the new world of dramatic form, the play's indifference to its own interruption is its most disturbing quality. But the longing for completion is "strictly conceptual" too.[16]

The problem of subjectivity is central to the play, but in most un-Pirandellian fashion it is not a problem to itself, only to the spectator, who feels as if she is falling through space. The play asks: What is a person? Can one "have" an identity, "own" one, achieve "self-mastery," the highest evolution of subjectivity under the old paradigm? Or does identity consist of continuously changing personae with no inherent self? And if the latter, is the role-playing subject a new adaptation to a world in accelerating mutation, as the play in part suggests? Or is its appearance merely the truth that "always already," as Derrida likes to say, lay beneath the mask of self-sameness that (as the play also in part suggests) was destined to be stripped away? Issues of cultural transition and subjectivity are joined in the play's sexual politics. The old order is presided over by the Beaverish boy scout Dennis, believer in a law-and-order masculine authority and its unitary self. In the course of the play, this identity paradigm collapses in unequal contest with a rising female power practicing a multiform self and its new ways of improvisation and masquerade. This gendering of the epistemes in McAnuff's play is a double-edged vision, however: a new feminine order is seen as inevitable, but it is rendered in the fearful terms of the reptile (lizard) as cold-blooded, subtle, and dangerous.

Thus, while the play brilliantly summons a vision of cultural transition, it is itself a transitional work, lodged in traditional representation (both dramatic and cultural) even while it brings that very attribute into question; and alternatively in the rupture of traditional form, coupling play and rock concert in uneasy harness. In this and other respects, the play evinced the aesthetic claimed for postmodern works even before it was fully articulated: an aesthetic of breaks and gaps, surfaces and masks, objectless in its irony, without closure, speaking a strange synthetic language packed with sly quotations and a myriad of references to pop culture. The transition the play enacts at many levels—in its story, its characters, its very gesture of transit between performance media—is the story of a disappearance: the movement from governance by rules and grounding principles to governance by an unstable if vital theatricality. (The attempt of the *New York Times* to stabilize the action in the earlier, more recognizable paradigm of modernism with the headline "Of TV Survivors, Clinics and Drug Addicts" was amusingly representative of the cultural confusion the play depicts and enacts.)[17] Its fluid and mysterious theatricality is key to the play's postmodern sensibility, and touches my concluding theme in chapter 8: the intrinsic connection between postmodernism and theatricality.

I could wish that of the two terms—postmodernism and theater—the latter at least would summon up firm and undisputed definition as a complement to the unavoidable slippage of the former. But in the past twenty-five years the term "theater," floating far from its old associate "drama," has itself become a proliferating source of meanings. New terms have sprung up in efforts to distance new performance modes from dramatic theater or to associate formerly distinct performance modes with theater. Performance, performance art, art performance, solo performance, the "performance piece," even *performance theater* have arisen, all with different shades of meaning intended to edge them differently away from association with the more closed and traditional forms of a dramatic theater; paradoxically, the terms music theater and dance theater have come into currency to edge traditional opera and dance back toward what in the contexts of these arts becomes the more heterodox, open, and welcoming performance mode that is also "theater." Some have claimed for performance art, particularly, the spark of *le vrai postmoderne*, though it has never been clear to me why performance art, with its collapse of real and theatrical time and space, is not in fact the heir to or at least the echo of the modernist avant-garde performance tradition. But here again one would have to make discriminating judgments between art performance as practiced in the 1970s in galleries and in the 1980s in theaters and clubs. In any event, none of these contemporary theatrical and performance variants is the exclusive locus of a postmodern theatrical genre, practice, or style. Rather, evidence of the new epistemological and ontological currents circulates through all of them.

How then to limit the terrain on which I link theater and postmodernism? The following chapters are the result of a decision (perhaps attraction is the better term) to stay close to that practice in the theater that is itself most interested in defining itself by measuring its distance from the long practice of traditional, dramatic theater. Thus the Wooster Group, whose performers are actors and whose deconstructed material is often drawn from classic theatrical texts, would fall within my sphere of interests here, while the no less interesting, no less postmodern, and highly theatrical performance style of, say, a Frankfurt

Ballet under William Forsythe would not make an appearance in these pages because the tradition it is measuring its specific distance from is not theater but dance. Similarly, the postmodern pastiche and "landscape" plays of a Suzan-Lori Parks are linked in many ways to traditional theatrical forms, like Greek tragedy, and inspired by earlier theatrical mentors, like Gertrude Stein and Samuel Beckett, while the performance pieces of a Laurie Anderson, no less postmodern, would still measure their distance more from the popular concert format and performance art, than from the practice of theater as defined here. The themes I take up respond to another pole of attraction as well: behaviors in the world that theater peculiarly illuminates. This will constitute a sort of subdominant in the book.

These two prongs of interest may appear at times to be quite separate. For instance, chapter 2 deals entirely with what I regard as a submerged genre of modernism, the "mysterium." Alternatively, the final "Reviews and Articles" section contains a piece on the AIDS Quilt as cultural performance. But in my own understanding these two approaches—reading into the theater, and out from it—comprise aspects of a single, symbolizing form of knowledge, or form of acquiring knowledge, that regards theatrical performance and cultural theatricality as markers of consciousness, to be read symptomatically, as visible if difficult to decipher tracks of where-we-are-now. Thus chapter 6, "When Bad Girls Play Good Theaters," and chapter 7, "Theater as Shopping," pursue both approaches at once. My title signals this simultaneous pursuit in the sense that "character" as a term of dramatic art can never be independent of contemporary constructions of subjectivity. It is to the continuing thread of "character" in the book that I should turn now.

Character is the theatrical "element" (as Aristotle says) that best represents the "standing in" invitation that endows theater with this double fullness of meaning. By standing in I mean what Bruce Wilshire describes: that in a theatrical event "an actor must stand in for a character . . . and through this standing in the audience member stands in for this character . . . ," to which continuum of involvements I would add playwright and director on the theatrical side of the interface between theater event and world, and the community at large on the other, for which in a sense the spectator "stands in."[18] Thus, reading "symptomatically" and beyond the individual stage event, each epoch of character representation—that is, each substantial change in the way character is represented on the stage and major shift in the relationship of character to other elements of dramatic construction or theatrical presentation—constitutes at the same time the manifestation of a change in the larger culture concerning the perception of self and the relations of self and world. "Character" is a word that stands in for the entire human chain of representation and reception that theater links together.

My first attempt to explore this nexus, its raveling and unraveling, came in the article that gives this study its title, "The Death of Character."[19] There I suggest that one of the meanings of "postmodern"—its psychological formation, I would say now—was a dispersed idea of self, and that this dispersal was represented in many different ways in the contemporary alternative theater. (We still don't know what to call it: avant-garde, experimental, alternative, deconstructive, postmodern, "new." All of these terms may be used, and none is wholly satisfactory, perhaps least of all "avant-garde," with its early twentieth-century associations.) I had no intention at the time of pursuing its themes further, but to my very great surprise, the article occasioned an eruption of interest and even controversy. Attacked in the *San Francisco Chronicle*, republished in the magazine of the Guthrie Theatre, published again in the Belgian theater journal *Alternatives théâtrales*, published one last time in the Polish journal *Dialog*, it seemed to catch for a moment the sense of change experienced by many in theater communities, and at the same time to locate the new theater work it discusses on a recognizable, even classical, theatrical spectrum. Re-reading the article, I am struck by its idealistic tone: it is still within the first wave of deconstructionist postmodernism that conceived a new cultural climate based on the lifting of closure and the principle of "free play." The dystopic postmodernism of the second wave (as for instance in Jameson) finds its way into the essay more as a threat than as an inevitable "cultural logic." In a third wave—beyond the horizon of the original article—materialist feminist theorists made an alliance with postmodern theory in their effort to expose the concealed misogyny in conventional narrative structure. This returned the poststructuralist sources to their early potential for political resistance.

The "death of character" idea started out as a spark of insight ignited in alternative theaters and fanned by the various poststructuralist "deaths" announced in the late 1970s and 1980s (of Man, the Author, the Subject, the Work, the Book), but another important tributary came from my own readings in Buddhism. I was especially interested in the correspondence between the poststructuralist emptying out of the subject and the Buddhist idea of *anatta* or "no-self," the denial of a continuous self that is a corollary of the Buddha's precept that all human suffering arises from the grasping for an illusory permanence. The turn of the cultural wheel that might result from Buddhism rooting itself in the West has been contemplated by many, including Toynbee, who is often quoted as claiming that the encounter between Buddhism and Christianity would prove to be the most significant event of the twentieth century.[20] Poststructuralist thinking, especially the negative regress of deconstruction, might be a harbinger, it seemed to me at the time of my own early article, of a shift from Western to Eastern metaphysics. In the theater, this speculation was supported by the aversion of so many advanced theater practitioners to the idea of autonomous character—for instance in the work of Robert Wilson, Lee Breuer, Meredith Monk, and Elizabeth LeCompte—combined with the strain of formal Eastern influence in their theater.

Yet when I returned to "The Death of Character" a few years after it appeared, I was more inclined to regard the loss of grounding principles in postmodern culture as transitional. The turn to the East seemed only one source of several, not all of them anti-foundational like Buddhism, from which new thinking about the self and character could evolve. Cybernetics, ecology, feminism, a totalizing capitalism, fundamentalism, were clearly among the active contending forces. Chapters 4 through 7 of Part II, "Theater After Modernism," explore signs in the theater that point in some of these directions.

The original article did sketch many of the themes around which individual chapters eventually gathered; in fact all three themes of Part I, "Modern After Modernism," find their origin there. Chapter 1, which concerns itself with the treatment of character in dramatic theory up to the end of the nineteenth century, traces in some detail the trajectory Aristotle–Hegel–Nietzsche, briefly outlined in "The Death of Character." The deindividualizing impulse that appears in the final decade of the century in Mallarmé, Maeterlinck, and Yeats, along with the dehumanizing attack of Jarry, may indirectly signal the inhumanity that was to characterize ideology in the twentieth century. It points directly to the particular problem the human figure presented for advanced dramatic and theatrical practice in the next decades. "It's difficult to act in your play," Nina tells Treplev, "there are no real living characters in it."[21] This was the challenge that some playwrights could sense at the turn of the century. To compensate for the reduced station of character after its Hegelian apogee, something else, some other "element" must occupy the dramaturgical center and carry the burden of narrative. Allegory, metatheater, and Brecht's critical dialectics— three methods that lift the spectator's focus from character to the relationship between levels of dramaturgy—became the principal vehicles of this shift.

In chapter 2 I follow the destiny of character into the mysterium, an allegorical modern dramatic genre that can be traced from Strindberg through Beckett and beyond. In the mysterium the spectator follows an unfolding on two planes: a quotidian plane on which little may happen, and a mythic level which mysteriously drives and governs quotidian event. These modern mystery/morality plays typically reduce the autonomy and dramatic range of their protagonists, but at the same time attach them to fables of great eschatological sweep, as in *To Damascus, From Morning to Midnight*, and *Waiting for Godot*, where the spectator follows the working out (or not working out) of recognizable metaphysical patterns.

Chapter 3, also devoted to a retrospective consideration of modern drama, returns to Ibsen, with the implicit question: What does the drama of realist character look like from the perspective of its representing a closed dramaturgical epoch? By which I do not mean that such plays may not continue to be written, but that there is no more revelation in the form. Bringing the perspective of the postmodern to realist readings of *Hedda Gabler*, I find that what has long been taken to be psychological character study par excellence has been complicated, made less "decidable" as to form, by recent allegorical readings of the play. Re-reading *Lady from the Sea*, I make a similar discovery, but from the other direction. What modern critics, liberating themselves from the realists, have taken to be a symbolic drama about the destiny of humankind is complicated by, even pitted against, the story of Ellida and the two daughters. This story solicits a feminist reading and resists allegory almost ideologically. Postmodern readings of realist and modern plays, I conclude, encourage difference, not only the differences brought out by reading for gender, race, and other class divides, but formal differences that become apparent in texts when the demand for unified interpretation is lifted.

Part II, "Theater after Modernism," includes four perspectives or angles of vision on the theater and culture of postmodernism, and a fifth chapter that might be thought of as a perspective on those perspectives. Readers hoping for a general survey, an overall view of postmodern theater, will not find that expectation met here. At one time I myself thought the work would take that form. Seeing that it persistently refused, I supposed that it was either too early to create such a survey out of the appearing and disappearing evidence of theatrical postmodernism, or that creating such a survey was basically uncongenial to my own mind. In any event, such an overview tends to be the result of the application of general principles to specific cases, whereas my work was to a considerable extent the opposite, the seeking of general principles to account for specific cases encountered in the theater. Finally, the resistance to totalizing thought that is in the very nature of postmodern art and theory would probably have defeated such a "master"ful approach had I persisted in the attempt. The approach of this book, as its subtitle signals, is consciously perspectival.

In a loose sense, this entire project has been tutored by deconstructive thinking; that is, by an understanding that seemingly solid constructs and accepted hierarchies tend to dissolve under scrutiny. So, for instance, I urge in chapter 3 that directors seek ways to bring onstage the conflicting meaning systems that are always lodged in a complex work. Similarly, in chapter 6, I permit myself uncomfortably to see, in response to experiences in the theater, that I can no longer sustain the opposed categories of "good girl" and "bad girl" into which I was long ago indoctrinated. In chapter 4 I make an experimental effort not simply to engage deconstructive thinking, but to apply Derrida's early deconstructive theory to contemporary theater. My project here is to align his attack on metaphysical presence with the undermining of theatrical presence. The subversive agent is in both cases the same: writing is Derrida's worm in the apple of metaphysics, and in contemporary theater it is the entrance of reading and writing onto the stage as an element in the performance that interrupts the illusion of presence. In the work of the Wooster Group, for the past two decades the most experimental theater group in the United States, actors may read books aloud, play scenes with colleagues represented on video screens, or quote taped lines spoken elsewhere rather than enact them. This chapter attempts to assess the implications of such means for the future of a theater of presence.

Still indirectly following the career of character on the postmodern stage, chapter 5 explores contemporary staging with the question: What happens to the presentation of time and space when we are no longer in a theater of character, when the human figure is no longer the single, perspectival "point" of stage performance? One answer, traceable to the symbolists and to Gertrude Stein, is the landscape stage. The landscape stage may include the representation of an actual landscape, as is often the case in the stagings of Robert Wilson. But the meaning of landscape derived from Stein, whether natural or not, is conceptual. Unlike the usual developmental narrative, the landscape play, as Thornton Wilder wrote in his journal, is "a thing held full-in-view the whole time."[22] Another way to put this is that on the landscape stage time is emptied into space. This spatial stage is almost a necessary consequence of the waning of interest in character moving through narrative. The stagings of directors Reza Abdoh and Tina Landau, and the play settings of playwright Suzan-Lori Parks, to name only a few theater artists working in this way, present dispersed fields of activity where many time periods may be represented simultaneously. There are, of course, human figures on these natural/conceptual landscapes, but the landscape itself is the central object of contemplation. The result could be seen as a new kind of pastoral, one appropriate to an ecological age when the human figure is no longer the measure of all things.

While the various themes of these chapters evolved over a long period of seeing new theater, reading, and thinking, only one, chapter 6, is intentionally caught at a particular moment in theatrical history. This moment abruptly ended when the National Endowment for the Arts came under attack in the late 1980s for funding "obscene" art—first Mapplethorpe, then Serrano, then the performance artists Karen Finley, Holly Hughes, Tim Miller, and John Fleck.[23] I had become interested in the early 1980s in the proliferation of sexually offensive performances by women in New York performance spaces customarily reserved for art performance of one kind or another. I became especially curious about the discomfort that some of this performance created in me as spectator, discomfort that was evidently shared by others in the audience. This unease suddenly vanished for the audiences that frequented these performances, however, when the performers were attacked by Senator Jesse Helms and his allies. It then became the obligation of politically progressive New York spectators to experience only positive feelings for this work. Three and a half years after my first Karen Finley performance, when audiences at The Kitchen sat uncertain and numb at "The Constant State of Desire," she performed "We Keep Our Victims Ready" in the Serious Fun Festival at Lincoln Center to a sold-out throng of sudden insiders, who continuously laughed in a knowing way and applauded as at a political rally. Finley and the other de-funded performers were now in harmonious league with the very spectators they had tried to challenge and put on edge. The problem internal to the work was shifted onto Washington and the right.

What is now chapter 6 was written at a moment when the discomfort and ambivalence stirred by women's obscenity in the theater could still be sifted in an environment free of external restraint. Its affronts therefore challenged the deep inner restraint of feminine socialization, which I became convinced was not an accidental by-product but at some level the intent of the work. The "death of character" theme was suddenly pointed at the divisions in my own character formation. If the frightening gulf between good and bad (heterosexual) women on the basis of sexual practice, a gulf that has scarcely entered into male psychology, were to become merely historic, incalculable social change would result. In a transitional period there are signs in Western culture that such change is evolving; there are powerful reversing currents as well; and there are even contrary signs that class division by sexual behavior is for the first time beginning to scorch men in public life. It is not surprising that theater, where the body as sign is so immediately displayed, has become a flash point for these conflicting norms and ideals.

In these chapters, I oscillate between seeing in theater a reflection, or even a vehicle, of some gradually evolving, hopeful new formation in the social domain that could result from the obsolescence of "man"-centered thinking; and, alternatively, seeing the possibility that the long tradition of Western theater itself could fail to survive the effects of other currents in postmodernity. In chapter 7, I locate in a number of recent theatrical events an esthetic of "shopping" that points toward such a fatal consequence. These events have emerged in very different theater cultures but they have in common the surge of the spectators, or of the stage event, across the magical line that—notwithstanding the environmental theater experiments of the 1960s, as well as occasional efforts to revive a medieval-type festival theater—has held the two apart for centuries. Walter Benjamin sees in the orchestra pit the physical emblem of this division, calling it the "abyss which separates the players from the audience as it does the dead from the living."[24] The mingling of the active event and the formerly passive spectator in an exciting arena of free choice and co-performance, even though the freedom is somewhat spurious and the choice strictly controlled, is what I call "shopping theater."

Theater such as *Tamara* or *Tony 'n Tina's Wedding* activates a passion for acquisition and incorporation hitherto unknown in the theater. It is curious in fact how many such events actually include a meal, as a kind of talisman of the "real" experience that shopping theater claims to offer. The spectator who seeks this heightened reality is not the spectator who gazes across Benjamin's orchestra pit ready to absorb the event into a spiritual and psychological interiority. The shopping spectator is in a sense a de-interiorized being in the theater, whom the experiences of hearing and seeing that the functions "audience" and "spectator" suggest cannot satisfy. The shopping spectator requires an embodied relationship to the experience. This new version of Benjamin's *flâneur* portends the end of classical spectator/spectacle relations in the theater, and the spread of a postmodern theater peopled entirely by players, whether paying or paid. This, the reader will recall, was precisely the internal dramatic situation of *Leave It to Beaver Is Dead*, where both clients and proprietors, to mutual profit, enact the mysterious performance called "The Show."

"The Show" is in a sense where these reflections come out. In my concluding chapter, "Postmodernism and the Scene of Theater," I undertake to explore what might seem at first to be a minor literary curiosity, the persistence of the theatrical metaphor in many of the texts that offer the theoretical grounding of postmodernism. There I actually make a discovery, that many theorists—for instance, two as unlike as Derrida and Baudrillard—project a narrative of Western culture that is divided into two phases: a stable, grounded, non-theatrical past, and an increasingly theatricalized present. French feminist theorists such as Cixous and Irigaray similarly adopt the theatrical metaphor, but in the service of a reversed cultural trajectory. Here, traditional patriarchal narratives from Plato to Freud are derided as theater (and mocked with theatrical flair), but the feminist future projected is a post-theatrical one that has acquired new foundational principles grounded in previously suppressed realities. Though the cultural trajectories described by the male and female theorists I cite move in opposite directions, they cross quite precisely in a present moment that is a virtual theatrical arena, a metaphorical "scene" of theater where Western culture plays itself toward different possible narratives. Theater appears in these readings as the very content of the postmodern transition itself. It offers an ontological lifeboat in a period when foundational principles have lost their authority. Or put another way, a cultural "death of character"—shorthand for an explosion of doubt about ontological grounding—necessarily brings about an expansion of the theatrical term. The theatrical becomes a protected arena for the exploration and playing out of difference, a kind of substitute grounding for the postmodern soul.

This book begins and ends in theatrical performance. In the section, "Reviews and Articles, 1979–1993" following chapter 8, I have gathered nine pieces from the many I wrote in that period. Most of these supplement the foregoing chapters by giving an immediate sense of what productions by some of the more significant contemporary theater directors looked and felt like on the stage. I hope that this section will be useful to students of theater, for whom the play of ideas can never be separated from the experience of images, gestures and language in performance.

The final piece, on the AIDS Quilt, returns to the theme of "cultural performance" that has surfaced intermittently in the preceding chapters, especially chapters 7 and 8. Cultural performance is my general term for the hyper-theatricality and self-performance that emerged from new directions, or in new and larger ways, in American culture of the 1980s. In a period in which social and economic forces were moving toward the undoing of theater as a formal, artistic practice, theatricalism was leeching into every cell of the national mind. Some of these cultural performances were arranged for state aggrandizement, like the (Statue of) Liberty Weekend extravaganza orchestrated by the Reagans and commercial interests. Others were mass charity events, none more startling in its theatrical implications than Hands Across America, the experiment in postmodern desubstantiation and auto-intoxication in which millions of people paid millions of dollars to perform, and be spectators of their own performance, as links in a human chain stretching from New York to California. Spun from a swirling hub of entertainment and news, social event and social statement, the event was also pure utopian theater of the mind. The chain, if realized (which it was not), could have been witnessed from no other vantage point than the imagination.

The AIDS Quilt occupies a unique position among the cultural performances of contemporary America. It is at once a cultural expression with roots in traditional, rural, American artistic and social life, and an act of countercultural resistance, related to the guerrilla theater "die-ins" staged by Act Up. Its four complete appearances in Washington, D.C. were theatrical at every level, from the material details of performance stitched into its panels, to its mode of presentation, to the ways, both sublime and subversive, in which it linked communities of gay and straight, conservative and radical, living and dead. It makes, I believe, a fitting coda to these perspectives on "theater after modernism."

The thinking embodied in this book began in the early 1980s. At that time almost nothing had yet been written about theater and postmodernism. In an important pioneering book, Bonnie Marranca had organized some new theater (which others later called "postmodern") under Aristotle's least and last term, Spectacle, as a "Theater of Images."[25] But where to go from there? How to account for the changed relations of spectacle to character and narrative? How to give an account of *that* account's relationship to what we once confidently called "modern drama," or to the earlier avant-gardes? And what relationship could be traced between the artistic practice of theater and the almost obsessive theatricality that was surfacing in all forms of postmodern culture? During the period in which I considered these questions and the ideas here accreted, a typical postmodern "disappearance" began to be worked on the term itself. The reader may thus want to ask whether we are not now *post* the postmodern.

Those who never caught up with the "p" word at the height of its notoriety will be glad to think it has passed like a fever, and the patient has survived. Others who embraced it early on have wearied of it and, the better to discard it, shrunk its scope. I am reminded of DeMusset's amusing satire on the word "romanticism," written in 1836:

> Cotonet and I decided to . . . come to grips with the schisms polarizing so many sprightly minds. We were well schooled. Specially Cotonet, who is a notary and whose hobby is ornithology. We believed at the outset, for two whole years, that *romanticism* in literature was applicable only to the theater, and that it differed from the classical in doing without the unities. . . . From 1830 to 1831, we believed that romanticism was the historical mode. . . . From 1831 to the following year . . . we thought it was the *intimate* manner, that was being much discussed. . . . From 1832 to 1833, it occurred to us that romanticism could be a system of philosophy and political economy. . . . From 1833 to 1834, we believed that romanticism meant not shaving and wearing waistcoats with large lapels starched stiff. . . . The following year we believed nothing, for Cotonet had gone to the South to see about an inheritance, and I myself was very busy mending a barn damaged by heavy rains.[26]

Romanticism survived its own protean reach. Ultimately, in my view, postmodernism will acquire lasting value as a cultural marker.

A nuanced answer to the question of postmodernism's survival has to be searched out on many tracks, geopolitical, societal, and aesthetic, and within these its trajectory in each art and discipline. The stunning collapse of communism and retreat of democratic socialism destroyed the compass by which most nations in the twentieth century organized themselves ideologically, whether for or against, willingly or under compulsion. The much longer trajectory of modernity, with its system of imperial states organized into defensive alliances against external enemies, now offers little guidance in solving the many agonizing predicaments being played out in the century's wreckage. Geopolitically we are perhaps in the early phase of postmodernism that Americans experienced locally a decade and more ago—the confusion that comes with the collapse of boundaries and the dissolution of the *grands récits*, which Jameson and Craig Owens tellingly translate as the "master narratives." Of course, the entire planet does not move together. In some areas of the globe societies are struggling to enter modernity from pre-modernity, and some are struggling to reverse modernity back to pre-modernity. Yet all are forced to acknowledge and respond to the irresistible advance of transnational economic and electronic forces.

In the United States, we are passing from the confusion of postmodernism into the somewhat deflated conviction of postmodernity. Deflated because it is now deeply feared that the horizon of economic growth and social amelioration—components of "progress"—is being permanently shut down. The blurring and crumbling of seemingly impermeable boundaries that stood as the external sign of the postmodern have now become normalized in some parts of the society. Where this is so, normalization has involved the recognition of "difference" as a social and psychological good, a recognition that Derrida's emphasis on *différance* promoted and helped to theorize.

It is generally understood in the quarters where the ethos of difference prevails, for instance, that the heterosexual binary that was virtually the only way of thinking sexuality out loud as late as, say, 1960, has been opened up into distinctions between sex and gender, or among sex, gender, and sexual orientation, which now define a spectrum of identifications and behaviors that are not regarded as the declension of a central term. The erosion of generic boundaries has opened a space for differentiated thinking in many fields, such as the relaxation of boundaries, to take a very different example, between canonic and previously peripheral literature to reflect a range of literary differences. Identity politics, multiculturalism, then interculturalism, emerged in this period of evolving postmodernity as new perspectival bases for social and cultural organization. The very word "difference" has if anything become the somewhat banalized slogan for a postmodern politics that is, as I write, under intense reactionary pressure. One of the forms this reaction predictably takes is the hardening of multicultural divisions themselves into fundamentalist nodes. The entrenched reaction back towards foundational principles in their most narrow and even paranoid form is itself a phase of postmodern politics.

In the field of theater, similar discriminations must also be made. The Wooster Group's, or Mabou Mines's, deconstructive methods of working on many simultaneous tracks are now well understood by audiences. Multitrack thinking has invaded the entire aesthetic sphere. In theater performance that is not organized around opposing systems of value, it is in effect the appreciation of difference that is asked of audience. The Foreman or Wilson sorts of emphases on perception gleaned through repetitions with small incremental changes, harking back to Stein, comprise a principal method of difference in the theater. In the theater of difference, each signifying element—lights, visual design, music, etc., as well as plot and character elements—stands to some degree as an independent actor. It is as if all the Aristotelian elements of theater had survived, but had slipped the organizing structure of their former hierarchy.

But even if the theater that most often came under the rubric of the postmodern in the last decade has in a sense also been normalized, it has not in any sense become the norm. Playwrights and directors whose work expresses a sense of the postmodern divide are few if notable; theater has retreated with the frightened mood and straitened fortunes of the country. Yet this by no means signifies some passage back across an epistemic fault line. Even a theater work as accessible as *Angels in America* vaults easily between supernatural mystery play and soap opera, tragedy and camp. Its postmodern awareness is especially signaled in its elegiac organization around the very experience of cultural *passage*.

The Angel tries to save the earth and the human species by stopping history. There must be an end to human migration. AIDS is carried by the human flood, and in its turn carries away psychic and moral floodgates. The 1980s, the decade the scourge enters history, become a historical transition in the play, a sensed marker between epochs in part defined by the collapse of progressive modernist credos. Recall the speech, late in Part II, by Kushner's Aleksii Antedillovianovich Prelapsarianov, the world's oldest surviving Bolshevik. Kushner's own nostalgia for a lost age is unmistakable:

> And *Theory?* *Theory?* How are we to proceed without *Theory?* . . . You who live in this Sour Little Age cannot imagine the sheer grandeur of the prospect we gazed upon. . . . We were One with the Sidereal Pulse then, in the blood in our heads we heard the tick of the Infinite. . . . And what have you to offer now, children of this Theory? What have you to offer in its place? Market Incentives? . . . The snake sheds its skin only when a new skin is ready; if he gives up the only membrane he has before he can replace it, naked he will be in the world, prey to the forces of chaos. . . . Have you, my little serpents, a new skin? Then we dare not, we cannot move ahead.[27]

Ideology, Althusser taught, is any symbolic system that permits the human subject to become a subject, to wield the "I." The sense of being adrift on the planet without a guidebook, without a skin, in effect the theorylessness of the (nonetheless highly theorized) postmodern, continues to shake the "I" of this time. In a brilliantly playful essay of the early 1970s, Hélène Cixous used theater to undermine unitary versions of the self. The "I" must stop purporting to be a "true subject" and reveal itself as a succession of masks. "I," she wrote "must become a 'fabulous opera.' "[28] In a more grounded mood, Dr. Robert Jay Lifton has written that a new, flexible, multiply-defined personality whom he calls the "protean self" is the creative adaptation required of human development in the contemporary period.[29] This book suggests some of the ways theater has predicted, reflected, and perhaps guided such an adaptation.

PART I

Modern after Modernism

1

The Rise and Fall of the Character Named Character

IN 1960, the Polish playwright Tadeusz Rozewicz published a short play entitled *The Card Index*. The play has a Hero and a Chorus of Elders, ironic references to a vanished classical dramaturgy. In that dramatic world, unlike Rosewicz's and our own, plays proudly bore the names of their protagonists. For Rosewicz's "Hero" one name is as good as another; he submits to several in the course of the play. From time to time, as the playwright suggests in his stage directions, he may even wander offstage to be replaced by another actor. He is as anonymous as the serial card catalogue that gives the play its title. Yet the Hero is onstage every minute of the play, even if he spends it mostly lying in bed, occupying in his relative absence the very center of attention that heroes of an earlier day commanded by their presence.

In a wry comment on the inaction of this un-hero, the Chorus of Elders declaims mock-heroic verses celebrating Heracles:

He who in childhood cut off Hydra's head . . .
Will in his youth the blood of Centaurs shed . . . [1]

This parody of the art of a golden, mythic age is matched elsewhere by a parody of formalist modernism, as the Chorus gravely recites the alphabetical catalogue of the title ("Guatemala, goulash, guzzle . . . " etc.). The Chorus attempts to rouse the Hero to a sense of his symbolic role in the drama.

CHORUS OF ELDERS:
Do something, get a move on, think.
There he lies while time flies.
    (HERO covers his face with the newspaper.)
Say something, do something,
Push the action forward,
At least scratch your ear!
    (HERO is silent.)
There is nothing happening
What is the meaning of this?
. . . .

There must be action on the stage,
Something should be happening at this hour!

HERO:
Isn't it enough when the hero scratches his head and stares at the wall? . . .
I don't feel like doing anything.

As a last resort, the Chorus pleads a higher cause.

CHORUS OF ELDERS:
But even in a Beckett play
somebody talks, waits, suffers, dreams,
somebody weeps, dies, falls, farts.
If you don't move the theater is in ruins.

Stubbornly, the Hero refuses action.

HERO:
Today a flea circus is performing *Hamlet*
leave me alone
I am going away.

Rozewicz has created an amusing political allegory on the impotence of
the postwar generation in Poland and the paralysis of the bureaucratized subject. But he plays not just with political and social dead ends, but with theatrical
dead ends as well. In the universe of *The Card Index*, all theatrical traditions are
portrayed as exhausted—classical, renaissance, and avant-garde alike. If Hamlet, the hero who would not act to redeem his father, is reduced to performance
by a flea, why should his contemporary descendant bestir himself merely to save
the theater? The only thing left to do, as the Hero says, is to "go away."

Could that threatened departure be a clue to a new poetics of theater? In
this chapter, I will follow the career of the dramatic "element" Character up
to a crucial turning point, circa 1890, when symbolist playwrights all but formally announced their loss of interest in the principle of character as the motor
or agency of dramatic structure. I shall turn to this moment of change at the
end of this chapter, and conclude by suggesting some of its dramaturgical consequences for twentieth-century modern drama. At present I am interested in
the history of character's changing representation in dramatic theory. Like a
good Aristotelian, I shall attempt my account of Character, by studying its
changes of fortune. I want to know, What is the story those changes tell?

Each generation of modern students puzzles afresh over Aristotle's discussion of Plot and Character as primary and subordinate elements of tragedy.
They approach the *Poetics* with the assurance that the rounded, inward character of the psychological stage has always been fundamental to the dramatic form

and to the human mind. When we explain that to read *Antigone*, say, for the psychological subtext is anachronistic, they may be tempted to counter that Freudian psychology itself is based on her parents' relationship. Yet the topic, Aristotle on Character, presents problems to even the most sophisticated modern scholars. I quote the disputed text at length, first from Butcher's well known translation of chapter VI:

> For Tragedy is an imitation, not of men, but of action and of life, and life consists in action, and its end is a mode of action, not a quality. . . . Dramatic action, therefore, is not with a view to the representation of character: character comes in as subsidiary to the actions. Hence the incidents and the plot are the end of a tragedy; and the end is the chief thing of all. Again, without action there cannot be a tragedy; there may be without character. . . . Again, if you string together a set of speeches expressive of character, and well finished in point of diction and thought, you will not produce the essential tragic effect nearly so well as with a play which, however deficient in these respects, yet has a plot and artistically constructed incidents. . . . The Plot then, is the first principle, and, as it were, the soul of a tragedy: Character holds the second place.[2]

Some translators have softened Aristotle's dismissal of character. Where Butcher tells us there may be tragedy "without character," Grube has "a tragedy without characterization is possible."[3] Some now believe Else's more recent translation with the blunt plural, "without characters," to be closer to Aristotle's meaning. The crucial passage above, "Dramatic action, therefore, is not with a view to the representation of character . . . ," has been the occasion of particular dispute. Else's translation of the passage becomes a wilderness of lost antecedents, "Hence they are not active in order to imitate their characters, but they include the character along with the actions for the sake of the latter."[4]

In an important 1960s commentary on the *Poetics* that overturned a century-long idealization of the "tragic hero," John Jones brought an almost ruthless clarity to the passage, "And so the stage-figures do not act in order to represent their characters; they include their characters for the sake of their actions."[5] To Jones, Aristotle saw tragedy as expressing no conception of autonomous character.

> [Aristotle] is not saying, or he is saying only incidentally, that character is less important than action. This crucial inflexion of argument has not been acknowledged, either in close professional analysis, where stress falls on the "subordinate significance" of character and on the "superiority of activities over states," or in the general and popular expositions with their antithetical talk of Plot and Character, those capital-letter fixtures of commentary. It needs to be said that the plot-character dichotomy is radically false to Aris-

totle's understanding of Tragedy, that character, like colour [in painting], must be denied even the most primitive autonomy.[6]

According to Jones, the "tragic hero" may inhere in the "omnipresent consciousness" of a Hamlet, but the Aristotelian figure is one of "bare doings" touched with ethical coloring, not an inner man at all as we understand the "no doubt transient self of the modern West." The sum total of "doings" amounts to character. "(N)o potent shaping spirit lodges aboriginally behind the face," he writes, in an allusion to the power and function of the tragic mask. "By the erosive flow of action the individual features are carved out."[7]

In the twenty-five years since Jones's powerful intervention (albeit prepared by Bruno Snell and other, especially German, critics), a series of re-revisions by scholars of tragedy has emerged in the effort to recuperate a somewhat more continuous, psychological notion of character for Aristotle. Nonetheless most of these critics—Christopher Gill, P. E. Easterling, John Gould, and Simon Goldhill—acknowledge the importance of Jones's "no character" position. As recently as 1992, Elizabeth Belfiore, in perhaps the most substantial re-reading of the *Poetics* since Jones, reaffirms his basic orientation. "Because Aristotle . . . insists that plot is essential to tragedy while *ethos* is not," she writes,

> his views on the nature of tragedy differ radically from those of many modern readers and scholars, for whom character is the center of interest. . . . A bias in favor of character has often led scholars to attempt to find a "psychological realism" in Greek drama that the dramatic conventions of this genre did not allow and that the extant tragedies do not display. The inappropriateness of the view that agents in drama are psychological entities much like their real-life counterparts is now widely recognized, as scholars from Tycho von Wilamowitz to Thomas Rosenmeyer have argued. . . . There are, as John Jones remarks, no further realities lying behind the masks.[8]

It is not difficult for actors to discover for themselves, without benefit of sophisticated philology, that imagining an Oedipus at the level of individual psychology does not so much enhance him with lifelike detail as dissipate his moral force. On the contrary, it is the actor's difficult task to inhabit the actions of an Oedipus with such concentration that, in effect, no "excess" character is left over. The actor seeks the actions, not the coherent personality that commits them. The inexhaustibility of the great Greek tragic roles lies precisely in this mystery, that their tragic actions do not appear directly to be anchored in the recognizable contexts of psychological and material life. By contrast, Shakespeare's characters seem to the reader/spectator to exist not only within but outside the dramatic narrative that gives them life. It is possible to imagine a Hamlet apart from his tragic circumstance. Or put another way, we imagine an extended "whole" in which we place the only partially visible Hamlet of the text. In contrast to the Greek roles, the inexhaustibility of Shakespeare's tragic roles lies in the permission they give actors to make new wholes of the feeling and thinking dimensions suggested by the text.

It is difficult today to be certain whether the move to "denature" Shakespeare's psychological depth by such critics as Francis Barker and Jonathan Goldberg springs from modernist dehumanist/semiotic moves retrospectively projected, or whether they are uncovering the transitional, proto-psychological Shakespeare on whom later generations projected their growing commitment to depth psychology.[9] Clearly, however, from the eighteenth century on, theorists looked almost exclusively to Shakespeare as they began to advance a standard of inwardness for character, and, as a parallel development, began to revise the Aristotelian assimilation of character to plot.

Aristotle developed his ideas on dramatic structure in the century after the work of the great tragedians. Similarly, it was only in the late eighteenth and early nineteenth centuries that a new theory of tragedy arose in response to the forms that emerged in England two centuries earlier, and to a lesser extent in the playwriting of the Spanish Golden Age. Well before German romantic critics announced the new Shakespearean synthesis, however, eighteenth-century critics like Luigi Riccaboni, Marmontel, and Lessing began to link character, actor, and spectator in a mutual play of subjectivity (intended here in its allied senses of consciousness of self and of spiritual inwardness).[10]

Lessing, though he was a modified classicist and adherent of the ideal of artistic "objectivity," struck a peculiarly modern note by finding in Aristotle's enigmatic remarks on catharsis the center of Aristotle's theory of tragedy. The authenticity of a tragic work turned for Lessing primarily on its ability to stir, and then to purge, an emotional or inward state in the spectator.[11] With the German *Sturm und Drang* movement in the last quarter of the eighteenth century came a wholesale collapse of the classical ideal. *Sturm und Drang* strove to replace external representation with the turmoil of the inner world of feelings. These "romantic" values were clarified and pushed forward at the end of the century by the young Friedrich Schlegel and his circle (Novalis, Schleiermacher, Schelling), for whom the inward, or subjective, was elevated to a transcendental principle. As Schleiermacher wrote in 1800, "As often as I turn my gaze inward upon my inmost self, I am at once within the domain of eternity. I behold the spirit's action, which no world can change, and no time can destroy, but which creates both world and time."[12]

The application of romantic theory to dramatic literature was systematically carried out by Friedrich Schlegel's older brother, August Wilhelm, in the famous Vienna lecture cycle of 1808. There he leaves no doubt that romantic subjectivity in art is a concomitant of the inward and mystical bent of Christianity, which, unlike polytheism, "claimed an authority over the whole inward

man and the most hidden movements of the heart."[13] Like Herder and
Friedrich Schlegel in their earlier formulations of romantic theory, Wilhelm
identified Shakespeare as the emblematic "romantic" poet. And the emblematic talent of this artist, according to Schlegel, was characterization ("Never
perhaps was there so comprehensive a talent for characterization as Shakespeare"[14]) considered in its multifarious aspects as behavior, passions, and structural element in a dramatic scheme. Quoting Goethe, Schlegel links Shakespeare's brilliance in characterization with the admired quality of inwardness:
Shakespeare's characters are comparable to "watches with crystalline plates and
cases, which, while they point out the hours as correctly as other watches, enable
us at the same time to perceive the inward springs whereby all this is accomplished."[15] Yet Schlegel distances himself from the naive mechanicism of the
simile, preferring to identify as the secret of Shakespeare's gift for creating
characters a near-mystical capacity to transport himself into every human being.

In G. W. F. Hegel's lectures on aesthetics and the fine arts of the 1820s
came the apogee of a trend that had grown steadily in romantic critical
thought: romantic inwardness raised to the power of religious revelation.[16]
Hegel based his distinction of the classical from the European post-medieval
(or romantic, in the generic sense) form of art almost entirely on the hypothesis
of a shift from a self-enclosed objectivity to absolute subjectivity, or the "absolute inner." Classical art, while setting the model of the beautiful, suffers from
a "deficiency of inner subjectivity." It is not present to itself, as evidenced by
the fact that classical sculptures are sightless. By contrast, "the God of Romantic art appears seeing, self-knowing, inwardly subjective, and disclosing his inner being to man's inner being."[17] The Incarnation becomes both the animating force and model of all romantic art: hence the centrality of character, which
Hegel locates as "the proper center of the ideal artistic representation" because
it stands at the nexus of the absolute inner and manifest, material particularity.[18]

It is a matter of some delicacy in Hegel to distinguish the relative weight
of character in classical and romantic art, specifically drama. At times Hegel
appears almost unaware of the anti-Aristotelian implications of his principal
insight into romantic art. He can read classical forms in entire consistency with
Aristotle, even citing without comment the much-worried passage from the
Poetics, quoted above, stating that characters are included "for the sake of the
action."[19] At other times, he appears to collapse his own distinction between
classical and romantic from the other direction, reading back into classical
drama his romantic enthusiasm for character: "[I]n drama the inner will, with
its demands and intentions, is the essential determinant and permanent foundation of everything that goes on. The things that happen appear to be entirely
the result of a character and his aims. . . . "[20] In this passage, Hegel comes close
to replacing the Aristotelian "soul" of tragedy, Plot, with another soul, Character. Hegel even goes so far as to say, in his third chapter on the romantic form

of art, that "At the stage we are now considering . . . the achievement of the action is *eo ipso* a further development of the individual in his subjective inner life and not merely the march of events."[21] For Hegel, character was the only artistic vehicle that could give material form to absolute spiritual subjectivity.

If Hegel subjectivizes conflict in romantic tragedy, locating it fundamentally within character rather than between characters (which he associates with classical tragedy), he also sets limits on that process. What he approves in Shakespeare he despises when, as he believes, it is carried to extremes in the work of his contemporaries, Schiller, the young Goethe, and later (and worst of all) Kleist. The subjectivity of romantic tragedy and the inversion of conflict are no sooner achieved than, like the broom of the sorcerer's apprentice, subjectivity splits and splits again until the dichotomous notion of inner conflict is lost in a welter of subjective aspects. "But what is worst of all is to exhibit such indecision and vacillation of character, and of the whole man, as a sort of perverse and sophistical dialectic and then to make it the main theme of the entire drama, so that truth is supposed to consist precisely in showing that no character is inwardly firm and self-assured."[22] Finally, Hegel resists the "modern principle of irony" which, in contrast to the motives of a Shakespeare, "has seduced poets into bringing into characters a variety that does not come together into a unity, so that every character destroys itself as character."[23] Just as Aristotle derived the principle of unity of action from the Greek tragic poets, Hegel extrapolates from Shakespeare not only the primacy of character, but a principle of unity of character as well.

The last major philosopher to express sustained interest in the dramatic form was Friedrich Nietzsche, whose resonance in modern and contemporary theater has not even now been fully accounted for. Writing half a century after Hegel, Nietzsche leaves intact, and even builds on, the great idealist's promotion of the aesthetic to the rank of "absolute" philosophic concerns. "Art is the highest human task," Nietzsche proclaims in his 1871 introduction to *The Birth of Tragedy*, "the highest task and the truly metaphysical activity of this life. . . . "[24] Hegel's linkage of the Absolute with subjectivity results in a quasi-sacralization of dramatic character (which partakes of the absolutes of art and of subjectivity). But Nietzsche breaks the Hegelian connection between character and the Absolute. Individual subjectivity now becomes not a gateway but a barrier to deep connection with universal psychic forces.

Nietzsche's radical new theory of the tragic describes not so much a concrete dramatic form with articulated constituents as an archeological stage in human self-understanding. The stage of "tragic culture" was a moment suspended between self-consciousness (represented by the Apollonian plastic forms), and an earlier stage of primordial self-abandon, now sublimated in the aesthetic (represented by the Dionysian element of music). The devotees of Dionysus at the tragic festivals, Nietzsche argues, understood that "a world

torn asunder and shattered into individuals" was the very definition of suffering, and celebrated art as "the joyous hope that the spell of individuation may
be broken in augury of a restored oneness."[25]

To Nietzsche, this moment of balance between separation and oneness begins to erode in Attic culture with the advent of the "demon" Socrates and his
theatrical proxy, Euripides. Nietzsche accuses Socrates of introducing to human
culture the self of optimism and reason, whose concern it is to understand itself
as a separated, self-conscious individual. From this moment on, "theoretical
man," cut off from his roots in Dionysiac surrender, begins to loom on the
psychic horizon of the West. The Greeks knew better than to "suffer individuals
on the tragic stage,"[26] but character begins already to be sickly individualized
by Euripides, and ancient drama rapidly deteriorates into psychological refine-
ment. This falling out of the Dionysian prepares the way for the "Alexandrian"
period of analysis and reference, the period of the "librarian and corrector of
proofs."[27]

At the material plane of actual works for the stage, it would follow,
Nietzsche has nothing but contempt for the representation of individuated dramatic character. Among the most damning charges Nietzsche can level against
the post-mythic drama produced by "theoretical culture" is "character representation." Character is above all the fatal flaw of the "death leap into the
bourgeois drama."[28] At the threshold of modernism, Hegel's defense of the
individualistic "romantic" hero has curdled into Nietzsche's revulsion against
all that smacks of the individual and the "characteristic," projected backward
over nearly two and a half millennia of Western history.

In this first book, published at the age of 24, Nietzsche foreshadows modern and postmodern movements in theater with three simultaneous moves that
might be seen as rippling out in successive waves of influence. The most immediate repercussion, probably a direct influence, appeared in the attacks by playwrights and critics on dramatic character that ensued in the decades immediately following the publication of *The Birth of Tragedy*. These I will discuss
presently. The next, more general foreshadowing can be found in Nietzsche's
own theatricalism. Nietzsche does not outline a formal theory of dramatic art
in *The Birth of Tragedy*, rather he expresses the primacy of the aesthetic *through*
the aesthetic (one could even say the primacy of the dramatic through the
dramatic), through resort, that is, to an enactment or staging. In Nietzsche's
philosophical metatheater is played out the myth of the struggle between
Apollo and Dionysus, their accommodation in tragedy, and, in a sequel,
tragedy's violent undoing by the demonic force of rationalistic individuation.
Nietzsche lifts Hegel's account of Greek tragedy as a collision between two
ethical imperatives up from the level of discursive content in tragedies to
the level of a metaphysical "dramaturgy" first generating, then destroying,
tragedy.[29] The self-conscious theatricalization that can be seen not only here,

but throughout Nietzsche's literary career in his prolific role-playing, anticipates the fascination with metatheatrical strategies that is one of the distin-
guishing features of modern theater.

But there is another motion in *The Birth of Tragedy*, which might be
thought of (after Foucault) as "archeological."[30] In his youthful theory of the
evolution of ancient theater, Nietzsche goes beyond positivistic theories of artistic change from period to period to suggest that artistic differences can be
understood fundamentally as differences in the nature of human subjectivity,
of its understanding to itself of itself. Nietzsche implies that cultural change
can be read not merely as a series of shifts in what is known, but as shifts in
the knower, in the very ground of knowing. "Tragic" man/culture is interrupted by optimistic "Socratic" man, who decays into "Alexandrian" or "theoretical" man, who just might again be succeeded by "tragic" man.[31]

Foucault declared the debt of his own historiography of discontinuous
epistemes to Nietzsche, although to the much later *Genealogy of Morals*.[32] But
The Birth of Tragedy, with its assertion that tragedy (in effect) died with the
creation of the individual, already seems to hint at what was perhaps Foucault's
most startling archeologic assertion: that the modern, humanistic notion of
Man is itself culturally limited, a passing historical phenomenon.[33] To trace the
links between Nietzsche's hint of a periodic human subjectivity in *The Birth
of Tragedy* and the proliferation of postmodern theories of the discontinuous,
even arbitrary, nature of the "subject" is well beyond the reach of the present
chapter,[34] as are the links between such theories and the de-ontologized representations of character in postmodern theater. I return to a nearer subject, the
change I located at about 1890, when what our own generation has debated as
the "death of the subject" begins to emerge in the dramaturgical theory of the
symbolist movement.

The term "symbolism" was first suggested in an 1886 manifesto published
in *Le Figaro* by critic Jean Moréas. Symbolism, he said, was the method of that
poetry which "seeks to clothe the Idea in a tangible form."[35] Ten days later,
Gustave Kahn, the editor of the French journal *La Vogue*, explained, "The essential aim of our art is to objectivize the subjective (the exteriorization of
the Idea) instead of subjectivizing the objective (nature seen through an individual's temperament)."[36]

Symbolist playwrights and their theorists soon took up this same enthusiasm for de-individualization in favor of the Idea. The chief obstacle to achieving
this ideal, they realized, was character as represented by the living actor. Writing
in 1889 in *La Wallonie* about Van Lerberghe's short play *Les Flaireurs*, the Belgian poet and critic Albert Mockel stated that "*le drame idéal*" should have two
planes of significance, a plane of reality and a plane of irreality. Similarly, he
wrote, its characters should have two selves, one accessible, the other distant.
In 1890, Mockel returned to the theme in the same journal, urging a drama-

turgy that was not bound to a particular period, and a performance style that
would solve the problem of the live presence of the actor onstage who could
mislead the audience into focusing on the merely "anecdotal and the individual,
not the eternal history of man."[37]

Maeterlinck echoed Mockel in his distaste for the "violence of the anecdote." He called for an "interchanging of the roles" in drama that would bring
"the mysterious chant of the Infinite, the ominous silence of the soul . . . nearer
to us, and send the actors farther off."[38] In an effort to scour his plays clean
of a certain human materiality, he conceived of his early one-acts as plays
for marionettes, mysterious "inhabitants of two worlds," as Bettina Knapp
writes.[39] Elsewhere he spoke of the disruption to symbolic understanding that
the corporeal actor creates.

> There is a continual discord between the forces of a symbol and the forces of
> a man; the symbol of a poem is a center, the rays of which stretch into infinity;
> and these rays . . . have an importance that is limited only by the might of an
> eye following them. But an actor's eye oversteps the sphere of the symbol. . . .
> If man enters on the stage with all his faculties and his whole freedom, if his
> voice, gestures, attitude are not veiled by a great number of synthetic condi-
> tions, if even for a moment the human being appears such as he is, there is
> not a poem in this world which could stand that event.[40]

The rejection of the human image was not limited to Belgian and Parisian
symbolism. In a lecture on "Nationality and Literature" in 1893, W. B. Yeats
expressed the view that in every culture, character belonged to an intermediate
literary paradigm, now past. The classical divisions of Epic, Dramatic, and Lyric
had played themselves out in the history of English (and one presumes, Western) literature. First there were Mallory and Chaucer, the Homers of the English, but "as time passed, men became more and more interested in character
for its own sake, until at last they were ripe for the great dramatic movement
of Queen Elizabeth's reign." But later still,

> (T)he dramatic gave way to the lyrical. . . . The great personages fell like im-
> mense globes of glass, and scattered into a thousand iridescent fragments,
> flashing and flickering in the sun. . . . Character, no longer loved for its own
> sake, or as an expression of the general bustle of life, became merely the mask
> for some mood or passion. . . . In other words, the poets began to write but
> little of individual men and women, but rather of great types, great symbols
> of passion and mood. . . . When they tried, as in Byron's plays, to display
> character for its own sake they failed.[41]

Anton Chekhov could not be claimed by the symbolists of his generation,
yet he has Treplev advance some of their ideals, and not without respect, in Act
One of *The Seagull*. The central issue is character. When Nina complains that

the play is difficult to act because it has no living characters, Treplev rejoins, "Living characters! We don't have to show life as it is, even as it ought to be, but as we see it in our dreams!"[42]

Perhaps nothing measures the distance of symbolist theater from the theater of character better than Mallarmé's notes on a production of *Hamlet*, first published in November 1886 in *La Revue Indépendante.* "Even the finest of [individual] qualities," he writes,

> must remain relatively unimportant in a story which dwells solely on an imaginary and somewhat abstract hero. Otherwise the reality of the atmosphere created by the symbolic Hamlet will be disintegrated like a curtain of mist. Actors, it must be so! For in the ideal stage performance, everything must be carried out *in obedience to a symbolic relationship of characters.* . . . Whoever hovers around an exceptional character such as Hamlet, is merely Hamlet himself.[43]

Hamlet, one of Hegel's chief examples of a tragedy of character, has here moved into a realm of abstraction that borders on allegory, with all characters functioning as symbols, aspects, or projections of an "imaginary and somewhat abstract" hero.

Thus at the entrance to theatrical modernism, there are clear signs that autonomous character is in retreat from its Hegelian apogee. One immediate sign perhaps was the avoidance of the actor through experiments with puppets, marionettes, and various kinds of mask-work by some 1890s playwrights and directors. Even if the live actor was never seriously threatened by such experiments, character—the chief business of the actor—was undergoing a radical transformation. It was giving up a piece of its ontological ground to the abstract play of philosophical or ideological levels; or, put another way, it no longer served as the adequate container of such ideas and positions. In Aristotelian terms, if once Plot was the "soul" of the tragic play, and later Character moved into that place of preeminence, in twentieth-century non-realist theater, Thought began to assume a newly dominant dramaturgical position, shadowed by the slighted Aristotelian category of Spectacle as ideas became manifest through a quasi-allegorical use of space. I do not, of course, mean merely that within the dramatic fiction characters were represented as being overpowered by forces beyond their control. Rather, I am pointing to the emergence of dramaturgical and performance strategies that deliberately undermined the illusion of autonomous character.

Though my intention in this chapter has been to sketch a theoretical "career" of Character up to the *fin-de-siècle* moment of what John A. Henderson has called the "first avant-garde,"[44] I venture beyond that moment to suggest the three major directions I believe this process of the dissolution of autonomous character has taken in the modern period: allegorical, critical, and theatricalist. Strindberg, Brecht, and Pirandello provide the seminal examples. A word here about the use of the term "allegory." Mockel's description of the ideal drama as manifesting character on two planes, one near ("anecdotal") and one distanced ("eternal"), can be seen as describing not only symbolist dramaturgy and the proto-expressionist Strindberg, but much of the non-realist avant-garde theater that follows in the twentieth century. This dramaturgical layering is fundamentally allegorical in structure.[45] The term as I use it here describes both a specific line of development linked with the medieval mystery and morality, and also a general tendency in modern drama.

Strindberg's *To Damascus*, Part I, marks the beginning of a modernist tradition of quasi-allegorical mystery plays, going up to and past Beckett, in which character is presented as material to be molded by great forces in the universe. Here Saul's journey to Damascus and the stations of Christ's journey with the cross, combined by Strindberg into a Dantean meaning-saturated landscape, provide the patterns that shape the Stranger's "character development" from anger to contrition. The Stranger is not only molded from the outside in this way, but hollowed out from the "inside" in the sense that aspects or fragments of self are represented as a series of haunting figures who appear as his doubles. Whether we understand the Stranger as a being whose changing inner life is projected onto successive landscapes and onto other characters, or as a blank tablet whose subjectivity is the sum of these encounters, it is clear that we are not reading character perspectivally, with "inner" and "outer" in seamless alignment. Rather we are reading allegorically: horizontally as a series of aspects, and vertically through multiple levels of interpretation. This mode of reading is called into play by expressionists and later playwrights who continued Strindberg's revival of medieval dramatic forms.

Brecht's depiction of character on simultaneous levels requires of the spectator another kind of allegorical reading, not primarily idealist and metaphysical, like the later Strindberg, but ironic, dialogic, and analytical. It can emerge only in actual performance, through the critical and conscious relationship of actor to character. The actor should not adopt "another's facial expression at the cost of erasing his own," says the Dramaturg in *The Messingkauf Dialogues*, but "show the two faces overlapping." The split image may be brutally disjunct, as suggested by the Philosopher's preceding comment, "The classics say that apes are best understood from the point of view of their successor in the evolutionary process, man."[46] The actor/character uncoupling permits the spectator a critical understanding of the ideological construction of the social subject, and provides in some sense a scale model of it. Yet taken as an aesthetic construct, the actor/character split can also be compared to the dual-aspect portraiture of a Picasso who wants to break down humanist norms of perspective painting.

The political controversy surrounding Brecht's *Lehrstück* (learning play),

Die Massnahme, has tended to obscure the fact that it is one of the most extreme experiments of the modernist turn against character. Brecht goes beyond his earlier theme of mutability of self, as in the world of *Mann ist Mann*, where continuous character can be given up when it becomes an unaffordable luxury. In *Die Massnahme*, the autonomous self is not merely a bourgeois illusion, but has the moral weight of a crime. The analytical separation of actor and character is itself part of the fiction, as the Four Agitators impassively take turns playing their "disappeared" fifth comrade.

This fictive presentational style mirrors the story they tell about the Young Comrade, whose romantic humanism must be suppressed in the interest of the revolutionary work of the group. The Young Comrade must be persuaded to give up attachment to his identity and consent to his own execution. In a final level of remove from personal identity, his very face must become unrecognizable. Just as his features melt away into the white of the lime pit, so all traces of individuated character dissolve into the dramaturgy of the play. In an ideal presentation, the actors would not even be set apart from spectators with the usual heightened identity, for the "culinary" line between spectator and actor was to disappear in the enactment of Brecht's didactic plays.

There is a radical Aristotelianism, subordinating character to plot, in Brecht's supposedly "anti-Aristotelian" dramaturgy. In his notes on the Street Scene, Brecht comments that "the demonstrator [the actor] should derive his characters entirely from their actions." He charges the traditional theater with pleading something akin to the circular orphan defense, in which a man who murders his parents pleads clemency on the grounds that he is an orphan. The theater bases "the actions on the characters," who are then exempted from criticism because the actions are "an unavoidable consequence deriving by natural law from the characters who perform them."[47] Brecht's analytic dramaturgy is a direct challenge to psychological acting techniques and their essentialist appeals to a transcendent human nature.

Among the three tendencies I have identified in modern theater as distancing themselves from character, the metaphysical strand, with its ties to the mystery and morality play, is closer to traditional allegory than the Brechtian parable with its ironic relationship between actor and character, society and fable. The theatricalist play, the third, has among its antecedents the allegorical *auto* of Calderón, *The Great Theater of the World*.[48] In its modern incarnation, it still maintains a memory of allegory, as it were, in the interface of micro and macro worlds. That interface is no longer a transparent relation of transitory to eternal, as in Calderón's religious allegory, but a paradoxical relationship in which lesser and greater realities can no longer be clearly determined. Because of its ability to hold two or more planes of reality in ambiguous suspension, theatricalism has emerged in the twentieth century as a favored dramatic mode to express the relative and multiple nature of self-identity.

In *Six Characters in Search of an Author*, Pirandello drives a wedge between actor and character, as Brecht in a very different way was to do later. John Willett speculates that the Reinhardt production of this play in Berlin in 1924 may in fact have inspired Brecht to rethink the relationship.[49] But whereas in Brecht's production dramaturgy it is the actor whose consciousness is wider than, and superior to, the character's, in Pirandello's text it is the characters who see more than the actors. As the Father explains to the Manager of the theater troupe in Act Three:

> Well, sir, if you think of all those illusions that mean nothing to you now, of all those things which don't even seem to you to exist any more, while once they *were* for you, don't you feel that—I won't say these boards—but the very earth under your feet is sinking away from you when you reflect that in the same way this *you* as you feel it today—all this present reality of yours—is fated to seem a mere illusion to you tomorrow?[50]

By reifying the characters in *Six Characters*, Pirandello paradoxically makes it impossible for the audience to extend to his stage figures the customary passport of a free-standing ontological base. In place of the illusion of definability, substantiality, continuity—all springing from the illusion of unmediated and spontaneous life—character here is split into two unsatisfactory halves, each being granted one or another of these essential traits. The six characters are definable, substantial, and continuous, but become strangely truncated aesthetic objects through their very exaggeration of these traits. The others, the actors, seem to have the attributes of unmediated and spontaneous life, but at the same time are undefined and insubstantial. Ironically, both groups can accede to a state of "living" character only in the moment of theatrical enactment, a theme Genet picked up later in the century. In *Six Characters* Pirandello defined a set of reflections that later playwrights, among them Beckett, Handke, Heiner Müller, and others, could assume and build on. It is the theatricalist *Ur*-text in the modern period, demonstrating that character no longer offers the spectator ontological assurance, but embodies an unsolvable ontological problem.

The "dehumanization of art," as Ortega called the move away from the human subject in cubism, futurism, and other art movements, was foreshadowed by advanced theater artists at the end of the nineteenth century. Still, theater's basic material was the actor, and unlike painting and sculpture, its practical response to the new theoretical insight could not have been a total abstraction that left behind the human form.[51] Yet it is not quite correct either to say, as Michael Goldman does, that because of the live actor dramatic character "survived what we think of as the particularly modern disassemblage of the concept of character."[52] One must still ask what it is that survived, and what constitutes survival. If characters become walking experiments in disassemblage, are dislocated or trapped by the artifacticity of character, as are Brecht's Galy Gay or Pirandello's Enrico IV, are they evidence of character's survival or of its newly-problematic status?

Modernist character comes to the stage partly de-substantiated. The various means to accomplish this have in common a kind of layering that breaks apart the integrated image of human identity. The burden of signification (the answer to the question, What are we following?) begins to shift from the unfolding of character and plot to the more abstract interest of the play of ontological and ideological levels. Yet the very act of putting character into question still marks its place as central. This strikes me as a core dilemma of modernist drama, which repeatedly introduces *as a humanistic problem* its own very questioning of the human image on the stage. If there is any clear watershed between modern and postmodern in drama, it is that the postmodern normalizes and shrugs off as "merely conceptual" the sense of terror (or novelty) associated with posthumanist thinking.

2

Pattern over Character

The Modern Mysterium

IN THE PARIS of the 1890s, as Strindberg observed, the Middle Ages seemed to be "coming again to France. . . . Young men don the monk's cowl . . . dream of the monastery, write legends, perform miracle plays, paint madonnas, and model Christs."[1] In theater, medievalism ranged from revivals of religious forms to atmospheric evocations of a remote time out of time. Maurice Bouchor's charmingly naive mystery plays, performed by the Petit théâtre des marionettes, developed almost a cult following in the early years of the decade.[2] In 1893, Maeterlinck's *Pelléas et Mélisande*, set in a mysterious and other-worldly Middle Ages, launched Lugné-Poë's Théâtre de l'Oeuvre. Mallarmé greeted the work as the "paradigm of the theater of the future."[3]

As Strindberg had reason to know, the medieval craze was closely related to the hermetic revival—centered in, but not limited to, Paris—of the last decade and a half of the century. Many interlaced figures, heirs for the most part of the recently-dead great mystic and kabbalist Eliphas Levi, or perhaps converts to the Theosophy of the recently-arrived Mme. Blavatsky, contributed to the occult movement as priests, organizers, and editors. Among avant-garde artists and writers of the symbolist generation, it is no exaggeration to say that "every symbolist was a mystic, more or less a Rosicrucian, an occultist,"[4] including French writers as diverse as Jarry[5] and Claudel, the Belgian Maurice Maeterlinck, Yeats in Ireland, Micinski in Poland, and Bely in Russia. Hofmannsthal had no clear cult affiliation or attraction, but described himself as a "mystic without a mystique."[6] Strindberg's journey into the Parisian occult is rendered in *Inferno*, an account of his experiences of 1894–97, when he gave up playwriting, performed (al)chemical experiments, spiraled into spiritualism, and hoped to become the "Zola of occultism."[7]

Turning away from realism, materialism, and positivism, this generation stumbled afresh into the *mysterium tremendum*, and sought corresponding art forms. Their cry, as Mallarmé wrote in 1887 in the *Revue indépendante*, was *"Remplacez vaudeville par mystère."*[8] In the theater, "mystery" shortly became a loose designation for any play that regarded human life *sub specie aeternitatis*, ranging in form from Van Lerberghe's fable on the coming of death, *Les*

Flaireurs, to Claudel's comparatively realistic saint play *La jeune fille Violaine*, to Maeterlinck's static dramas of everyday life, to neo-romantic occult dramas by Edouard Schuré and Péladan. Strindberg called his 1898 religious fairy-tale play *Advent* a "mystery."[9]

By the early years of the century the mystery play was being conceived not only as any play of a mystical bent, but as a performance mood and also as a distinct dramatic type.[10] Meyerhold wrote that "the performance of Maeterlinck is a *mystery*," which must be performed with a "mystical vibration . . . conveyed through the eyes, the lips, the sound and manner of delivery."[11] The Russian poet and budding Nietzschean philologist Vyacheslav Ivanov conceived the mystery as a dramatic genre, central to a new "prophetic" Theatre of the Future; this third theater would be the modern analogue to the choric tragedy of ancient theater and to the comic form of medieval religious theater.[12]

Not long after Ivanov made his prediction, World War I and the Russian Revolution put the esoteric fascinations and mystical longings of this *fin-de-siècle* generation into eclipse. "To use the word spiritual in the late 1930s and 1940s . . . was near-heresy and dangerous to an artist's career," writes Maurice Tuchman.[13] Modern critics now assigned the occult and mystical movement in art and literature to an unhealthy romanticism, and set themselves the task of rescuing artists' modern innovations in form from outdated romantic content. We sense John Gassner's discomfort as he alludes to the "weirdly penumbral" writing of *To Damascus*, a play Richard Gilman concedes is a formal "turning point in the history of the stage" but whose "Biblical quotations and occult verbiage" are "not always appropriate materials."[14] From a perspective on the other side of modernism, however, not wedded to mid-century critical assumptions, modern drama never shed the mystery impulse. It continued to be expressed in the dramatic texts of expressionism and surrealism, in revolutionary Marxist theater, in the metaphysical theater of the absurd and beyond, evolving as a distinct, twentieth-century genre.

I attempt in the following chapter an initial survey of this modern dramatic form, which I call the mysterium to distinguish it both from the medieval Christian mystery, where it finds its roots, and from the symbolist mystery play, in which it immediately originates. First emerging in Strindberg's late pilgrimage plays, it evolved in part as a revival of allegorical methods, however dislocated by a self-conscious, modernist irony, and also continued to bear the stamp of *fin-de-siècle* symbolist occult aesthetics. Representative of this latter influence were Péladan and Maeterlinck, for both of whom Strindberg expressed uninhibited admiration.[15]

The Catholic occultist "Sar" Josephin Péladan, novelist, personality, and co-founder in 1888 of the *Ordre kabbalistique de rose-croix*, was a significant public force in aligning art with the mysteries of the universe in the Paris of the early 1890s. Péladan envisioned the "revival" of a Rosicrucian brotherhood in a flash of intuition while witnessing a performance of *Parsifal*. In 1890, Péladan's Catholic wing of the new movement broke with the occult kabbalistic wing, and announced the foundation of a Rosicrucian art society that would produce an annual salon. All art shown there would be dedicated to the three important criteria of great art Péladan had set forth a decade earlier when under the influence of Florentine primitive painting: the Ideal, the Redemptive, and the Italianate.[16] Péladan's own Wagnerian occult dramas were performed at the salons in conjunction with the art exhibits.

In *Le Trésor des humbles*, a collection of essays on spiritual and humanistic themes published in 1896, Maeterlinck traced a theory of "mystery" that asserted the reality of an unseen, eternal plane. "The Tragical in Daily Life" called for a theater that would show not merely gross physical action and the "violence of the anecdote," but "the mysterious chant of the Infinite, the ominous silence of the soul and of God, the murmur of Eternity on the horizon, the destiny or fatality that we are conscious of within us, though by what tokens none can tell. . . . "[17] Maeterlinck saw the time approaching when souls would communicate directly without recourse to external appearances. The ineffable was gathering critical mass. Thus even an indifferently gifted turn-of-the-century playwright could have "glimpses of a secretly luminous life" that was not yet available to a Shakespeare or a Racine.[18]

From the mystic drama of everyday life of Maeterlinck and the esoteric Ideal of Péladan we can begin to piece together an occult poetics for the symbolist mystery play. The two approaches are consistent with the general prescription for symbolist dramaturgy by the Belgian poet, critic, and Mallarmé disciple Albert Mockel cited in chapter 1. Mockel saw the *drame idéal* as operating on two levels, a plane of reality and a plane of irreality, or perhaps superreality. Similarly, he wrote, its characters should have two selves, one accessible, the other distant. Mockel urged a dramaturgy that was not bound to a particular period, and a performance style that would solve the problem of the too-material actor, sparing the spectator the temptation "to perceive on the stage an anecdote and an individual and not the eternal history of man."[19] Mockel aptly described the intent of all symbolist playwriting that has continued with the modern mysterium: to escape the merely anecdotal and individual through recourse to another plane of existence, whether suggested by myth, legend, or a heightened reality.

All these prescriptions for a cosmic dramatic form led inescapably to a revival of the allegorical methods found in the medieval epics and morality plays, a revival already inspired by the nearer examples of *Faust* and *Peer Gynt*. The renewed interest in Calderón at the end of the century was another sign that this revival was underway. Allegorical methods helped playwrights move beyond the symbolists' favored dramatic form, the one-act play encapsulating a timeless moment. Yet even Maeterlinck's own one-act mysteries, especially "The

Intruder" and "The Blind," demonstrate the inevitable role of allegorisis in a theater of cosmic aspirations. It was the allegorical, morality/mystery that persisted as a genre past the symbolist era, while the symbolist mystery in the atmospheric sense remained primarily a turn-of-the-century phenomenon.[20] I do not, however, describe the works I shall discuss as "allegories," as I want especially to avoid the implication that they can be submitted to what Rosamund Tuve dismisses as a "slicing machine" capable of separating ideas from concretions, or that they are a "disguised form of discursive writing."[21] By and large, I prefer to say that they are "allegorical," or conditioned by "allegorisis." Unquestionably, they use the scenes and methods of allegory—quests, pilgrimages, symbolic landscapes, meaningful cycles of time, typology, and, on occasion, personification.[22] Perhaps most important, they reflect the central allegorizing turn of mind that confronts absolutely, as Walter Benjamin puts it, the transitory and the eternal. Whatever this mind picks up, Benjamin says, "its Midastouch turns . . . into something endowed with significance."[23]

Allegory as a procedure makes "reference to man's ultimate destiny or meaning . . . usually in some ancient similitude or element accustomed to bear this burden of reference."[24] The mysterium as I define it is by no means simply a modern reworking of forms that traditionally make such reference, or a return to the figures that may lie behind them. Rather, the mysterium typically uses its models with a cunning irony, simultaneously embracing and distancing, even subverting, their eschatalogical force. *To Damascus*, Part I—the play, according to Egil Tornqvist, that marks the inception of truly modern drama—is the first dramatic work clearly of this type.[25] Here we see not only a wealth of allegorical tropes, but Mockel's "ideal drama" of two selves, eternal and individual. We see the esoteric dimension forcing itself upon everyday life, though not precisely in the manner of Maeterlinck. And finally we see, remarkably, all of Péladan's Rosicrucian criteria of artistic excellence. Both in its religious mysticism and in its abandonment of a mimetic, realistic action for an artificial, highly patterned form, it partakes of the Ideal; in its penitential teleology it is Redemptive; and in its debt to Dante's *Divine Comedy* it is Italianate. Further, it bears the title, whether by chance or as a quotation is not known, of Péladan's second published work, *Le Chemin de Damas*.[26]

The medieval mystery plays told the sacred history of the world; the moralities, based not on history but on doctrine, recapitulated this universal form through a central figure's progress toward salvation. In a conflation that became the model for all modern mysteria, *To Damascus*, Part I, is a mystery within a morality. Its underlying structure is that of the progress, the central narrative device of late medieval allegory from Dante's *Divine Comedy*, to Guillaume de Deguileville's *The Pilgrimage of Human Life*, to *Everyman*.[27] Within the progress or journey form in *To Damascus* lies the imprint of another medieval dramatic structure, the passion play, depicted here as a path of sorrows and rejections (later described by the Mother as the Stations of the Cross) leading to a death-in-life in the asylum scene. The "resurrection" that follows is the Stranger's rebirth in contrition.[28] Strindberg's combination of the morality and the passion play inspired a string of related experiments in the early part of the century, such as Andreyev's *The Life of Man* and numerous dramas of the expressionists. The basic pattern—a progress within which are contained other biblical motifs and structures—appears in every mysterium I shall discuss.

Though Strindberg later called *To Damascus*, Part I, the first of his dream plays, the statement has perhaps been understood in a too concrete psychological sense. Christian allegories, such as *Piers Plowman*, frequently presented themselves as the dreams of their authors, while the *Divine Comedy* is a vision depicted as an awakening from the dream of life. In his *Letters to the Intimate Theatre*, Strindberg spoke of the pilgrimage theme as allegory in *To Damascus*. There are many other parallels between *To Damascus* and medieval allegory, such as character fragmentation, typology, magical causality, the cyclic treatment of time, the use of an emblematic landscape, and the representation of sin as illness. Many of these elements also appear in later mysteria.

The journey we take in both the modern mysterium and its medieval forebears follows the moral education and purification of the morality play's typical protagonist, the naive traveler. (As the Stranger says in Part III of the *Damascus* trilogy, "I'll gladly go with anyone who can teach me something.")[29] In medieval allegory this traveler is a universal figure, struggling with the great human issues of sin, guilt, death, and redemption. Strindberg's protagonist, named with proper allegorical abstraction the Stranger (literally from the Swedish, the Unknown One), is similarly caught in the eschatalogical net, as are the protagonists of other mysteria.

But the Stranger—and here is Strindberg's version of Mockel's two-level drama—is also endowed with a very particular biography: he has a publisher, a lawsuit, debts, a marriage, a mother-in-law. Each of these circumstances is both individual and the occasion for an eternal teaching: particular events are not merely likened to cosmic events, they are their conduits of manifestation. Yet when looked at closely, this layering has an ironic quality. Almost because he is magnified with typological reference, the Stranger is diminished by domestic problems.

The Stranger's biography is of course quite nakedly Strindberg's own, a distinctively modern, disturbing invasion of the fictional fabric. But even this blatant self-revelation can be seen as a modern continuation of the narrative device of medieval religious allegory in which the real Dante, or the real William Langland, claims to be the narrator of the poem. As Paul Piehler writes in *The Visionary Landscape*, this poet-dreamer is "by no means a mere private individual" interested in a personal fantasy life, but a type of priest or prophet concerned with a "crisis of the spirit."[30] While most mysterium protagonists are not depicted as writers, all of them serve the vatic function through the reenactment of the sacred history of mankind as revealed in scripture or an alternate system of belief.[31]

The Stranger's journey begins in an emblematic town, "on the street, between the bar, the church and the post office,"[32] the secular space that recurs in many mysteria as a place of sin or spiritual indifference. It moves from the city to the sea to the ravine to an increasingly tangled wilderness. The movement from the human society of the town to the lonely wilderness as a place of moral teaching is frequently found in allegory.[33] On this psychological landscape the Stranger is temporarily "lost," most of all to himself. A number of different journeys is simultaneously inscribed on the terrain of Strindberg's play, including that of the fallen Adam in search of redemption, of Saul/Paul on the Road to Damascus, and of the suffering Christ approaching Golgotha. The conversion of the vengeful Jew to the repentant Christian is the figure which subsumes all other figural allusion in the play. In this double journey, from Adam to Christ, and from fallen to redeemed, the Stranger is again like Everyman and like the hero of the *Commedia*, both types of Adam and Christ in their progress from sin to redemption. Notwithstanding the power of this combined figure, it is important to note that the Stranger is neither redeemed nor redeemer, but remains stubborn in his skepticism. He will "pass through" the church, he tells the Lady. He will "definitely not" stay. This ironic resistance to the ordained pattern appears over and over as a basic structural element in the modern mysterium.

The mysterium characteristically contains, as an interior structure, some part of the biblical cycle. In Georg Kaiser's *From Morn to Midnight*, which is "broadly based on the medieval and sixteenth-century German tradition of the Mystery Play,"[34] the Bank Cashier begins as a naive Adam admiring the charms of the rich Lady, whom he mistakes for the naked Eve in a Cranach painting of the Fall of Man. That he will also become a type of Christ is ironically forecast with the ruse he employs—his hoarse, "Fetch—glass—water!"—to flee the bank with stolen money.

The Cashier's journey, like the Stranger's, can be read on more than one plane. His social journey leads from the stultifying safety of his petit-bourgeois job and marriage through all the illusory pleasures of high society. His universal journey starts as he encounters the grinning skull of death and takes him, in the winnowing style of *Everyman*—where illusory values are progressively discarded—on a search for "goods worth total investment." His cosmic journey follows in the sacrificial and redemptive steps of the Passion, including the "stations" of the Last Supper and the Crucifixion, represented here in the Cashier's suicide against the cross sewn on the curtain of the Salvation Army stage. The eclipse in Christ's last hours and the earthquake at the moment of his death, recounted in *Matthew*, are recalled in the electrical short that explodes the bulbs of the overhead chandelier. Interpreters who read this ending in wholly sacramental terms, however, miss the ironic, double-tiered structure of the modern mysterium, in which salvation may be proffered, but is always put into question by the "anecdotal."

Christian allegory proceeds along spatial trajectories that imitate the progress of the soul. The Cashier's progress from the small town to the big city is both an awakening from untested innocence and a descent into sin. Similarly, Christian allegory moves in emblematic cycles of time that directly represent or imitate Christian eschatology. Typical movements are from Creation to Last Judgment, from Nativity to Passion, from a summoning by Death to the promise of Eternal Life. MacQueen points out that religious allegories can also echo the sacramental pattern by taking the form of a completed natural cycle, a day and night for instance, or a year moving through all four seasons.[35] *To Damascus*, Part I, has both kinds of cycles, the spiritual journey to and from "Damascus," and a natural journey from spring to spring, the season of rebirth. The return to a starting point leaves us free to conceive the journey as a single moment of psychological or spiritual illumination, a dream in that sense. Characteristically, the mysterium adopts this cyclical movement, but is ambivalent about its completion. Thus the Stranger's rebirth is provisional at best. The return to an exact starting point is always open to the interpretation that nothing at all has happened. *From Morn to Midnight* announces a cycle in its title, but a cycle that is broken or disrupted. The Cashier dies a midnight death without the dawn of redemption that would complete the Christian pattern. Ambivalently, the play gives a contrary signal by completing a numerological cycle in its seven "stations," seven being symbolic of perfect order, a complete period or cycle.

At the very heart of the "classical" avant-garde, in Artaud's miniature biblical cycle play *The Spurt of Blood*, the mysterium pattern recurs. Another universal protagonist or "Everyman," this time the Young Man, is placed in the footsteps of Adam, courting his Eve like the Stranger and the Cashier before him. The opening scene is a paradise of love: "I love you and life is wonderful," he exclaims. The line is repeated four times with mounting intensity and finally shame. Sexual desire invades their innocence. There is a moment of climax: "We are intense. Oh what a well-made world!"[36] But sexual knowledge is punished here, as in *Genesis*, by a terrible expulsion, described by Artaud literally as a Fall—the sickeningly slow descent of body parts, colonnades, porticos, and scorpions of the famous stage direction.

Artaud now introduces the urban scene—the place of sin, as in Kaiser—along with the profane family who populate the "lower" level of his play. The Young Man describes the town, a kind of Everytown not unlike the Stranger's in *To Damascus:* "Here are the main square, the priest, the shoemaker, the vegetable market, the threshold of the church, the lantern of the brothel, the scales of justice." Strindberg and Kaiser similarly present the city as antipode to some mysterious teleological space or climate in which life's depth of meaning can be revealed. Yet what is disturbing to the divine plan is not the urban setting itself, but the modern will of the characters, to whom the pattern is often invisible and irrelevant. Thus the Knight and the Wet Nurse, cartoon figures opaquely reminiscent of Jarry's Père and Mère Ubu, now bustle onstage quarrelling about food and sex.[37]

Strindberg's Stranger sought reconciliation, Kaiser's Clerk sought a purpose in modern society, but the Young Man's search is more absolute and uncompromising: like a campaigning Caesar he seeks purity in a filthy world. "I saw, I knew, I understood . . . I can't stand it any more!" The Priest with the Swiss accent chides the Young Man for his attraction to God, "But that's out of date. . . . We must be content with the little obscenities of man in the confessional. And that's it, that's life." True to the type of the naive traveler, the Young Man is "very impressed": "So that's life! Well, everything is a mess." But now the play, which has already represented a version of the earliest catastrophe in the Bible, the Fall, moves to an enactment of the final biblical catastrophe, the Apocalypse. The similarity between Artaud's imagery and that of *Revelation* is striking. Both depict earthquakes and blood in the sky. In both are represented the Great Whore, exposed in hideous nudity. In Artaud the Whore's hair catches fire, in John, her flesh. In both there is a plague of scorpions—emblem of death, the Fall, sexual license, and treachery.

The correspondence goes beyond imagery to structure. In both are three women, Mother, Virgin, and Whore. The Whore of Babylon and the virginal New Jerusalem may be likened to Artaud's Bawd and his virginal young Girl. The mother in *Revelation* is the Woman Clothed in the Sun of chapter XII. Artaud's grotesque version of the mother "clothed in the sun" is none other than the Wet Nurse, the Young Man's mother, whose vagina "swells and splits, becomes vitreous, and flashes like the sun."

Artaud's text shares with *Revelation* the reverse symmetry of chiasmic structure.[38] Of the five major divisions in Artaud's play, the first is a scene of love and idealism shading into adult sexuality; the last is a grotesque representation of adult sexuality shading into a restoration of the ideal state of the opening; the second and penultimate scenes represent cataclysms; the third scene, with the village square at its center, depicts the fallen world. At the end of *Revelation* comes the New Jerusalem, the shining city of purity. At the end of *The Spurt of Blood* the Girl, "flat as a pancake" and left for dead, revives, exclaiming "The virgin! So that's what he was looking for." Beginning the play as a virginal Eve, she now appears to be the virgin again, and identifies the Young Man's journey as a search for the innocence of Eden—a type of cosmic virginity. "The shape of history implied by [the] Revelation is a circular one which constitutes 'one great detour to reach in the end the beginning,' " writes M. H. Abrams, quoting Karl Lowith. "The *Endzeit* [is] a recovery of the *Urzeit*. The heaven and earth that God in the beginning had created he ends by recreating."[39] However, Artaud alienates the Christian myth even as he invokes it, for the Young Man does not assume his triumphant place with the Bride but is last seen running offstage with the Whore.

In adopting *chiasmus*, it is possible that Artaud intended to echo as well the central structural device of *To Damascus*. Or perhaps both authors independently recognized the form as an invocation of biblical redemption. Whatever the source, the coincidence points to a general characteristic of the mysterium, its structural artificiality. The mysterium arrays itself against what realistic drama portrays as natural causality. In realistic drama, characters control, or hope to control, events. In the mysterium, characters are guided, chastened, and surprised by cosmic interventions; the dramatic events, over which the characters have little or no control, are the medium by which these forces manifest. The spatial-temporal world of the mysterium subsumes its characters in an overall design that in effect designs them. Character has not yet been dispersed, made see-through or disposable, as will occur in postmodern theater, but much of its signifying power has been taken over by abstract patterns.

It is a commonplace of cultural criticism that between the "irrationalists" and the "materialists" the plate of modernism is licked clean. To each fall opposing traits, movements, and heroes: to the irrationalists, dreams, madness, religious longings, sexual ecstasy, pessimism, apocalyptic fantasies, symbolism, surrealism, Dada, the "theater of cruelty," the "absurd"—and of course, Nietzsche, Freud, the existentialists; to the materialists, the revolution, optimism, technology, progress, realism, futurism (at least Russian futurism), behaviorism, constructivism—and above all Marx and Marxists such as Brecht. Though much is omitted from this game board of modernism (and the enormities of the Third Reich and the Stalinist terror mock its somewhat mechanical clarity) the division does illuminate certain lines of artistic influence throughout the century. My discussion of the mysterium thus far would seem to support a claim that the modern mysterium developed as the peculiar form of theatrical irrationalists (even though a current of social amelioration runs through the form in the hands of German expressionists like Kaiser). However, theater writers such as Toller (in *Transfiguration*), Mayakovsky (in *Mystery Bouffe*), and even Brecht were also drawn to the mysterium form, as implausible as the project of dressing Marxist doctrine in Christian eschatology might seem at first glance.

Brecht wrote *The Baden Play for Learning* (*Die Badener Lehrstück vom Einverständnis*) as the dramatic text of a cantata to be performed at the 1929 Baden-Baden *Neue Musik* festival.[40] The composers associated with *Neue Musik* had two socio-musical goals, to create and promote functional, or applied music (*Gebrauchsmusik*: music for use) and amateur, or community music (*Gemein-schaftsmusik*). Each summer, artists were invited to attempt specific forms that served these ends. In 1929, participating artists were invited to contribute radio works and cantatas (the basic model for the latter being the Lutheran church cantata). Working with Weill and with Hindemith, Brecht contributed one of each.[41] Through these exercises, he crystallized his own theory of the didactic *Lehrstück*. He also ended up pushing the aims of the festival organizers toward a much more radical politics than contemplated by their goals of disseminating music through technological collaboration and active participation.

In *The Baden Play for Learning*, a group of airmen, three Mechanics and a Flyer, report the triumph of human flight late in the second millennium. "We have arisen," they hymn, but presently suffer a crash to earth. In the second scene, titled, with obvious intent, "THE FALL," they lie on the ground asking for help. Already the combined mystery/morality structure is evident. The collective protagonist has become a seeking Everyman or Mankind figure, while the action, ostensibly related to aviation, appears to be a techno-futurist version of human history according to Scripture. Suddenly the tone shifts. Like the street episode of Artaud's *Spurt of Blood*, the clown dismemberment scene of Brecht's middle section—the "Investigations" into the question "Does Man Help Man?"—now adds a brutally secular and comic level to the text. The text then concludes on the earlier tone of sublime didacticism.

It is consistent with the aims of the revolutionary mysterium that Brecht would have a collective protagonist. (Mayakovsky similarly creates a group of seven "Unclean" in *Mystery Bouffe*.) Brecht's protagonist group now divides along class lines, providing an ending that recalls the medieval Last Judgment plays, where the saved exited at one side of the stage to eternal life, and sinners left at the other to Hellmouth. The three airmen cry out to be saved from death. In response, the Leader of the Learned Chorus offers a mystical, part-Buddhist, part-Marxist teaching in the parable of the "Thoughtful One," who weathers the storm in his "smallest size." "He knew the storm and agreed with the storm," says the Speaker. Despite the apparent allusion to the Buddhist doctrine of non-attachment, the scene also recalls the climax of *Everyman*, in which the doctrinally naive protagonist learns that Good Deeds is the only companion who can follow him to salvation.

THE LEARNED CHORUS:
> And we ask you
> To change our motor and improve it
> Also to increase its safety and speed . . .

THE FALLEN MECHANICS:
> We will improve the motors, their safety and speed.

Unlike the three Mechanics, the fourth Fallen One, the Flyer, cannot relinquish his individuality and his name. He is burdened by self-importance, cannot agree to "die" into the masses. His individualism ultimately damns him to death and oblivion.

Brecht's Mechanics, like Mayakovsky's Unclean, learn that they must create "heaven" themselves through class consciousness and work. What is the purpose, then, of drawing so faithfully on Christian dramatic forms? Hardison writes that in the mystery cycles, "every event has a past extending back and future extending forward to eternity."[42] The mystery form permits Marxist playwrights to attach a merely human historical process to a Christian sense of time. The Revolution is figured as an eschatological event, standing outside history even as it occurs within it. In *The Baden Play for Learning*, the apocalyptic course of Christian history is assimilated to a revolutionary techno-futurism, even as the airplane, the great secular cruciform of the twentieth century, is haunted by the cross it hopes to replace.

Whether the themes that motivate them are crypto-religious or revolutionary-Marxist, mysterium characters are always in some form governed by an "ancient similitude": in the mysterium, human life can never be, as Wedekind's Marquis von Keith remarks from the vantage point of his own improvised career, "a series of switchbacks." Or not until Beckett. In what we could call the existentialist mysterium, it would almost seem that Beckett has combined the religious allegorical tendencies of the genre with precisely the "one thing after another" dramaturgical philosophy of Brecht. The resulting ambiguity provides the ground on which the mysterium's own oblivion could be staged.

Notwithstanding Beckett's animadversions on allegory in *Proust*, the by now familiar lineaments of the mysterium form are evident in *Waiting for Godot*.[43] Didi and Gogo easily become the journeying Everyman morality figure who appears in every example of the form. Presented as a pair, they stand somewhere between the male couple of traditional comedy and the collective protagonist of the revolutionary mysterium. As the metaphysical Everyman, the collective consciousness of this protagonist dwells on salvation—he/they inhabit the inscrutable realm of "Being" that suffuses traditional allegory.[44] As the "unclean" Everyman, they live in the intractably material body. Their bellies are hungry, their feet are blistered, their kidneys are weak—as if their running jokes on the body also signaled the materialist consciousness of the revolutionary mysterium without its will for change.

Every mysterium I have discussed has contained elements of the biblical mystery cycle—Creation, Fall, the Passion, Last Judgment. *Godot* is suffused with the hope, and the reproach, of the Passion. So much has been written about the level at which the Christian symbolism in *Waiting for Godot* is intended, that there is little merit in re-playing the debate here. The mysterium does not in any event provide evidence of an author's doctrinal commitment; on the contrary, it characteristically uses Christian theatrical models and imagery in such a way as to sustain the image of an ambiguous, thus deeply mysterious, universe. It may suffice here to point to the Passion as a continuing motif in *Godot*, and to Didi and Gogo now as intermittent types of the suffering, abject, and forsaken, Christ; now as his brackets, the two thieves.

In earlier mysteria, two levels of meaning, held in an uneasy, ironic relationship, appeared in the same play, either through the ambiguity of the dramatic treatment, or through discrete dramaturgical elements—a "high road" of religious or mystical import combined with a profane "low road," ranging in style from naturalism to farce. In *Godot* the pattern manifests in a persistent, ironic undercutting, most evident in the "fourth dimension" of theatrical self-reflexivity. This self-observing consciousness operates at the level of the characters' canny awareness of their own role-playing ("at this place, at this moment of time," says Vladimir, "all mankind is us, whether we like it or not"),[45] and also at the structural level, where the reality of characters in their existential situation flickers on and off into the reality of performers in their theatrical situation. Thus the hat tricks, insult routines, and other "numbers" of the music hall. Even the emblematic setting of the play is ironically punctured by reminders that we are, after all, in a theater. In Act One, when Vladimir stumbles offstage to relieve himself, Gogo directs him, "End of the corridor, on the left."

At the level of high seriousness, however, *Waiting for Godot* shares with other mysteria a scenic terrain whose metaphysical import is signaled in the opening directions, "A country road. A tree. Evening." "A road," Per Nykrog writes of this stage direction, "is the archetypal metaphor for a movement, a development, a 'progress.' "[46] Beckett's road, unlike Strindberg's road to Damascus, has lost the metaphysical property, or faculty, of shaping personal redemption. The human journey is no longer a progress. It has become an enormous paralysis of waiting, or is mechanically reversible, as it is for Pozzo and Lucky. The progress is not progressive; redemptive suffering does not redeem. These are represented only by interruption, by their not taking place.

This failure to fulfill the so strongly projected Christian pattern is perfectly imitated in the version of dramatic cyclicality that Beckett alights upon. Though there is, in the Pozzo-Lucky reversal, an echo of the inverse parallelism of the earlier mysteria, Beckett's overall form is that adopted by Kaiser, the diurnal progression. Beckett's day-to-night cycle, with its attendant weight of "standing-for-something," is savagely undermined, however, by the transparently simple stratagem of repeating it. The series of two, like Marx's tragedy of history repeated as farce, conclusively defers redemption by doubling the search. (The move parallels the comic turn that exchanges the mysterium's

Christ/Everyman protagonist for Beckett's two thieves/clowns.) The mysterium structure is set forth in *Godot*, then cut off, and negatively persists like a phantom limb.

Arguably, the metaphysical strain in modernism inaugurated by the symbolists at the turn of the century culminates in Beckett, after whom one might expect it to have played itself out.[47] Yet the mysterium neither terminates at this point nor is confined to Europe, as evidenced by the many mysterium-like performance pieces created by the American postmodern avant-garde, such as Breuer and Telson's *Gospel at Colonus*, the Wooster Group's *Frank Dell's The Temptation of Saint Anthony*, Richard Foreman's *Eddie Goes to Poetry City*, and Meredith Monk's *Atlas*.

One of the most ambitious of the late modern mysteria, and here I conclude my discussion of the genre, is David Cole's *The Moments of the Wandering Jew*.[48] Written in the late 1970s, influenced by both Hegel and Shaw, it is a "chamber epic" that follows the figure of the Wandering Jew from the moment after his alleged affront through two millennia of Western history. The mysterium pattern of the questing Everyman emerges clearly. Cole acknowledges the roots of his form in medieval theater by setting Part III at the site of an Oberammergau-type religious festival play, but modernizes the reference by staging a rehearsal in which different versions of a Wandering Jew play are tried out. The play culminates in a scene of the Last Judgment, represented as a theatrical performance in heaven. However, the Jew's inability to take part, a compound of his historical choice and his historical necessity, results in the cancellation of the supreme eschatological event.

As in earlier mysteria, the motif of the Passion runs through the play, but here it has taken the form of an anti-Passion, created by the Jew in his very act of self-withholding in biblical Jerusalem, and forever recapitulated. The Jew is condemned, and now all humankind with him, to go on forever, neither in, nor outside of, history. With *The Moments of the Wandering Jew*, Beckett's despairing insight, that the journey is endless and redemption eternally deferred, becomes an obstinate faith. The skeptical, ironic dimension of the mysterium no longer subverts its metaphysics; it has become its metaphysics.

Like its medieval prototypes, the mysterium is a metaphysical play whose subject is salvation. The event it seeks is not the recognition of tragedy, the reconciliation of comedy, or the victory of melodrama, but a mysterious transubstantiation: characters shed, or want to shed, the dross of individuality and sometimes corporeality—whatever stands as their particular, painful separation from the larger plan. Anxiously these characters seek a transforming understanding, the "cosmic view of the intrinsic relationships of all objects and beings" as Edwin Honig says of allegory in general.[49] Some of the mysterium's traits may be found in other types of modern plays, but where they coincide, other genre designations—for instance tragicomedy—do not account for them as a totality. What distinguishes the mysterium from its medieval origins and makes it a distinctively modern genre is its ironic self-undermining, sometimes experienced by characters as radical doubt or ambivalence, and often expressed as a structural subversion by the dramaturgy of its own cosmic pretensions.

In the late 1960s, critics and scholars of modern painting began to revalue the occult and spiritual elements in such formative abstractionists as Kandinsky and Mondrian.[50] In an intriguing catalogue article for the 1972 Hayward Gallery retrospective of symbolist painters in London, art historian Alan Bowness suggested an "alternative tradition" of modern art, leading to abstraction not through the impressionists but through Puvis de Chavannes, Moreau, and Redon.[51] The 1986–87 exhibition, "The Spiritual in Art: Abstract Painting 1890–1985," widened the theme, attributing the decades-long tradition of twentieth-century abstract painting not to the purely aesthetic, formalist concerns championed by Alfred Barr and Clement Greenberg, but to the mystical and spiritual intuitions of such pioneers as Munch, Kandinsky, Kupka, Malevich, and Mondrian, and to the "cosmic imagery" of the alchemical, kabbalistic, and occult traditions that lay behind some of their beliefs.[52]

In this chapter I have suggested the possibility of an alternative tradition of modern drama, leading not through the highway of Ibsen's social drama and Zola's naturalism to the dominant realistic tradition, but through the mysteries of the symbolists to the fallen religious world of *Waiting for Godot*. This alternate tradition relied on the allegorical methods of medieval theater and more immediately on the mystery impulse, with its mystical and occult overtones, of *fin-de-siècle* theater.

I have come some distance from the central idea of chapter 1, the decentering of character in the modern theater, yet the connection should by now be clear. The decline of interest in the psychological depth and substantiality of character toward the end of the nineteenth century made room for the emergence of dramaturgies that were not character-generated. I am not suggesting that mysteria are like Treplev's symbolist playlet in *The Seagull*, in which "the bodies of all living creatures have turned to dust." The question is not whether there are living creatures on the stage, but what it is we are following when we engage them. Inwardness and its attendant conflicts, so important to the post-Shakespearean development of modern character, especially to the Romantics and Hegel, have been eclipsed by an abstract teleological patterning. What we follow in the mysterium, its true agent, is the unfolding of the pattern (or, as in *Waiting for Godot*, its failure to unfold).

It is more than a little uncanny to find Cole's Wandering Jew consciously aware of the extent to which he is constituted by such a pattern, and, one might add, by his fundamental need to perceive reality through pattern-making itself. In Cole's play, the Jew's great offense, for which he was exiled to his no-man's-land between history and eternity, was to suddenly see in the passing Christ-staggering-beneath-the-cross an abstract geometric figure. When questioned about his disengagement from "the greatest event in human history," he responds, "Shrank from the encounter? Missed my moment? I tell you, no one ever drew nearer to Him than that!" The Jew's eternal wandering evolves as an effort to discover through the faculty of making patterns in general his own relation to that particular pattern. But in becoming the one to carry the figure for all eternity (when the Christ has left it behind), the Jew becomes its definition. In some sense he *is* the figure; to be a separate, autonomous being who "believes in" meanings that attach to this iconography would merely separate him from them.

Cole's play makes explicit a tendency present in the mysterium from the beginning, the emptying of psychological character into the archaic sense of character as inscription, the making of, or merging with, a sign. From Strindberg's Stranger, whose world is a *via dolorosa* of mysterious inscription, to Beckett's tramps, who scour the trackless waste for a sign, any sign, of order or security, the world of the mysterium is a world of absent presences, represented by the mysterious signatures they leave on time, space, and all relationships. It is in this most fundamental sense that the mysterium owes a continuing debt to the occult revival where it began.

Notwithstanding its place at the front of theatrical modernity, the mysterium often seems to express nostalgia for a lost epoch of human faith. But I see the mysterium in a predictive light as well, as a preparation for the branch of postmodern theater whose concern has been the making of patterns and even the creation of a theatrical geometry. To hear a Robert Wilson, as I have on many occasions, "explain" one of his productions in terms of the relations of dark and light, verticals, horizontals, and diagonals, is to see realized a certain mysticism of visual form already implicit in this twentieth-century genre. In the mysterium, in fact, the shift away from character as an inner essence and the over-arching concern with pattern find expression in a new centrality of the visual. Cole's version of this trait is his character's obsessive tracking of a geometric figure whose meaning cannot be restated in the dramatic text. Beckett's tree on the planet, Artaud's sky-writing in blood, Strindberg's strange repeating beehive—to name only a few of these prominent, yet non-illustrative, images—point in the direction of the post-textual, visual dramaturgy of Wilson, or the occult stage environments, crowded with untrackable meaning, created by Richard Foreman.

The mysterium is a genre that reaches back to the cosmic medieval theater on one end, and forward to the postmodern theater of hyperspace on the other. The mysterium's return to the allegorical via the great allegory of the "perennial wisdom" of the occult is not merely a recuperative gesture, but also a radical new detachment from meaning at the level of the sign. Demonstrating that a witnessed reality is nevertheless not immediately knowable, the mysterium prepares the way for a theater whose audience willingly abandons the demand for a shared known. The mysterium is thus in part a station en route to the new allegorisis of postmodern "conceptual" performance, in which the spectator becomes the organizer and interpreter of patterns, but now without the mediation of a shared set of references, however fractured.

3

Counter-Stagings

Ibsen against the Grain

WHAT HAS CUSTOMARILY been called "modern drama" has long embraced two general lines of critical reading, realist and modernist, along with their respective traditions of theatrical production. Realist criticism and productions have stressed the illusionistic presentation of social and class issues, and, especially in America, of psychological character. Turning away from psychological character, modernist criticism and productions have tended to follow varying combinations of the three routes I sketched in chapter 1: allegorical, critical, and theatricalist.

Ibsen and Strindberg, virtually the inventors, between them, of realism and modernism in the theater, provide in their plays a terrain contested between these two types of criticism. This chapter concerns itself with re-readings of two such classic modern texts, both by Ibsen, from a "post-modern" point of view, *Lady from the Sea*, frequently claimed by the modernist allegorists, and *Hedda Gabler*, still claimed primarily by the realist critics. I momentarily insert a hyphen in the vague yet indispensable word "post-modern" to suggest my use of the term here to emphasize a chronological as well as stylistic connotation: the readings are post-modern to the extent they are no longer engaged within the long-standing realist/modernist quarrel of modern dramatic theory and criticism.

The following readings see the poles of this divide not as doctrinal alternatives, but as coexisting aspects of structures under tension. No value is placed here on resolving these tensions. I would rather see the contradictions suggested by a text struggled over on the stage than find them handily resolved in some smoke-filled theatrical back room. In the case of *The Lady from the Sea* this procedure means reaching back from the Olympian heights of contemporary allegorical readings to revive the realist, character-based, and strongly feminist reading that now "doesn't fit." In the case of *Hedda Gabler* the procedure is very nearly the opposite: to show how the still dominant realist reading has been put under attack by forms of the allegorical and theatricalist thinking I associated with theatrical modernism in chapter 1. Though the arguments I make can be seen as contradictory, my object is consistent: to keep alive in both readings conflicting aspects of the dramatic text. The category of conflict in drama is not exhausted by conflicts between characters.

There has always been a *Lady from the Sea* problem: for a drama of the immaterial, it is too material. Allegorical/realistic, philosophical/psychological: to critics, it has often been too much of the one to be enough of the other. If early critics such as Lou-Andreas Salomé could solve the tension by basically ignoring the symbolic implications of the Stranger, or like Henry James could wish part of the play away ("One winces considerably" at the "pert daughters"), recent Ibsen scholars have attempted to redeem the play with readings that account for both tones of the play, the two water levels (open sea and carp pond) of Ibsen's dramaturgical landscape.[1]

In a brilliant analysis, the Hegelian Brian Johnston has rationalized the play's structure by working all strands of the play through a central philosophical dilemma. This might be stated: the highest yearnings of the human spirit for freedom are in tragic conflict with the demands of organized society.[2] The *pas de trois* among the three central characters—Ellida, Wangel, and the Stranger—becomes a sort of allegory dialectically working out this problematic. But what to do with the "pert daughters"? In Johnston, they become emblems of the human community.

> The community depicted in the play is one animated by yearning, by longing for release from confinement and finitude. It is restless, discontented (Boletta), unhappily malicious (Hilde), or, like Ellida, subject to extreme disorder.[3]

In the end, the "community" cannot stand too much freedom. Thus, "Humanity chooses to remain earthbound, to reject the lure of absolute freedom, and to remain *this* side of the third empire of spirit."[4]

In this resolution, as readers may notice, something gets lost on the way to the universal signifier. The gender of the female characters of the play—degendered here as "community," "it," "humanity"—has become invisible. Johnston is not alone. Perhaps falling into a pathetic fallacy, critics doing "supertextual" readings of the play treat Ibsen's dramaturgy here in much the same way the men in the play treat the women.[5] That is, the women are invisible as autonomous individuals, but flourish as idea, force, symbol, embodiment of desire. As Teresa de Lauretis writes, "In other words, only by denying sexual difference (and gender) as components of subjectivity in real women . . . can the philosophers see in 'women' the privileged repository of 'the future of mankind.' "[6]

In these allegorical readings, Ellida Wangel is caught in a philosophical contest between two opposing forces. These have been figured Freedom vs. Contingency, the Erotic vs. Love, the Infinite vs. the Bounded: all imaged as an opposition of Sea and Land. However it is figured, this central conflict is seen as being embodied in the two men contending for Ellida's allegiance. The central interpretative quarrels about the play concern the opposed values we attach to these men, and the valuation of those values. In such readings, critics discuss the play as if it concerned "The Being from the Sea," the "Species from the Sea," "Modern Western Man from the Sea," and so forth. Ellida Wangel becomes chiefly interesting as the instrument through which certain values triumph and others are crushed.

But there is another, devastating battle of opposing forces below the surface of the action. In this battle the men assert authority and the women struggle for autonomy. *The Lady from the Sea* may be Ibsen's most painful play about the fate of women in male society. It is not only a play about freedom in the metaphysical sense, but about freedom within marriage, and about the way abstract ideals must be shaken when confronted with the bondage of half the race.

Without negating the philosophical debate at the loftier reaches of the play, I would like to restore its concrete social dimension, its gendered specificity. A gendered reading of *The Lady from the Sea* brings many surprises. In it, the transcendent turns ironic, male opponents suddenly appear as allies, and Bolette, the pertest daughter, becomes a figure of near-tragedy. Such a reading starts by acknowledging that the "*fruen*" of the *Fruen fra havet*, Ibsen's Norwegian title, means not just the implied madonna or mermaid (*havfrue*) of the English translation, but also, at the more concrete end of the spectrum of possible meanings, the woman or wife, the just plain Frau from the sea.

Reading for gender, we can see an absence not otherwise visible. Ibsen literalizes (though of course *avant la lettre*) the discovery of feminist semioticians that in narrative structure the subject position of woman is vacant, and "spoken" by men.[7] In the world of Ibsen's play, there is an eerie vacuum in woman's place, even her place as object or other. Wangel lost one wife and can't quite materialize the second. The Stranger lost a fiancée and never recovered. Lyngstrand lost his mother and for consolation lives with the local midwife. Desperate to marry, Arnholm will lie and cheat to get a woman. The Wangel girls need a mother. Ellida's own mother died long ago. The women who do inhabit the starved, male air are almost fleeing their own bodies: Hilda would rather be a boy, Bolette is miserable as a girl, Ellida wants to be a mermaid. Ellida's self-vacancy encourages men to want to own her, sculpt her, possess her will and her speech.

In Ibsen's story, Ellida Wangel's troubles began years ago with the appearance of so-called "Freeman." Most critics uncritically associate Freeman with freedom. Read for metaphysics, Freeman's "freedom" may be a spiritual challenge for the human race, as embodied in Ellida. But read for gender, this freedom turns into compulsion. Ellida had "no will of [her] own" when she was near him, but became engaged because "He said I must."[8] In a trance, she permits herself to think that two rings thrown to sea—his idea, not her agreement—constitute an actual engagement: it was "fated to be."

Years later, she flops out of this commitment and falls into another, apparently just the opposite, but from a gendered perspective very much the same. With Wangel, it is more "he said I must" and "no will of my own." In Act One, Wangel enlists Arnholm, behind Ellida's back, to help the "poor sick child." This is the right approach: "I'm sure of it." Like the Stranger, he ventriloquizes Ellida and induces Arnholm to do the same. In the next scene, Arnholm "helps" Ellida by demanding a kind of speech control. "You must tell me more about this!" he exclaims, and a moment later, "There's no other way: you've got to tell me everything," and still later, "You *must* tell me your troubles, freely and openly."

The act culminates in Lyngstrand's account of the "betrayal" of the American sailor Johnson (alias "Freeman") by his fiancée. "She's mine, and mine she'll always be"—so Lyngstrand recalls Freeman's outburst on the merchant steamer—"And if I go home and fetch her, she'll have to go off with me." Lyngstrand may be weak and young, but never too young and weak to enjoy the dominant discourse. Thus Lyngstrand has fantasies of an archetypal scene of erotic domination on the sailor's return: he "stands there over her bed, looking down at her . . . dripping wet." Deftly, Lyngstrand attributes his own sexual fantasy to the sleeping woman. Her guilt, not his desire, has summoned this spirit from the vasty deep.

In Act Two, Ellida attempts to explain Freeman to Wangel, while her kindly husband continuously resorts to unconscious condescension or compulsion. Full of mistaken certainty, he says "I think I understand."

"But you don't" she exclaims.

"Yes I do," he perseveres. He has "seen the whole thing, down to the bottom."

"Don't be too sure," she protests.

"You can't bear these surroundings," he insists, "We're moving away."

Over her objections, Wangel has decided. "It's all settled now." Ellida forces him to listen to her story. After a moment he jumps in again, "I begin to understand."

"No dear, you're wrong!" she corrects him, but finally he is sure again—this time that she's crazy: "much more than I thought," and heavily adds, more "than you can possibly know."

In Act Three, the scene changes from a vista of the distant sea to a close-up of a stagnant carp pond. Critics have likened the contrasting scenography to the difference between the landlocked Bolette and her sea-free stepmother, or between the two Wangel sisters. The women of the play may be at sea or on a pond, but as the old joke has it, they are in the same boat when it comes to the struggle for female autonomy.

Poor, maligned Bolette—whom Francis Fergusson calls "green" because she doesn't want instantly to marry the manipulative Arnholm![9] Bolette carries all the duties of the Wangel household patiently, but wants more than anything in life to learn, to attend the university as Father once promised. At last she permits herself to flare, "I have obligations to myself!" for which Prof. Fergusson dismisses her as "self-absorbed."[10] Disingenuously shifting onto Bolette responsibility for her own predicament, Arnholm assures her she can have anything she wants if only she wants it enough. "It depends completely on you," he tells her, "The whole thing is there, right in your own hands." But Bolette sees where the power lies. "[Put] in a good word for me with Father," she implores Arnholm. Bolette's freedom must be arranged, like—and probably through—a marriage. There is no such thing as an unmediated freedom, a freedom by birthright, for a woman. All the women share this knowledge. Even Hilda, young as she is, knows the facts of women's lives. The road to freedom is paved with husbands, preferably dead ones. In fact (Hilda's famous bridal fantasy), why not attend your own wedding in widow's weeds?

Arnholm has two excellent chances to speak to Wangel about Bolette, but knowing that any guarantee of independence will scotch his marriage plans, he does just the opposite when the opportunity presents itself. "You hardly need to worry about Bolette," he tells Wangel, who says he would make any sacrifice for his daughters, "if I only knew what." When Bolette asks whether he has talked over her needs with her father, Arnholm flatly lies: "Yes, I've done that . . . you mustn't be counting on any help from him." So powerful is the momentum of the supertextual for Johnston, however, that he must disregard this evidence and beatify Arnholm as a practitioner of "self-sacrificing" Christian love.[11]

For Arnholm, and all the other men, autonomy for women is literally unthinkable, at least until Act Five. In this world woman cannot be figured as other than a spirito-erotic furnishing of the male mind. Thus even when Bolette explains that Arnholm was mistaken about her supposed passion for him, he says, "It's no help, Bolette. Your image—as I carry it within me—will always be colored by those mistaken emotions." And so Bolette is maneuvered into marriage. She tries to negotiate a narrow zone of self-determination. "I can study anything I want," she reminds him, after dubiously rising to the bait at the edge of the carp pond. He answers, ever so smoothly, "I'll teach you, just as I used to." No sooner has a stutter of agreement to marry this unsavory person, at least sixteen years her senior, crossed Bolette's lips, than he slides into an obtuse intimacy, "Ah, wait till you see how easy and comfortable we'll be with each other," he murmurs, his arm oiling around her waist. "The progress of their affair," writes Fergusson of this gynicide, "is hardly worth the clear, sober light, and the long stage-time, that Ibsen devotes to it." Chekhov, he says, knew how to handle such commonplace love affairs "by presenting them very briefly, and without asking the audience to take their outcomes too seriously."[12]

Orley Holtan thinks "five alternative ways of life" are offered in the play, each represented by a male figure.[13] Laying aside Holtan's uncritical assertion of male signifying power, one must at least conclude that he misses Ibsen's savage irony. Thus Holtan believes Arnholm's adaptive "realism," rather than Bolette's crushed life, is Ibsen's interest. Holtan also thinks Ibsen ridicules Lyngstrand as a "helpless dreamer," as if his "dreams" were not supported, however parodically, by a solid foundation of far from helpless male privilege.[14] If the Stranger, Wangel, and Arnholm all hold inflated, narcissistic views of male power in marriage, Lyngstrand differs only in his inability to act them out. "Marriage," he confides to Bolette,

> has to be accounted almost a kind of miracle. The way a woman little by little makes herself over until she becomes like her husband. . . . A woman must feel a profound happiness in that. . . . That she can help [her husband] to cre-ate . . . that she can ease his work for him by being there and making him comfortable and taking care of him and seeing that his life is really enjoyable. I think that must be thoroughly satisfying for a woman.

Apart from their own slowly awakening powers, the only hope for women in this play is Dr. Wangel. Ibsen shows how hard it is for Wangel to learn, how excruciating the pressure must be for him to learn even a little, and what a victory it must be accounted when he makes even the first step. In Act Three the two contenders for Ellida's allegiance meet face to face and debate to whom she "belongs." The Stranger is as peremptory as ever—"Be ready to travel to-morrow night"—but he throws Ellida a lifeline in the form of a new idea: "Imagine," she marvels, "he said I should go with him of my own free will." It has never occurred to her that she had such a thing to exercise. Overnight, the idea grows. She didn't enter marriage of her own free will, she sees. "Every-thing came together in those words—like a beam of light—and I can see things now, as they are." Wangel is melancholy. "You've never belonged to me—never." The standard of possession is the opposite of the standard of personal freedom that Ellida is proposing. She wants an unequivocal return of her freedom of choice. Wangel cannot do it. Or, he'll do it tomorrow, after the danger has passed. But by then, Ellida cries, "The future I was meant for may have been ruined—a whole, full life of freedom ruined, wasted. . . . "

We must understand what these words mean coming from a woman. Holtan recounts the story told by Ibsen's biographer Halvdan Koht, that shortly before writing *The Lady from the Sea*, Ibsen "heard of a local girl who, appar-ently out of frustration and unfulfilled longing to get out into the world and be a poet, had shot herself. This incident so fascinated Ibsen," he goes on, "that he called at her home, obtained pictures of her, read the books she left behind, and even visited her grave."[15] If we persist in reading Ellida as a universal being (that is, as a man), we cannot understand her sense of terrible injustice, what it would mean to suffer "a whole full life of freedom ruined, wasted." Hers will be an abstract plaint, philosophically interesting perhaps, but which of us achieves absolute freedom in a human life? But read for gender this cry states the anguished preoccupation of Ellida, Bolette, and most women who reflect on their condition: they want *their* possibility of freedom, not only humanity's in some abstract sense.

One of Ibsen's great spiritual traits is that he never gives up on human growth. Wangel undergoes a phenomenal growth for a limited and decidedly unheroic man. In a remarkable breakthrough at the last instant, he dissolves the contract. "Now you can choose your own path—in full freedom. I mean it—with all my miserable heart." Ellida is amazed, "You can let this be?" "Yes I can. Because I love you so much." That does begin to sound like love; that is, reverence for another consciousness. It is, in its homely way, an expression of a man's love for a woman unparalleled in dramatic literature. And then the words with which Ellida grows past her inchoate drive for freedom. Wangel: "Now you can choose in freedom—on your own responsibility."

We recall Ellida's new knowledge of Act Three: that she might exercise her own free will. Again, Ellida is incredulous. "Responsible to myself! Responsible! How this—transforms everything." Throughout the agonized attraction to the Stranger, Ellida didn't have a self to be responsible to. No wonder she was terrified. Romantic transcendence may be fine for an Egmont, stuffed and wearied with self, but Ellida Wangel, gendered as a woman, can't become nobody without being somebody first. For the woman, if not the symbol, choosing land represents growth.

Now comes a telling detail. It is only after his great renunciation and Ellida's assumption of self-responsibility that Wangel for the first time in five acts actually asks Ellida what she wants instead of announcing what she needs. "Will you be coming back to me Ellida?"

The decision Ellida has made is as much about the girls as about her husband. The relationship with Wangel will be far from perfect. (Notice his regression when after all he's learned, he tells Arnholm that Ellida is not leaving for Skjoldvik because "We changed our minds this evening.") But the relationship with the girls has the promise of creativity, especially with Hilda, for whom Ellida finally reaches out.

There was an earlier scene of female alliance, the only other one in the play. At the beginning of Act One, Bolette and Hilda joined briefly in a secret birthday celebration for their dead mother. But this alliance also demonstrated a rift between women; keeping faith with the girls' first mother meant deceiving their second. Women do not again join forces in this woman-depleted environment until the final moments of the play, when Ellida is able to offer Hilda the "one small expression of love" Bolette says she has been longing for. (How different from the behavior of Wangel and Arnholm, who easily support and consult each other at every turn.) Almost all contemporary critics regard the ending of *The Lady from the Sea* as a choice between philosophical positions embodied by male figures; many note as well the comic device of the coupled ending. The same-gender reconciliation at the end of the play has largely escaped critical notice, despite the fact that the connection between Ellida and Hilda represents a significant realignment of affections in the world of the play.

I do not offer the feminist exegesis as a replacement for Johnston's or others' readings. I think the play is most interestingly served by keeping alive its contradictions and conflicts. I would even argue that in the opening scene of Act One, Ibsen sets us off in both directions at once. When Wangel discovers his daughters' secret observance of their mother's birthday, Bolette explains with a wink and a nod, "Can't you imagine how we went and did all this for Mr. Arnholm's sake. When such a good old friend comes back to visit. . . ." Apparently, there are alternate possible readings of the festive signs of flag and flowers that decorate the stage. These readings correspond to narrative types that have their immemorial gendered associations. One is a variant of the hero's return (even if the "hero" is only Arnholm, and his hero's journey is only a modest progress from southern town to northern sea resort). The other concerns a domestic ritual commemorating the dead and celebrating family lineage through the maternal line. Perhaps these readings can be taken as trail markers, set out by Ibsen to point a somewhat more complex route through the play than either its admirers or its detractors usually take.

Like the Act One celebration, the play too has its heroic and its domestic signs, its universalizing "cover story," and its concrete, gendered reality. In a gendered reading of *The Lady from the Sea*, a subtext boiling with woman's struggle for autonomy itself struggles to be recognized against the claims of Ibsen's "supertext," which enacts the clash of freedom and contingency worked through scenographic opposites and male antagonists. In the supertextual reading of *The Lady from the Sea*, the debate between Sea and Land, with their manifold associations, becomes a romantic search for a transcendent principle to govern human existence. Both the question the play puts and the dialectic through which an answer emerges fall into the binary logic of the metaphysical inquiry.

Feminist critiques of such "logocentric" argumentation have been levelled in many fields. One of the first was published by Hélène Cixous in 1975:

> Everywhere (where) ordering intervenes . . . a law organizes what is thinkable by oppositions (dual, irreconcilable; or sublatable, dialectical). And all these

pairs of oppositions are *couples*. Does that mean something? Is the fact that logocentrism subjects thought—all concepts, codes and values—to a binary system, related to "the" couple, man/woman? We see that "victory" always comes down to the same thing. . . . Subordination of the feminine to the masculine order. . . . Now it has become rather urgent to question this solidarity between logocentrism and phallocentrism. . . . What would happen to logocentrism, to the great philosophical systems . . . if some fine day, it suddenly came out that the logocentric plan had always . . . been to create a foundation for . . . phallocentrism, to guarantee the masculine order a rationale equal to history itself. *So all the history, all the stories would be there to retell differently.* [Emphasis mine.][16]

Ibsen's play is among the myriad stories "there to retell differently." The play's gender conflict makes no ontological claims and asserts no inalienable first principles. The questions it poses are who has power, over whom is it exercised, and how should the balance be righted. Does the gendered reading supplant the metaphysical, or can the two readings coexist? It seems to me possible that Ibsen, the withering ironist, in a deflationary move, may have intended to set ontological freedom and women's freedom in conflict. He pits the abstract "truth" of "man's" longing for freedom against the social fact of female subjection, the uncomfortable detail that puts the idealist vocabulary into question.[17]

The modern champions of Ibsen, determined not to let their man sink into realism's banalities, have based their readings on transhistorical symbolic systems: Orley Holtan reads Ibsen against myth, Brian Johnston reads him against Hegel. I don't want to supplant these mythic or metaphysical readings, but I do want to put them into the context of a fresh dialectic, undermining their "truth force" while allowing them to stand as a stage in the archeology of culture that is never, in any event, far from Ibsen's dramatic concerns. My own reading permits conflicting elements of Ibsen's dramaturgy to emerge, and even regards such conflicts as deliberate rather than as the playwright's "failure" to totalize his dramatic scheme by reconciling its contradictions.

Critics marvel at the reversibility of *The Lady from the Sea*: we can read it as an argument for the sea values or for the land values, and it works either way! Of course it does, operating within the overdetermined dualities of the systematic reading. But the play does not merely embody "signs against signs," as Arnholm says of Wangel's predicament in Act Four, it embodies sign *systems* against sign systems, advancing an ironic, mutually relativizing, bi-focal vision of human culture. Charles Lyons has written that Ibsen habitually puts his protagonist into "a situation which reveals his divided consciousness."[18] It is a step beyond that to find the structural consciousness of the play more divided than that of the protagonist.

To Johnston, Ibsen marks in this play a human defeat, a moment when mankind shrinks back to the land, with all its associations of boundedness. Much evidence in the play supports such a conclusion.[19] Yet suppose we set against that ending another ending and a different moment in human history, when woman finally emerges from the waters—from the amniotic fluid, the Imaginary, the consignment to the pre-oedipal—and begins the process of discovering her own subjecthood. Different evidence in the play supports this conclusion. Indeed, relying on this evidence, realist critics (affirming marriage and responsibility) initially regarded Ellida's final decision as a positive act.[20] Such evidence doesn't destroy a supertextual reading such as Johnston's; but it relativizes it, revealing it as a carrier of the very values it discovers in the text.

If both readings can be sustained, the metaphysical and the gendered, the play would extraordinarily prefigure the postmodern paradigm collision of our own cultural moment today. Coincidentally, the *Lady from the Sea* "problem," with which this discussion began, would perhaps dissolve into a new historical perspective. M. C. Bradbrook's mid-century complaint that Ibsen had set his own poetic vision in opposition to itself, her criticism that "there is a contradiction at the basis of the play," becomes unwitting insight.[21]

Hedda Gabler would appear to be far less compliant than *The Lady from the Sea* with a "post-modern" reading. The play has typically been treated as Ibsen's drama par excellence of realistic character, as if Ibsen had set the critical mold for all time when he commented, in a letter written to Moritz Prozor shortly after the play's completion, "What I principally wanted to do was to depict human beings, human emotions and human destinies, upon a ground work of certain of the social conditions and principles of the present day."[22] But a journey through *Hedda Gabler* criticism, especially since 1970, will actually show the steps by which this play, once considered "realistic in a far stricter sense," according to the Norwegian critic Edvard Beyer, than any of the plays written since *A Doll's House*,[23] is being converted into a mythic allegory and a theatricalist play of masks, the very moves, as I argued in chapter 1, adopted by modern non-realist playwrights as they followed in the wake of Nietzsche's war on bourgeois character. This section of my discussion, then, is less a reading of the play than a reading of the readings that have been taking the play along this surprising but perhaps not altogether unforeseeable route.

Well after the post–World War II change in Ibsen criticism that Charles Lyons describes as the re-validation of "Ibsen the poet," *Hedda Gabler* continued resistant to the discovery of the symbolic landscapes, mythic actions, and romantic quests with which modern critics countered the social and psychological realists.[24] As late as 1970, Orley Holtan wrote of the play, "Here there is no mysterious duck, no shadowy world of the unknown, no white horse, no demon lover from the sea."[25] Still, Errol Durbach's first study of Hedda as assuming "Godhead as mysterious and profound as that of Oedipus in the grove at Colonus" was published in 1971.[26] By the mid- to late-1970s, many other critics were exploring the play from a substantially non-realist perspective, working out in considerable detail classical or other mythic structures of imagery and action.

My own contribution to this approach came in a paper read at the Ibsen Sesquicentennial Conference at the Pratt Institute in 1978.[27] There I argued that beneath the realistic and parodic surface of the play are being enacted the archaic mysteries: the fertility-rite sacrifice of the god-king and his replacement by another, presided over by the goddess in triple aspect. The three female figures involved with Lovberg's fate who constellate the "goddess" have newly assembled in the town at the time of harvest, September. They are Thea, nymph, far from sensuality on her mountain-top; Mlle Diana, orgiast, triumphant in the middle region of town and valley; and Hedda, crone and Hecate figure, drawn to the underworld and death, or as Ibsen noted, to "Subterranean forces and powers. . . . Woman as a mine-worker."[28] Other mythic readers have derived Brynhild and Ariadne narratives from the imagery of *Hedda Gabler*.[29]

It is not my purpose here to advance the cause of a particular mythic reading, or even of such readings in general, but to point to their common participation in what I identify in chapter 2 as the modern re-allegorization of drama. Wary of realism and its characterological focus, the mythic readers share the assumption that the interplay between mythic and realistic levels "creates an intelligibility for the play that neither alone sustains."[30] What had provided ample intelligibility for the first wave of Ibsen critics is sufficient no longer, a judgment on realism that these critics do not hesitate to project back onto Ibsen himself. As Nina da Vinci Nichols writes, "once granted its function as a scheme of organization, Ibsen's myth . . . releases him from the . . . obligation to provide his characters with rounded or psychological motivation."[31]

Seeking a new unifying aesthetic principle after realistic character loses its unquestioned dominance in the dramatic scheme, Ibsen's mythic critics appear to be fashioning here a version of the post-Nietzschean dramaturgy theorized by the symbolists and performed by the mysterium writers. They shift the unifying principle away from character per se and onto the synchronous relationship between or among levels of interpretation. Nichols underscores this allegoric principle of "intelligibility" when she says of Ibsen's technique in *Hedda Gabler*, "myth and form tend to *correspond* [emphasis mine] rather than oppose each other."[32]

Modern gives on to postmodern when the coherence of levels is perceived to break down. But surely *Hedda Gabler*, of all texts, would successfully resist this further descent into the maelstrom of postmodernism! What could a play of such romantic depth, and at the same time severe symmetries, have to do with postmodernism's blank play of surfaces, erasure of psychological character, and refusal of unity? Even for *The Lady from the Sea* only the latter was claimed. Yet as if appearing punctually for an appointment, Philip Larson offered just such a reading in a paper delivered at the International Ibsen Seminar in Munich in 1983. In "French Farce Conventions and the Mythic Story Pattern in *Hedda Gabler*: A Performance Criticism," Larson asserts that in Ibsen's plays, the "illusion of realism is the product of a highly detailed artifice." An "enormous repertoire" of "dramatic conventions and literary materials" permits the playwright to fashion texts that, far from engaging in a naive realism, are actually "written in code."[33]

Like the mythic and supertextual critics before him, Larson claims to be retrieving authorial intention. However, just as the influence of Frye is discernable in the earlier critics, the contemporary interest in intertextuality and Roland Barthes's "chattering of the codes" is apparent in Larson. He reads *Hedda Gabler* through an intercutting of two principal "texts" or genres. One is the narrative pattern of the Brynhild story from the *Volsungasaga*; the other is the structure and style of the well-made play in its variant as French bedroom farce.[34] Larson not only effectively sidelines the questions of psychological motivation and gender, but goes so far as to assert that serious production errors have been made by "imposing an alien theory of psychology on the characters."[35] Instead of searching for the deep motivation in Hedda, Larson sees her as pure surface, "based on the model of the masked actor." She is "an actress" of whom one could not say that "one style is more 'true' . . . than another."[36]

Larson is not quite clear on whether the heroine of saga functions on a track independent of the masked actress of the French farce, or whether, as masked actress, Hedda plays the saga heroine as one of her roles. If the former, the play's allegorical dimension continues, but now floats unmoored from its surface narrative level, a strangely disunifying step. And if the latter, the only place where all the central character's personae meet is on the ground of theater and performance, making this play of consummate realism into a kind of meta-theater. In my final chapter, I identify this "scene of theater" as the groundless "ground" of the postmodern transition.

Hedda Gabler provides an unexpected lens through which the stages of inward, romantic character's progressive de-realization can be charted. Indeed, the play has turned into a palimpsest of critical trends, to the extent that in exactly a century this drama, with whose heroine Lou Salomé could quarrel as if in a dispute with an ideologically incorrect classmate, has been transformed into a collision of formal genre quotations and stylistic surfaces.[37] At this point, many readers and spectators may be tempted to rejoin that despite the fashion show of critical paradigms, *Hedda Gabler* still appears to belong more to the world of Hegel and the inwardness and fullness of romantic character than the world of Nietzsche, with his allegories of gods and horror of "character representation." Yet *Hedda* was published in 1890, the very year I locate, in chapter 1, as a watershed between theatrical epochs, and further, the play does appear to be directly influenced by the very text of Nietzsche that I have associated with the new epoch, *The Birth of Tragedy*. To take one further step down this path, I am led to wonder whether the virus of Nietzsche's own cultural archeology in that essay doesn't lurk in the play, and whether that very hidden trait has not led to its constant re-readings.

No one knows how direct a relationship to claim between *The Birth of Tragedy* and *Hedda Gabler*.[38] No evidence has been brought forward that Ibsen actually read Nietzsche's original text. Evert Sprinchorn has argued, in a fascinating article, that Ibsen was almost certainly aware of the content of Brandes's introductory lectures on Nietzsche, delivered in Copenhagen in the spring of 1888, and of the furor they engendered through their dissemination in the Danish journal *Tilskueren*. The debate between Brandes and the liberal humanist philosopher Harald Hoffding over Nietzsche's "aristocratic radicalism" raged until May of 1890, concluding just before Ibsen's intensive work on *Hedda Gabler* that summer and fall.[39]

However, Brandes devoted only a paragraph to *The Birth of Tragedy*, and even there misleadingly claimed an "antithesis" between, rather than an interdependence of, Apollonian and Dionysian in tragic art. Further, Brandes makes scarcely a reference to the text's (even) larger theme, the epochal shift in Hellenic culture after Socrates and its contemporary consequences.[40] Perhaps the references in the play to Dionysus—the "vine leaves," the "orgy," the sacrificial dismemberment and scattering at sea of the manuscript, the "wild dance"—could have been spun from Brandes.[41] However, the contest between Tesman and Lovberg, which Sprinchorn reads as an adaptation of the Brandes-Hoffding debate, also suggests that Ibsen was writing from a direct knowledge of Nietzsche.

Like Nietzsche himself in *The Birth of Tragedy*, the male antagonists in *Hedda Gabler* study the "history of civilization." There could be only one outcome in a true intellectual duel between the plodding Tesman, student of the handicrafts of Brabant in the Middle Ages, and the visionary Lovberg, author of an original new work on the "civilization of the future." That contest, bruited in Act One, never comes to pass. Instead, the unstable Lovberg loses to the pedantic Tesman in the course of a single night, a settlement made irrevocable not by Lovberg's drunkenness, the loss of his manuscript, or even really his death, but by Hedda's ritual *auto-da-fé*, the burning of the manuscript. From that moment in the world of the play, the torch of civilization has passed from the future to the past, from the visionary, that is, to the philologist, whose thorough but unimaginative scholarship will become civilization's only means of access to an unrecoverable work of genius. The symmetry between the shape of this plot and the shape of Nietzsche's argument is startling.

In Nietzsche, Socrates represents the great watershed of Western culture.

Before Socrates, Nietzsche posits "tragic" or "artistic" culture, the cultural moment when the dream force of Apollo is poised in balance with the ecstatic energies of Dionysus. With the intervention of the great rationalist, however, comes a terrible "cheerfulness." His spirit "combats Dionysian wisdom and art, it seeks to dissolve myth, it substitutes for a metaphysical comfort an earthly consonance . . . it believes that it can correct the world by knowledge, guide life by science, and actually confine the individual within a limited sphere of solvable problems."[42] Nietzsche's settled term for this age and its human type is "Alexandrian," the man "who is at bottom a librarian and corrector of proofs, and wretchedly goes blind from the dust of books and printers' errors."[43] Tesman of course is just such a cheerful, optimistic Alexandrian, a "specialist" as Hedda contemptuously calls him, who likes nothing "better than grubbing around in libraries and copying out old parchments."

If Tesman is Nietzsche's Alexandrian man, does it follow that Lovberg is his Dionysian/Apollonian, the representative of tragic or "artistic" culture? Despite the combination in his name of the Dionysian vine and the Apollonian mountain, some critics see in him only the parody of his classic traits in drunkenness and teetotaling. Without denying that Ibsen mocked the archetypal pretensions of his characters, I am also willing to believe (and it makes the play more interesting to believe) that Lovberg's manuscript was truly "one of the most remarkable things ever written," as Tesman explains, remarkable precisely for arising from some direct experience of Dionysian abandon and Apollonian control.

In Nietzsche, the Dionysian/Apollonian moment, like Lovberg, "commits suicide," and not beautifully either, willfully abandoning its own authentic genius to the new ethos.[44] Nietzsche called the post-Socratic order "Alexandrian" because the later Hellenic culture excelled in science and scholarship, attainments symbolized by the city of Alexandria and its vast library. The Alexandrian spirit triumphs in *Hedda Gabler* after the burning of the manuscript, as central an event in the world of the play as the great fire that destroyed the library in the late third century A.D. The loss of Lovberg's work promotes the reconstructive effort that consolidates, like a turbid gel, the Tesmanite culture of earnest scholasticism.

In my discussion of Nietzsche in chapter 1, however, dramatic character, rather than cultural archeology, was central. Nietzsche's contempt for "the death leap into the bourgeois drama," and its world "shattered into [comic] individuals," may well lie in the background of this most ironically bourgeois dramatic structure and set of characters Ibsen ever created.[45] Is Hedda nostalgic for the archaic pre-shattered world when she inveighs against this "tight little world I've stumbled into. . . . So utterly ludicrous!"? "Alexandrian" on the surface, and "tragic" at a deeper level, manifestly populated by shrunken bourgeois and comic individuals on the surface, yet in its depths by the dying gods, *Hedda*

Gabler can almost be said to enact Nietzsche's encapsulated themes, the death of tragic drama through "character representation," and the decline of culture through the rationalistic spirit of inquiry. In this quasi-allegorical structure, psychological character is a normative theatrical language only within the cultural period it reflects. Indeed, the ability of critics in the past twenty years or so to see a sunken symbolic continent beneath the psychological plane, or a brittle play of masks on top of it, may itself signal a weakening of confidence in psychological subjectivity.

Hedda Gabler seems slyly to forecast what I have called the re-allegorization of modern drama, both through its own double structure, and the doubling of that structure in its reflection of an external text. The different cultural and structural pulls in *Hedda Gabler*, and its peculiar openness—for such an apparently realistic play—to various anti-realist readings, are implications of its quasi-allegorical design, winched out of its own obsessive concern, by turns nostalgic and remorselessly ironic, with the changing epistemes of Western culture. It is not so surprising after all that the play seems to have become a barometer of critical change.

The two "re-readings" of this chapter are intended in the most direct way to be understood theatrically: they are not meant as exercises in "Alexandrian" thinking. The plays of Ibsen have almost always been produced on the stage with an interest in consistency and unity to which many interesting issues of form have fallen victim. Perhaps it is time to de-classicize the works of "classical modernism." A postmodern approach would not only open plays to the entire perspectival range of postmodern criticism, but especially seek out in them clashes among perspectives that will keep audiences awake, and the works themselves alive.[46]

PART II

Theater after Modernism

4

Signaling through the Signs

Thus one can read above the portals of modernity such
inscriptions as . . . "Here only what is written is understood."

—Michel de Certeau, *The Practice of Everyday Life*[1]

I reswallowed an alphabet.

—Richard Foreman, *The Mind King*[2]

MY TITLE BORROWS of course from the great mystic-theorist of the theater, Antonin Artaud, who wrote that artists must be "like victims burnt
at the stake, signalling through the flames."[3] Near death, the victim is never
more intensely alive. Her entire Being is compressed into this moment only.
And in this moment she sends her message. She has no leisure for mere speech,
she is past speech, or perhaps pre-speech. She relies on the urgent, mute signal,
on the total signifying power of her pain-vivified body. And we, who seize upon
this signal, likewise have only this single moment in which to grasp it, for it
cannot be repeated. The artist-victim's absolute presence is almost unbearably
intensified by proximity to its other, the absolute absence of death. Compacted
in Artaud's unforgettable image is the entire aspiration to presence in the theater, and by extension proposed in it also, under cover of an end to dualism, yet
another "solution" to the long struggle in Western metaphysics between body
and mind, action and reflection.

Thirty years later, in the 1960s, a new generation of theater artists—Jerzy
Grotowski in Poland, Peter Brook in England and Paris, Julian Beck and Judith
Malina wandering Europe, Joseph Chaikin, André Gregory and Richard
Schechner in the United States (the early Meredith Monk might be included as
a transitional figure)—created theaters and theater pieces that took on this vi-
sion as instructions for actors. The Living Theatre and its *Paradise Now!*
Schechner's *Dionysus in '69*, Grotowski and his "actor-saint," and Chaikin's
Open Theatre in different ways sought Artaud's "culture without space or
time," the zero-degree revelation of an Artaudian presence.[4] Chaikin's 1972
book, *The Presence of the Actor*, uses the very term in its title. For him, too, the

image was fire: the theater event should seek to "burn into time as a movement cuts into space."[5]

The sense of presence in the theater has always had two overlapping, but still separable components, the "double 'now'" of which Thomas Whitaker writes:[6] one relates to the dramatic narrative as embodied in the total *mise-en-scène*. Here, the narrative becomes so present as to be happening *now*. The other has to do specifically with the circle of heightened awareness in the theater flowing from actor to spectator and back that sustains the dramatic world. But never before the 1960s generation of practitioners had the two realms so nearly merged, at least not in a secular theater. Never before, also, had the dramatic text been looked upon as the enemy, rather than the vehicle, of theatrical presence. Inspired by Artaud's rejection of the "masterpiece" and by Grotowski's training, many theaters came to regard the author's script as an element of political oppression in the theatrical process, demanding submission to external authority. *Ex tempore* speech, or even better, pure sound that bubbled up from the depths of the actor, was more trustworthy than the alien written word. Chaikin describes an acting project in 1968 that involved escaping from the restrictions of "beautiful" and "natural" speech in order to "be in touch with parts of ourselves which are as yet unformed."[7] The turn away from the perceived restrictions of language led to attempts to slip the constricting knot of rational language altogether, such as Brook's famous *Orghast* experiment, Serban and Swados's re-invention of a chanted, primitive Greek in their *Fragments of a Greek Trilogy*, or Meredith Monk's syllabic vocalization in her *Education of the Girlchild*. Above all, there was a belief that the self, plumbed deeply enough, contained all mysteries. "I have reached into my entrails and strewn them about the stage in the form of questions," wrote Julian Beck.[8]

Critics and scholars who followed in the wake of such theater in the 1970s extolled theatrical presence as had no previous generation, presenting it in almost religious terms. In *The Actor's Freedom*, Michael Goldman identifies presence as the unique informing attribute of all theater. In the theater, he writes, "we find a present beyond the limitations of the present, a selfhood beyond the limits of self. . . . We identify with actors because the self longs for clarification, because it longs to possess the present and possess itself in the present, in a way that ordinary space, time, and selfhood do not allow."[9] The exalted goal served by the actor was nothing less than the recuperation of full Reality, the true Presence of divinity. As Julian Beck put it, quoting Eric Gutkind, "God is absent because we are absent."[10]

One may wonder whether the cry for presence was not the cry of an endangered species; for this ontological theater of the unlimited, stripped-bare, sacred Self was already being superseded in the late sixties and early seventies by a new experimental theater that formalized the actor, broke off his ritual communion with the spectator, strictly controlled his effect in a total *mise-en-scène*, and in various ways went about interrupting the satisfactions of theatrical presence. In 1975, for instance, Mabou Mines brought before a New York theater audience the triple bill of Beckett stagings the group had been performing in galleries and museums since 1970. Instead of seeing three actors physically present in Beckett's "Come and Go," as the author's directions indicate, the audience gradually realized that it was seeing only their ghostly reflections. A mirror nearly the width of the stage, sunk slightly below platform level, then angled back and upwards, caught the images of performers who were actually located in a balcony above and behind the spectators' heads. Lee Breuer's staging frustrated traditional audience expectations of bodily presence and actor-audience contact, yet achieved through this bold stroke the spirit of the mystery and abstraction Beckett calls for in his notes to the play.[11]

In quite another way, Robert Wilson's marathon spectacles also moved away from the actor-spectator loop of realized presence. The fascinated spectators who attended a twelve-hour dusk to dawn *The Life and Times of Joseph Stalin* at the Brooklyn Academy of Music in 1973, for instance, were surprised to find that they were literally permitted to be absent: walking in and out of the performance, eating, napping, wandering visually, and daydreaming were all accepted behaviors in the theater. Further, Wilson used amateur performers who did not fill the aesthetic surface with the charismatic projections usually associated with stage presence.[12] Wilson's audience was learning to relinquish the psychological self that Goldman assumes (the self "longs for clarification") in order to become non-self, a porous receiver to a diffuse field of sensory impressions. (The landscape metaphor is more cogent for Wilson than the ontological.) In short, the old bargain of theatrical presence between spectacle and spectator was being re-thought on both sides of the "curtain."

There are many ways to think about the revision of the ideal of theatrical presence, and different arenas in which to examine it. My discussion here begins from a traditional base: my concern is primarily with dramatic form. I will keep in mind Keir Elam's definition of drama—"An *I* addressing a *you here* and *now*" (Elam's emphasis)—as the foundation of the effect of presence in that form.[13] My particular interest is the undermining of the presence-effect in contemporary plays and dramatic performance pieces through the infiltration of what has traditionally been the banished "other" of dramatic performance—the written text itself. My focus may at first seem almost dry and technical. Who really cares whether actors open books and read aloud onstage, or whether playwrights insert quotations from one of their works in the text of another? But I believe that the reading/writing topic provides an opening through which to glimpse the course of the postmodern tearing at the banks of dramatic form. The works that incorporate such forms of regressive (or, depending on one's point of view,

intrusive) discourse show in still another way the accommodation of theater to the de-authentication, the "absencing" in some sense, of the speaking
subject.

My approach has been influenced by discussions of "presence" in another
field entirely, the attack on the Western metaphysical tradition by the French
philosopher Jacques Derrida, especially in three major works: *Speech and Phenomena*, *Of Grammatology*, and *Writing and Difference*. I don't make the
claim that any of the playwrights or directors I discuss has been influenced by
Derrida, though both the encyclopedic Daryl Chin and philosophical omnivore
Richard Foreman are familiar with his writing. Rather, I see in Derrida a cultural indicator: his deconstructions were quickly grasped because the basic
metaphysical and, by extension, ontological assumptions they attacked had long
since been undermined, certainly since Nietzsche. Derrida's work both revealed
and accelerated the process. Almost incidentally, Derrida opened a theoretical
route to the new theater, where old vocabularies of plot and character had lost
their interpretative power. Thus these reflections could be thought of in part
as a thinking about theater both after and "after" Derrida. Though many of
my readers are by now familiar with Derridean deconstruction, I briefly rehearse
its main tenets here in order to prepare some of its implications for theater.

Well before the "aura" of theatrical presence, to use Benjamin's wonder-
fully resonant term,[14] came into question as a theatrical value, Derrida was submitting its philosophical base to relentless interrogation. "On the stage it is
always now," wrote Thornton Wilder half a century ago.[15] But Derrida challenged the assumption that it is within the power of human nature to enter a
Now, to become entirely present to itself. To Derrida, there is no primordial or
self-same present that is not already infiltrated by the trace—an opening of the
"inside" of the moment to the "outside" of the interval. "That the present in
general is not primal, but rather, reconstituted, that it is not the absolute, wholly
living form which constitutes experience, that there is no purity of the living
present" is the persistent theme running through Derrida's exegeses.[16] His close
readings characteristically take the form of "deconstruction," the discovery of
the worm of difference in the apple of wholeness or presence. In order to be
clear that the differences he discovers are temporal as well as spatial, Derrida
creates the French neologism "*différance*," which is intended to incorporate the
meanings of to differ, and also, to defer. "Trace-structure, everything always
inhabited by the trace of something that is not itself, questions presence-structure."[17] To Derrida, these "traces" and these "presences" are none other than
the conceptual oppositions on which Western metaphysics has staked its "logocentric" (by which he means not so much word-centered as centered on a first
or originating principle, centered on the *Word*) claims to presence for the past
2500 years.

In the binary structures of metaphysical argument, a single term—Good, for instance, or God, or Light, or Mind, or Reason, or Male, or White—becomes an essential or foundational principle, while its opposite (Evil, Satan, Dark, Body, Passion, Female, Black) assumes the role of the outsider, the banished other. These are what Richard Rorty calls the "final vocabularies" of metaphysical systems.[18] The preferred term in such pairings is associated with the idea of ultimate reality, or presence. "Presence" becomes another word for the divinity, or the monarch. "Presence chamber" was the name for a room in which a king received his followers and supplicants. The binary opposition that in Derrida stands for, and in his lexicon may even be said to demonstrate, all others is the opposition of speech and writing. Derrida sees the authentication of speech at the expense of writing, for instance in the thought of Saussure, but running back to Plato, as foundational to metaphysics. The human voice, writes Christopher Norris, explicating Derrida,

> becomes a metaphor of truth, . . . a source of self-present 'living' speech as opposed to the secondary, lifeless emanations of writing. In speaking one is able to experience (supposedly) an intimate link between sound and sense, an inward and immediate realization of meaning which yields itself up without reserve to perfect, transparent understanding. Writing on the contrary destroys this ideal of pure self-presence. It obtrudes an alien, depersonalized medium, a deceiving shadow which falls between intent and meaning, between utterance and understanding. It occupies a promiscuous public realm where authority is sacrificed to the vagaries and whims of textual "dissemination." Writing in short is a threat to the deeply traditional view that associates truth with self-presence and the "natural" language wherein it finds expression.[19]

Far from being secondary to speech, Derrida asserts, writing has "always already" infiltrated speech, could even be said to precede speech, if by writing we understand not only the formal graphic system but the entire linguistic structure he calls "*écriture*" that must precede any particular, limited manifestation in spoken utterance. Writing in this sense involves "an endless displacement of meaning" that places language "beyond the reach of a stable, self-authenticating knowledge."[20] If there can be no assurance of the bond between thought and speech, there can be no single moment at which utterance originates and no single point of origin; and if no originary principle can be identified, then such a thing as a self-same presence is merely a "self"-serving illusion. Thus Derrida's attack on "phono-centrism," the privilege accorded to speech in Western thought, has as its aim the entire "metaphysics of presence" that has been the focus of the Western metaphysical tradition since its Greek beginnings.

I suppose most theater-lovers who enjoy what they identify as the sense of presence in the theater don't have Derrida, "logocentrism," or the long tradition of Western metaphysics in mind. Still, even this short review suggests that what we mean by theatrical presence is deeply linked to metaphysical assumptions. When we read in Goethe that the spectator to the dramatic production should be transported in the theater into a realm where "even that which is narrated must be so placed before the eyes of the spectator as though it were actually taking place," we recognize the association of speech with presence in its most concrete form. Further, when we read that the spectator "must not pause to meditate, but must follow [this present action] in a state of passionate eagerness; his fancy . . . entirely put to silence,"[21] we recognize in the "putting to silence" of alternative currents, oppositional thinking, seeming digression, or meditation, precisely Derrida's quarrel with the binary terms—one present/ one absent—of metaphysical argument.

I realize that in welcoming Derrida as my guide to the "metaphysics" of drama—and since Platonism was incubated in the same century, society, and culture that gave rise to the dramatic form the connection between the two may run beyond mere analogy—I am indirectly opening a large question about their comparable fates. For now, however, I defer that question to return to the particular premise that dramatic performance traditionally imitates the hierarchy of speech/writing that Derrida locates in the Western philosophical tradition as a whole. Here I mean concretely writing as embodied in the dramatic text. That is, drama has evolved as the form of writing that strives to create the illusion that it is composed of spontaneous speech; it is a form of writing that paradoxically asserts the claim of speech to be a direct conduit to Being. Yet in a curious deconstructive implosion, numerous plays and performance pieces beginning in the 1970s project writing back onto the stage performance in a "literalization" that any previous generation of theater-makers would have rejected as untheatrical. This literalization or textualization of the theater event has appeared in a number of forms, as subject, as setting, as stage business. Writing, which had traditionally retired behind the phonocentric texture of performance, in a surprisingly large number of works now declared itself the environment in which dramatic structure and theatrical performance are situated. The price of this emergence, and perhaps its aim, has been to complicate the spectator's experience of theatrical presence. This has important implications for dramatic character, which begins to re-assume its cursive, pre-psychological meaning—character as impression or inscription.

In the most general way, the entire tradition of self-referential irony in both the novel and the theater (in which, for instance, the author of the piece appears on page or stage in faux-improvisation) lies behind the contemporary textualized theater. However, its immediate pre-history must include works of Brecht, Beckett, and Handke.

More than sixty years ago, in notes explaining his use of slides and screens in *The Threepenny Opera*, Brecht called for the "literarization" of the theater. He even envisaged the creation of theatrical "footnotes," anything to lift the spectator above the coercive tactics of identification and empathy.[22] I have deliberately not adopted Brecht's term literarization. The examples I will cite are at once more formally radical and more politically passive. Still, Brecht's explanation for bringing writing onstage, "Some exercise in complex seeing is needed," could serve all the playwrights and directors I will cite here.

Beckett's *Krapp's Last Tape* uses the mechanical device of the audiotape to rupture both the fabric of presence on the stage created by the actor's alignment of voice and gesture, and the seeming presence of life to itself with its seamless "now." The audiotape, an unsettling juncture between voice and writing, present and retrospect, saves voice as inscription, as writing, but also stands as an image of the problem of writing itself. "To EXPRESS something means you first killed it," writes Foreman.[23] With the tape recorder at the center of the dramatic action, how easily breached is Goldman's magic circle that enables the self, through performance, to "possess itself in the present." Krapp dwells on the literary remains of former selves who dwell on the remains of former selves in a ritual of regress. The trail is arrested by the memory of one moment of sexual connection, like a return to the maternal source.

> . . . my face in her breasts and my hand on her. We lay there without moving. But under us all moved, and moved us, gently, up and down, and from side to side.[24]

We learn, of course, that the couple had already agreed to separate before this moment. The remembered moment of fullness was already infiltrated by loss, and it is viciously alienated in the present by Krapp's manipulation of the writing/reading machine, the fast forwards, rewinds, and repetitions that ridicule the island of reconstituted presence. Beckett slyly raises the question whether the voice on the tape, seemingly so close to lived experience, was ever other than the self-conscious production of a prior writing, for when Krapp tries without success to make a new tape, he speaks not "from the heart," but reads from scrawled notes on the back of an envelope. This may serve as an ironic judgment both on the playwright's sleight-of-hand that creates a "now," and on the illusory "presence" of living itself.

In *Ohio Impromptu*, nearly twenty-five years later, Beckett returned in another way to the issues raised by *Krapp*—the impossibility of achieving or returning to a present Now (or for that matter a former Then). The shadow of writing falls across the illusion of presence. The Reader reads, and the Listener listens, to a story of the Reader reading, and the Listener listening, etc., etc. The substantial personhood of the figures recedes into the fiction, which in turn empties the figures back onto the stage. The very line between the living and the dead blurs in the shifting alignments we make between actors as present beings and actors as ghostly reflections of the Word, a blur encouraged by Beckett's stage directions describing the two senescent figures. Neither they, nor the Book, can lay claim to an originary force; both are shredded in the continually twisting Möbius strip of Beckett's conceit. Within the paradox is embedded yet a third, missing figure, the owner of the "dear name" and "dear face" who sent the Reader with his book to the Listener, yet "figures" in the book. This figure is indeed a *figure*, in the literary sense, of lost origination and undecipherability; all three might be said to be uncertainly poised between ontological and cursive character, character as mark, as a stroke in a configuration.[25]

Beckett with mordant wit names such a text "impromptu," a title suggesting the spontaneity and unrepeatability of play and improvisation. The breaking of frame within the theatrical impromptu that joyously returns us into the performance and reminds us of theater as activity and process is darkly echoed by introducing theater's shadow frame of writing. In this shadow frame, "nothing is left to tell," as the Reader's book has it, because everything has "always, already," in Derrida's famously nostalgic phrase, been said.[26]

If *Krapp's Last Tape* demonstrates an ontology sliding into textuality like an Escher print, Peter Handke's *Kaspar* shows ontology constructed from textuality, identity spun from sentences. Yet for both authors, the sense of loss surrounding the recognition of compromised Being is acute. *Kaspar*, taking up Brecht's theme in *Mann ist Mann*, attacks the sentimental idealization of an innate, in-dwelling presence of the self. Not only is Kaspar's self not "present to itself," but it actually seems to "long for" the inscription of socialization, the accumulated dead grammar of a civilization that by the end of the play leads back to the chaos out of which the unsocialized Kaspar emerged.

Kaspar's cobbled-together prayer of longing—"I want to be a person like somebody else was once"—is fulfilled by unseen "prompters."[27] The theatrical metaphor interestingly brings into the text the normally obscured relationship of the outer "book" to the inner representation.[28] The manner of speaking of the unseen speakers "should be that of voices which in reality have a technical medium interposed between themselves and the listeners: telephone voices, radio or television announcers' voices . . . of announcers of train arrivals and departures . . . of language course records." These make Kaspar into a person "like somebody was once" by drilling him in the text of instrumental language. *Kaspar* offers not so much a deconstruction of the speech/writing binary relative to theatrical presence, as its outright reversal. Character-identified speech, traditionally the central constituent of stage performance, is the mere by-product here of an anonymous linguistic accumulation, a voice of authority with no author. The entire aspiration to self-presence is mocked. At the end of the play Kaspar emerges into his "own" language, but it is only the smooth voice of the prompters. "I learned to fill all empty spaces with words," he says. His final words, "goats and monkeys, goats and monkeys," several times repeated, and uttered into a microphone against the cacophony of metallic scraping and the mocking repetitions of several other Kaspar-clones, are those of Iago.[29] The quotation represents a doubly despairing gesture: humanity's grim alternatives in *Kaspar* are the script, or the beast.

American playwrights of the 1970s and 1980s were well aware that the compact of theatrical presence, with all its associations conferred on both sides of the proscenium of authenticity, autonomy, and origin, was painfully thrown into doubt by Beckett and Handke. But when they turned to the motif of self as text, it was not for the most part as the tragedy of a lost presence, but as the expression of mediated culture. They are becoming postmoderns. Thus, for instance, Richard Nelson's madly-dictating U.S. senator in *The Vienna Notes* (1979) becomes the fictional invention of his own "memoir." And, in another register, Len Jenkin's *Dark Ride* (1981) concerns a text about a text composed of fragments of other texts which appear to embody yet other texts. Its central character, not surprisingly, is called simply the Translator. Here are two more extended examples.

The black and white of the title in Adrienne Kennedy's *A Movie Star Has to Star in Black and White* (1976) refers not only to images on film, but to print on paper, and above all to racial difference. The play is an autobiographical collage loosely focused on the hospitalization of Kennedy's brother after a car accident. Clara, described as the "bit player" but actually Kennedy's central character, writes continuously during the course of the action and reads to us from her (Adrienne Kennedy's) diaries and plays. Clara is so identified with writing, she tells us, that her husband says "my diaries consume me," and that "my life is one of my black and white movies. . . ."[30]

Popular films fill Clara's imagination. Famous white stars—Bette Davis in *Now Voyager*, Jean Peters in *Viva Zapata*, and Shelley Winters in *A Place in the Sun*—lead her life and speak her words, while Clara silently writes in her notebook. Kennedy returns here to the split racial consciousness of her first play, *Funnyhouse of a Negro*, but there has been a change in the twelve years between the two plays. Now the large issues of race and gender are refracted almost entirely through the activity, the artifacts, and the problem of writing. "Everyone says it's unrealistic for a Negro to want to write," says Clara, while images from the writing of white culture play all around her.

With rare exception, the dramatic fabric of *Movie Star* is not the relationship of "living" characters rendering the illusion of spontaneous speech, but is largely composed of quotations (Kennedy diary narrations and passages from her play *The Owl Answers*), spoken by Clara or refracted through the movie scenes and star selves. What we learn of the interactions of characters is read through the interactions of genres. Very rarely does the present time emerge in a scene of dialogue that creates the comforting "double now" of presence. The most significant such moment occurs between mother and daughter at the midpoint of the play. The issue between them—whether happiness consists of families living together, or a life of writing—could be translated into a debate between two kinds of dramatic writing, one in dialogue whose subject is conventional family struggles; the other "literalized" by the "black and white" of texts. The lighting directions, rather than the dialogue, resolve the issue: the mother-daughter scene is played in "constant dim twilight," positioned between the romantic shadows of the *Now Voyager* ship lights and the "dazzling" wedding-night lighting of *Viva Zapata*.

Kennedy's *Movie Star* is fascinating in its poise between a pastiche of texts and a drama of character. Daryl Chin's work in the theater is, or was (he stopped creating theater pieces in the mid-1980s), far more radically anti-theatrical in its rejection of the methods and affect of theatrical presence. Many of his plays not only incorporated long passages of art criticism or theory, but in themselves were instruments of criticism. *Act and the Actor*, produced in 1984 at the Theater for the New City, takes its title from a work of criticism, the book of the same name by art critic Harold Rosenberg.[31] The play begins with a reading of a paragraph from a 1966 essay in *Film Culture* by Annette Michelson, delivered by a character called, simply, the Reader. The Michelson quote essentially lays out the proposition that a fateful divide occurred in late 1920s cinema, where revolutionary formalism was split off from revolutionary political aspiration. "Politically oriented art at its best became a chronicle of absence . . . a formal statement of the impossibility of discourse."[32] This theme, so deeply related to my own in this exploration, in turn becomes the backdrop to Chin's own brand of formalism.

The prologue continues with the immediate display of a rather large absence. An actor reads the author's note about the origins of the play. It was derived, he tells us, from a more ambitious, unproduced play (as in so many of these plays, another text hovering behind or encroaching on the text being performed), that posed the question, "What would happen if there was a merger between Jacques Derrida and Preston Sturges?" The current play, the Prologue concludes, is an "attempt to analyze the problematic," whether American popular culture and mass medium conventions "can be called archetypes."[33] The play proper consists of an interweaving of dozens of scene fragments quoted from or inspired by film noir classics, interspersed with critical passages. The weaving of fragments never coalesces into an illusionistic reality with plot and characters, yet creates a sense of coherence because the intertexts are part of the spectator's cultural narrative. We find ourselves surrendering to the pleasure of the film noir stagings, a surrender that winkingly answers the critical question of their archetypal power raised at the outset of the play.

Chin thrusts texts at his audience: books, articles, films, fiction, criticism. His earlier *Apoplectic Fit* "fits" together various pieces of dance criticism with enactments of plots taken from Djuna Barnes's *Nightwood* and *Beauty and Sadness* by Yasunari Kawabata. Chin creates a thin, almost transparent dramatic surface of "character" and "plot" through which shines a discourse woven of and about a variety of texts. It is a distanced world of texts speaking to texts, not the dramatic world of speaking selves.

The group of faithful and talented actors who worked with Chin and his collaborator-director Larry Qualls developed a mode of stage speech quite different from the expressive, emotive speech, emerging from an inner depth, which is the norm for dramatic utterance. Rather, the Chin actors spoke quietly, hurriedly, and in flat tones, a kind of "zombie speech" that gave the impression of reading or quotation. Even in playing style Chin undermined the illusion of presence to remind us that his kind of live performance emerges out of the interaction of texts, whether "written" in frames of film or print. In his plays, Chin resisted the spectator's longing for a greater reality in an enhanced, fully conscious present; his greater reality was that of the immense penumbra of textuality surrounding and shaping human culture.

Act and the Actor was the next to last in the series of theater pieces Chin mounted in the downtown experimental theater world of the early and middle 1980s, but it was at the beginning of what in the late eighties and early nineties may be emerging as the part-read, part-enacted "theorized play," or "theory play." I am thinking of such experiments as Gayle Austin's feminist theory plays at Georgia State University, or the Molière *Don Juan* that Richard Schechner mounted at the University of Florida at Tallahassee in 1988, a production that was staged with periodic interruptions by a read counter-text of feminist criticism.[34] Joan Schenkar's one-act impromptu, *The Universal Wolf*, stages a rewriting of the "Little Red Riding Hood" tale, with interventions from such pop-up theoretical figures as Roland Barthes, Julia Kristeva, and Teresa de Lauretis. The layering of reading on enactment here performs the unusual move of asking the audience, during the entr'acte, to silently read an unperformed section of the text.[35]

With theater projects such as these, I have moved into that other realm of the American theater, the realm of "performance theater," inhabited by Richard Foreman, Robert Wilson, Elizabeth LeCompte, Stuart Sherman, and a small number of other artists.[36] Performance theater bears some similarity to the conventional theater of dramatic texts in situating the theatrical event in an imaginative world evoked by visual, lighting, and sound effects, and an ensemble of actors. Yet it is like performance art in two signal regards: in its continuous awareness of itself as performance, and in its unavailability for re-presentation. That is, the work is associated with a particular director or group of performers of such visual and stylistic originality that the text seems not to be

reimaginable even where it is presumably restageable. Just how valid the latter
distinction is may be debated—for instance, Richard Foreman's play texts have
begun to be staged by other directors. However, for purposes of the present
discussion, I affirm the distinction because performance theater artists have performed the literalization of the theater in a characteristically distinct way—they
perform "literally" what is still primarily an effect of the dramatic text in the
works discussed above. In the Prologue of Robert Wilson's *Alcestis*, for instance, a middle-aged woman worked her way slowly across the stage, her back
to the audience, miming the writing of an invisible script; or in the Cologne
section of *the CIVIL warS*, Wilson brought onstage writing figures, or perhaps
one should say figures of writing, in the eight Black Scribes, and in the immense
White Scribe, stylus slanting skyward, covered in curling scrolls of writing paper. Stuart Sherman was even more "literal" in his 18-minute silent *Hamlet*.
There, five actors playing Hamlet carried about copies of Shakespeare's text
while performing various gestures (including sitting and reading the play),
against a stage decor covered with pages from the play, cut and pasted into
dagger-like patterns. In his 1985 *Stuart Sherman's Chekhov*, a group of white-
clad performers commanded less interest than the grove of cut-out cherry trees
that were the piece's central feature. These were constructed from enlarged
pages of Chekhov's play texts and clearly readable by the audience. In a won-
derfully Derridean *coup de théâtre*, these toppled and fell at the end of the piece.
The very literalness of these images—presenting not characters writing, but
the activity of writing itself, and not allusions to texts, but the very texts themselves—opens a stranger gap in the structure, or the anticipation, of theatrical
presence than any we have yet encountered. Sherman, especially, by using the
names of classic plays, stirred up the entire expectation of present enactment
only to force the spectator to ask where—if anywhere—the "real" play resides.
The artists of performance theater don't merely haunt presence-structure with
trace-structure, they directly stage the traces. Writing becomes "presentable."
For the moment, I defer the questions raised by such a statement to turn to
two final, complex examples within performance theater of the staging of writing and reading.[37]

There is a parenthetical comment in Richard Foreman's first Ontological-
Hysteric manifesto that reads, "The actual making of the art object then becomes essentially a matter of notation."[38] The manifesto itself is festooned with
notations of various kinds, syntactically unincorporated bulletins that pierce
the page from every side. Foreman productions make more or less the same
move, presenting the spectator with a notational space that cracks open the
expectation of perspectively organized meaning. Such notation is at one level
like the pattern- or phrase-making of visual or musical art. It is evident, for
instance, in the replicative details of a Foreman set—the multiple clocks, skulls,
mirrors, flowers; or in sudden intensities of light blinding the spectators; or in

portentous music loops—whatever it is that by its repetition takes on significance; or rather takes on the aureola of significance, putting the audience into a state of heightened receptivity to perception. Our best response to such effects may also be one of bare notation, or taking note.

But most Foreman productions have also included notation in the more literal sense—having to do with legible phrases or combinations of letters decorating the stage space like a code whose key has been lost. Such examples of a literalized surround are legion in Foreman productions. Sometimes the notation is composed of words in English, like the "Poetic Theory" banner across the drawing of a woman's face in the 1991 *Eddie Goes to Poetry City*, or the "No Secrets" legend hanging from the perennial Foreman strings across the top of the set of *The Cure* in 1986. In the 1988 *Symphony of Rats* the money mottos, *Novo Ordo Seclorum* and *E Pluribus Unum* appeared on the set, quotations that, along with their distinctive designs, carry both political and occult associations. The most mysterious use of writing on the Foreman stage are the Hebrew letters that have appeared over the years, mysterious because unlike these other examples, they often have no allegorizable relation to the text. This silent presence in Foreman's plays hints of his long-standing attraction to Kabbalah. Kabbalah's elaboration of the theme of an esoteric, heavenly writing, the hidden text behind the text of life, distantly undergirds Foreman's notational theater. (His plays, *Book of Splendors*, Part I and Part II, are named after the central kabbalistic text, the *Zohar*, or "Book of Splendor," the great thirteenth-century compendium by the Spanish kabbalist Moses de Leon. Foreman disclaims any but a casual acquaintance with the *Zohar*, however.)[39]

To think of Foreman as kabbalist, at least in this analogical sense—as the rabbi of the world-as-text—is to confront at once his conflicted relationship to language and writing: on the one hand he literalizes his often-repeated conviction that we are trapped in the "prison-house of language," unable to express or experience more, or other, than our language system permits; and on the other hand he hints at the possibility of escape from the restrictions of instrumental language through a higher writing. The Hebrew letters strain to connect the entire theater event with the great mystery of signs and codes in the universe—or I should say, they have that effect to me. One can envision the outer reaches of Foreman's theatrical world lined with "traces prior to any entity of which they might be the trace," writing as pure cosmic notation.[40]

One might ask at this point whether the "kabbalistic" Foreman does not simply reverse, rather than deconstruct, theatrical presence; the immediate event is not simply decentered by text, but arguably subordinated to a higher text and a higher presence. This very issue was struggled to a stand-off in Foreman's 1989 play *Lava*, a conflicted exploration of Foreman's relationship to writing and its staging.

As anyone who has attended a Foreman performance knows, most of his plays have included the Voice, an omniscient offstage observer, played by Foreman, who questions and admonishes the onstage figures. Occasionally, as in *The Cure*, he is not heard from. In the early days Foreman was visible as he spoke the Voice, sitting downstage at the sound console. Now, and for many years, he has spoken the Voice's lines from the sound booth. *Lava* is unusual among Foreman's works in assigning nearly three-quarters of the lines to the Voice. The Voice is not an occasional interlocutor to the characters, but "their author, their director, their boss—even the voice of God."[41] That only partially ironic statement would seem if anything oppressively "logocentric." The Voice hangs over actors and spectators like a lid. Yet the Voice's continuous theme in *Lava* is the oppressive dome of language over his own head, and the paradoxical nature of any efforts at escape:

> Open, open the door . . .
> I don't see a door.
> Sure there is.
> The door out, is outside.
> The door in, is inside.
> Am I outside or inside?
> You wanna get out or in?
> I want to get out.
> That's where the door is.
> I want to get in
> Ah, that's where the door is.[42]

To stage the play, Foreman created a "reading" set, a "study hall, dominated by a large table on which a few books lie." (The table and books reappeared a few years later in the Talmudic *Mind King*.) Newspaper pages "in foreign, exotic script" are tacked to the walls. Three or four blackboards are visible, and all the actors scrawl on them from time to time. The onstage figures, three men and a woman, listen raptly, study large tomes, repeat the words of the Voice, and take studious notes. They are learning to ingest language, which fuses with their bodies:

> MATTHEW:
> I'm waiting here with pad and pencil.
>
> NEIL:
> As soon as you see one of the letters, rising from one of the back muscles . . .
>
> MATTHEW:
> I'll write down whatever I see.[43]

The idea is reminiscent of Handke, especially as the actors in *Lava* take on "the function of clowns" (for instance, at one point the three male figures are disguised as comic Talmudic scholars, hunchbacks wearing phony black beards and dark glasses). But unlike the stern external voices in *Kaspar*, which lead toward tragedy, the Voice in *Lava* is concerned with itself, now full of pompous self-importance, now naive in its longing for a "true self," now winking with self-deprecating irony. The Voice's words confusingly cancel each other out.

For instance, the Voice complains that language is unreliable and obscures truth—

> Hello to you all. I am here to minister and I shall . . .
> I shall drift into your very hearts.
> I shall heal you all . . .
> The truth is as follows. [And now the wink]
> It can't be said, the truth.
> Which, of course, renders even that statement questionable. Hum.

It falsifies feeling—

> I'm crying because there's no way to express my real feelings. [another wink]

And—a virtue for a change—language can shift ground every moment to outwit the "verbal police."

> . . . I have at my command, [a deflationary wink] not your guttural virtuosity,
> and therefore lack your nothing but preword-noise-network.
> I simply use statement:
> In the most perverse way possible . . . [44]

I have omitted until this point an interesting detail. Into this literalized environment with its language-obsessed text Foreman has introduced another intervention of writing, as direct as it is strange. Even before the lights have gone down, a "woman in red" has begun to write on a blackboard. "What she writes is the beginning text of the play that follows." Throughout the entire play she continues, positioned at a blackboard writing the text of the play, "skipping forward whenever she falls behind the Voice."[45] What does it mean to put in the same event these two representatives of the text: the invisible but voluble Voice which never stops talking, and the visible but silent woman who never stops writing? Do these two collude in their control of language and their oppression of the actors, or is this some kind of struggle for symbolic mastery between speech and writing? As I read it, or amuse myself by reading it, as there are no correct readings of Foreman texts, this continuous writing adds a wickedly ironic commentary—the biggest wink of all—to the lucubrations on language uttered by the Voice. Struggling to escape the dreaded mirror, the Voice seems to be represented as lagging after the Writer. The Voice may see himself as lava, pouring out warm, impulsive words from the hot center of his being, but the writing woman offers a cool riposte. He can finally only blather about language *in* language, like his actor who pathetically goes up in his lines in the part of the script that is about the actor's going up in his lines. And while the Voice grandly instructs his actors to, in effect, "repeat after me"— robbing them of their (already inauthentic) voices—he too is at some level engaged in repetition. The fact that Voice and Writer do not acknowledge each other adds a real, if arcane, poignancy to Foreman's parable of the doors.

The effect of Foreman's staged deconstruction of the speech/writing binary (where this discussion began), and of his many forms of notation, is not simply to disrupt the illusion of presence and of autonomous characters. Foreman's theater has long been free of any such illusions. ("Character," Foreman once told me, quoting Max Jacob, "is an error.")[46] His penetrating interest in Being, in the "ontological," is active sub-characterologically, attending to subtle shifts of consciousness and body sensation. To him, the fragments of writing that are given an illusory coherence by his actors are not "characters" but constellations of impulses ontologically inflected. When I write, asks Kate in *Book of Splendors/II*, "is it mind or body?"[47]

In the staging of *Lava* there were two elements, so far unmentioned, that perhaps dissolved writer and speaker into some larger environment. These were the electronic "hum" heard periodically over the speakers, and a tape with a different voice, not Foreman's, repeating at intervals the same random sequence of the numbers one through nine. When asked about the latter, Foreman said he thought of numbers as a " 'pure' language which is more concerned with Platonic forms than language-language, which is a degraded form of that." He has "thought of doing a play—and I'll never do it because it's too pure for me—a play with the dialogue all numbers."[48] Foreman also associated the humming sound with the "primal hum that precedes all socialized forms of discourse" that he mentions in his introduction to the play.[49] There is the subtlest of suggestions in these effects that Foreman is kicking the struggle for origination "upstairs" from the lower grades of conscious language to the high school of post-verbal metaphysics. There is always the hint that Foreman's is a kind of hermetic, religious theater. He speaks of such attractions frequently, but one must be careful not to over-materialize such suggestions in his work.

In Foreman's theater, to come to the largest implication of the "presence" debate, there is never an expectation of realizing the mystery, or becoming present enough, as in Julian Beck's aspiration, to make God present. "We lack a center, always," writes Foreman.[50] In Foreman's cosmogony, God is in the "cracks in our . . . systems of discourse," but will never pass through them.[51] We are not waiting for God. We are waiting for these cracks. Thus the liveliness he hopes the spectator will attain through opening herself to perception is always penetrated by the absence whose mark *is* the mark, or notation, whether of absence or of presence. There is a moment early in *Lava* where the Voice laments, "(W)hatever I say necessarily misses the mark." And again a moment later, "We have to talk, right? But whatever we say is . . . off the mark. Off the mark . . . Off the mark."[52] Seeking language to describe his wish to escape language, Foreman/Voice is driven to use a word that stands for language, written language. Somewhere, in the place where one transcends language, there is finally the right *mark*: we cannot imagine the very state we long for; the handle to the door is always on the other side. This is the dilemma opened by the always necessary deferral of the aspiration to presence, including divine presence, and its reflection in theatrical presence.

Finally, Elizabeth LeCompte's Wooster Group has not only made a practice of "re-reading" classic modern texts, but has done so staging the very mechanics of reading itself. From 1978, when they first performed *Nayatt School*, to 1991, when they substantially concluded their work on *Frank Dell's The Temptation of Saint Antony*, the Wooster Group introduced into their performance pieces variations on the performance of reading, the most persistent emblem of which was a 24-foot long institutional gray reading table. It ran nearly the entire width of the playing area in the Performing Garage, the group's home. In *Nayatt School*, the table was placed immediately in front of the high bleachers where the audience sat. At the beginning of the piece, the actors were seated at this table before microphones to read a section of T. S. Eliot's *The Cocktail Party*. At the end, this reading returned as an obscenity. The British cast recording was played from three portable record players placed on this table, with the actors— Spalding Gray, Ron Vawter, and Libby Howes—furiously breaking the records and pornographically squatting over the turntables, the men dropping their pants as if to defecate, or—with bare ass and dangling testicles—as if to scrawl the graffiti of "cocks" and "tails" over the polite British cocktail party chatter. In this piece the distance of reading and text-consciousness were played against the almost unbearable closeness of physical obscenity.

For several years after that, the table, and reading from and around it, persisted in LeCompte's stagings. It appeared, raked at a 30-degree angle, in *North Atlantic*, its surface bristling with electronic speech-distancing devices— phones, tape recorders, and the usual microphones. Roles were not so much played as announced; lines were spoken in an exaggerated manner, as if in quotation marks. The table was the central focus of *L.S.D. (. . . Just the High Points . . .)*, the group's complex investigation of the psychedelic era's messianic promise, excess, and ultimate repression. Trisecting the obliquely assembled narrative of Timothy Leary's drug experiments were two principal others: Arthur Miller's account of the Salem witch trials in *The Crucible*, and, under the heading "Miami," the Leary aftermath which involved him, after his release from prison, in several notorious debates with the born-again Watergate felon, G. Gordon Liddy. (The group took its text for some of this section from an actual debate between the two at SUNY-Albany in 1982.)

In what became Part II of *L.S.D.*, the actors managed to convey the entire action of *The Crucible* from the reading table—seated at it speaking from microphones, or standing next to it, lying on it, or even sliding under it. The entire performance was in this sense a reading. At a late stage of the struggle with Arthur Miller to obtain rights to perform *The Crucible* (ultimately denied, after which the entire piece was withdrawn), the cast converted the text to a gibberish that sounded like fast-forward tape. Ron Vawter, playing the inquisitorial Reverend "Hall" (Hale in Miller), and standing angrily before a microphone at the stage right end of the table, was responsible for the most extended such passage. This particular experiment in reading proved a revelation. From Vawter's performance, meaning and feeling emerged clearly, like the raised surface of a relief. Or perhaps the analogy is not precise, for the relief dispenses with fully rounded sculptural forms in order to attain a painting-like complexity of field. The flow of language here was more precisely analogous to contemporary speed-reading, in which language streaks by so quickly that the reader "sees" the text as a series of flashing images, space in effect exchanging for time. As audience to this radical distillation of "just the high points," I recall thinking that realistic, psychological enactment of the familiar Miller text would only have weighted the performance with a ponderous ballast.

At the beginning of Part I of *L.S.D.*, several male actors seated behind the table introduced themselves as the readers of certain writers whose work was important to the "drop out, turn on, tune in" generation, many of whom figured in the narrative of the piece—Huxley, Kerouac, Ginsberg, Koestler, Watts. The actors held up books, announced their intention to read passages at random from these texts, and proceeded to create at each performance an improvised collage of quotations. This experiment with chance—an avant-garde variation on "presence" since Dada—combined in a felt logical contradiction with the readings from books, where the fixed, printed text held priority of attention over the actors' performances. This scene, and the Rower narration, described in a moment, with their layerings of immediacy and mediation, are among the most interesting examples of the Wooster Group's deconstruction of the "metaphysics of presence."

For the production, LeCompte had taped an account by Anne Rower, Timothy Leary's babysitter in the Harvard/Millbrook period. Nancy Reilly played the role of Rower, or rather "read" it, by listening at each performance to Rower's taped words on headphones, and repeating them in precisely Rower's inflections without performing the least cosmetic "improvement" upon the halting, droning, memoir spaced with long "uh's" and pauses. Like the readings from books, the Rower material created a conflicted impression. Rower was doubly absent—once through Reilly's self-effacement in referring the spectator past the actress before them to the tape, and once through the fact of the tape itself, its disembodied voice lacking gesture and facial expression. But Rower was for these same reasons peculiarly present, more "real" for being presented in a form that resisted representation. The conventional aura of theatrical presence is suppressed in order to retain a pre-performed vitality. The Nancy Reilly "Anne Rower" is read over the "real" Anne Rower. Both are both absent and present.

The cumulative effect of the Wooster Group's readings-over—its graffiti over canonic theater texts, like *Our Town* in *Route 1&9* (or over naive and "sincere" representations of subjectivity, canonic people, as it were)—is to mount a resistance to the traditional positivism of theatrical representation. This resistance takes the form of a continuous, and continuously self-canceling, irony, a fierce nihilism in which the spectator is presented with obstacles to the alignment of seeing/hearing/thinking/feeling that is assumed in a theater cultivating "presence." Gertrude Stein thought this kind of alignment was fundamentally unobtainable anyway. Closely observed, theater was always uncomfortably "in syncopated time."[53] Stein abandoned the standard narrative techniques that made her "nervous," and set out to create a greater presence unfolding in a diffused "landscape" that did not require the audience to follow the temporal demands of a dramatic raveling and unraveling.[54] LeCompte on the other hand has for years actively sought syncopation almost at the molecular level. She is never what (or where) Stein extolled as "just there."[55] She strains to achieve narrative, or its simulacrum, but over chasms of broken connections. If Stein cultivated the relation of "any detail to any other detail,"[56] in a homogenous field, "disconnect, only disconnect" could be LeCompte's credo. In LeCompte's theater, reading in its many forms could be seen as a central emblem of the failure of "presence" not only on the stage but in the world, where barriers "always, already" exist between text and meaning, intention and reception, and between individuals.

LeCompte's reading approach to performance climaxed in the dense, hermetic *Frank Dell's Temptation of Saint Antony* (serially known as Part III of the retrospective trilogy, *The Road to Immortality*) whose title derives from Flaubert's immense dramatic novel of the same name. Up to this point in the group's work, and again later, LeCompte's principal deconstructive base, one might say, was always a classic modern play text, such as *Our Town, Long Day's Journey into Night*, or *The Three Sisters*. The Flaubert choice came about through the happenstance of Peter Sellars's interest in exploring this text in collaboration with the group. Sellars went on to other projects, however, and LeCompte continued the work, folding into its complex mix various other cursed, false, or occult "saint" narratives, including certain tapes of Lenny Bruce, the Bergman film *The Magician*, and the 1932 spiritualist tract *The Road to Immortality* by Geraldine Cummins, a book that had impressed Bruce before he died (as well as Eugene O'Neill thirty years earlier).[57] Ron Vawter, an actor who himself had sometimes been described in journalistic profiles as a "saint," played the central fictional role of "Frank Dell," leader of a seedy troupe of traveling actors, a figure composed of Flaubert's Antony, Bruce, and Bergman's charismatic magician. If this was a saint play, however, it became the group's most difficult *via negativa*. It was saturated with the anticipation of death, not only that of the desert saint, Lenny Bruce, "Frank Dell," and other characters alluded to in the text, but that of Vawter himself, whose advancing AIDS represented a collective anguish to the company. The piece was not only morbid and dark in this sense, but formally difficult, imbricated with unfamiliar references and determined—far more than in *L.S.D.* or in *Route 1&9*—to deny its spectators the satisfaction of stable meanings. (By which I mean not stable answers, but stable *questions.*) Unlike Stein's *Four Saints in Three Acts*, which permits spectators to loaf, "do nothing," and enjoy themselves just as Stein claimed saints did, this saint play forced the audience to its most severe and attentive effort in a LeCompte piece, straining for a narrative coherence always just beyond its range. Only when the bodies of her actors are engaged in the brilliant dances she sprinkles through this and other works, do the barriers for a moment fall.

For a theater troupe that had been exploring the boundaries among reading, textuality, and performance, the Flaubert novel was a strangely significant choice, for this is the novel that Foucault has described as a "fantasia of the library."[58] Foucault sees the novel as Flaubert's response to "a new imaginative space in the nineteenth century," a space in which the visionary experience arises not from "dreams and rapture," but from "the black and white surface of printed signs." Dreams are "no longer summoned with closed eyes," he writes, "but in reading; and a true image . . . derives from . . . the reproductions of reproductions." The imaginary "is born and takes shape in the interval between books. It is a phenomenon of the library."[59] Foucault celebrates Flaubert's *Temptation* as an anticipation of Mallarmé, Joyce, and Pound. It is "linked in a completely serious manner to the vast world of print and develops within the recognizable institution of writing. It may appear as merely another new book to be shelved alongside all the others, but it serves, in actuality, to extend the space the existing books can occupy."[60] LeCompte has linked her career to an analogous space for theater, not only the world of books and print, but the world of archival performance—of former dramatic and theatrical presences folded back on themselves as text. Whether her brilliant layerings are, as Foucault says of Flaubert, an extension of the space theater can occupy without simultaneously also working a contraction on the space that theater has traditionally occupied (specifically the Western space of drama)—this question, over these many examples, has doubtless been edging into view.

The appearance of these kinds of textualities on many different stages, their acceptance by diverse audiences (their being noticed by crrritics!)—all of this becomes possible when the "space" of speech in theater, with all its character(istic) associations of authenticity, origination, presence, has already begun to contract. Just as Derrida's work undermining speech appears at a historical moment when metaphysics is in retreat, so these theaters of reading and writing appear when, as Julian Beck declared, "The Theater of Character is over."[61] The work of early modernism, described in chapter 2 as a shifting of the center of signification from character to allegory, must in part be seen as a loss of confidence in the active, originary force of speech itself. Derrida, for all his retrospective universalism (so carefully installed as to avoid directionality, either of origination or of emancipation), seems to me finally the quintessentially modernist philosopher. His deconstruction of the speech/writing binary belongs in the company of such classic commentaries on modern culture as Benjamin's "The Work of Art in the Age of Mechanical Reproduction." The insight, and certainly the dawning of the insight, that speech was "always, already" in the shadow of writing, is less a transhistorical truth than a specifically historical development.

Writing after Derrida, and attempting just such a correction, Michel de Certeau puts in an anthropological/historical register what in Derrida is the transhistorical motion of language. Certeau's name for the large cultural tide whose individual eddies I have called "literal" in theater is the magisterial term "scriptural." We live in a "scriptural economy," he argues, whose reign stretches from the seventeenth to the twentieth century.[62] The scriptural economy has installed in every human activity the apparatus of writing with its own rules and discipline. "Scriptural practice has acquired a mythical value over the past four centuries by radically reorganizing all the domains into which the Occidental ambition . . . to compose history has been extended." Authority no longer resides in a discourse of an origin, but in the very production of texts themselves. "Progress" is thus inherently scriptural. "Reciprocally, the 'scriptural' is that which separates itself from the magical world of voices and tradition. A frontier (and a front) of Western culture is established by that separation. Thus one can read above the portals of modernity such inscriptions as . . . 'Here only what is written is understood.' Such is the internal law of that which has constituted itself as 'Western.' "

The transition to a scriptural from a more dominantly oral culture is marked by the change in the reception of the Bible sometime between the sixteenth and seventeenth centuries. Until then, Certeau writes, "The sacred text is a voice," and "scripture" is Holy Scripture, a written record pointing back to that voice. "The modern age is formed by discovering little by little that this Spoken Word is no longer heard, that it has been altered by textual corruptions and the avatars of history." Scripture is no longer a narrative of an origin in speech and act, but an activity in itself (it loses its "aura," Benjamin might say). In the world it invades, the virtual definition of mastery is the filling of the blank page. Ultimately Certeau foresees a society that has become the prisoner of writing: "The scriptural system moves forward on its own . . . trans-form(ing) the subjects that controlled it into operators of the writing machine that orders and uses them."

Certeau describes—just as in my view Derrida reflects—a vast shifting of the cultural tectonics that underlie local and particular manifestations of culture, a shift in which the proliferation of reproducible culture has made the attribution of "presence" suspect. Theater is similarly de-theologizing itself, doubting speech, voice, character, self, presence. We are looking at the end of drama and the emerging form of a post-metaphysical theater. What's theater to metaphysics, as Hamlet might ask. Is the dramatic form implicated in some generic way in the destiny of metaphysics, or only in proportion as all of Western culture is embracing (or lamenting) multiple perspective, "undecideability," and other post-foundational assumptions? Lifting the Derridean terms "speech," "writing," "presence" into theatrical analogy, must we also import their active principle, Derrida's attack on metaphysics? The most extreme form of this question is whether the great trajectory of Western drama—which found its origin in the century, culture, and society that incubated metaphysics—will prove to be roughly coterminous with it. The speech/writing pairing is only one prism through which to see that dramatic structures, more than any other poetic mode, reflect the dualism of metaphysical argument. I am not speaking only of dramatic conflict between antagonistic characters, but of drama's ravelings and unravelings; its bi-polar "themes" and imagery; its represented and unrepresented orders; its divided situation between spectator and spectacle, stage and auditorium. It will be protested that the dramatic form, so fundamentally ironic, is the subverter par excellence of metaphysical certainty. However, irony plays best against such certainty; ironic subversion is the obverse side of the *logos*. Drama doesn't have to be the appointed minister of metaphysics in order to be coterminous with its reign; even as court jester it would suffer the king's fate.

As I write, a review of an art installation in New York City appears in the *New York Times*. The artist, Ann Hamilton, has filled the floor of an immense loft space with horsehair, like a tangled sea. Hidden in various windows is audio equipment from which a male voice can be heard reading, or struggling to read with a slight speech defect, an indecipherable text. At the center a performer sits at a small desk "reading a book, burning away its words with a small heated implement." A smell of burnt paper fills the air. "The written word is eliminated with mindless, relentless ease," writes the reviewer, inferring from book and hair, perhaps, a Holocaust reference.[63] I am struck by the artist's use of both speech and writing in her installation, and that the speech, far from the transparent medium to Being that the stage has traditionally idealized, becomes a kind of background noise, distant and muffled. Because of the speech defect, the voice actually adds a barrier to the text. But the smell of burning paper is the very "stuff" of theatrical presence. Incontrovertibly, it is happening *now*, and cannot happen again or not in that way, for the burning object can only burn once. The "victim burnt at the stake" is neither saint nor actor, but text itself. But rather than lamenting the burning of text, the burning of writing, the artist may ironically be returning her audience to the experience of "presence." Unlike the 1960s avant-garde, however, which attempted to banish the absent oppressive text, Hamilton brings the text onstage "literally." The text has become an actor.

The text comes out from the wings as a separated theatrical element: the very impulse is a move away from the self-centered signification (centered on selves) that is still today the conventional if somewhat weary focus of the stage. Yet I find myself resisting the too inevitable implications of my own narrative. The narrative itself begins to demand a victim, and a loss.

What I describe in the postmodern theater of reading and writing is an experimental practice that takes little interest in theoretical debate, just as the theoreticians are less aware of actual theater than of any other art. This mutual oblivion is reassuring, in fact, for it elevates the parallel concerns of theater and theory to the level of cultural epidemic. But even if philosophy leads us to conclude that drama as we have understood it may be moribund, it cannot be certain where the human energies drama gathers together will settle next. In the games now being enacted in the electronic coils of virtual reality is emerging a much more radical theater of reading and writing than any performed on the stage, for it is a theater that presents no visual images to the eye, but only advancing scrolls of words. The players in these theaters are creating cybernetic dramas that push notions of "presence" into new, disembodied, territories. In these worlds, speech and writing, body and idea, presence and print, know nothing of former boundary disputes and appear in post-deconstructionist fusion.[64] Room must always be left in the story, finally, for new human adaptations.

5

Another Version of Pastoral

FOREMAN: I'd like to think that in happier, healthier times maybe I wouldn't even be an artist.

LeCOMPTE: Yeah . . . I've had a vision of just doing landscape architecture. It has to do with figuring out how to replant the earth the way it was. Returning it. You know. . . . Returning it to the way it might have been naturally.[1]

THIS IS A discussion of a type of staging that has become a signature style of contemporary experimental theater. In these performances, the human figure, instead of providing perspectival unity to a stage whose setting acts as backdrop and visual support, is treated as an element in what might be described as a theatrical landscape. Correspondingly the spectator's focus on this stage is no longer convergent: it is darting or diffuse, noting some configurations, missing others, or absorbing all in a heterogenous gaze. Heiner Müller wrote that the ideal "One-Person-Audience" for Robert Wilson's *Death, Destruction & Detroit II* "should have one eye that is attached to a pillar rising from the navel, circular and catholic, or turning with great speed as the eye of a certain reptile whose name I have forgotten. . . . "[2] Theater patrons who seek new forms in the theater have become accustomed, if not to the 360-degree staging of *DDDII*, to the multifocal scene and the diffused spectatorship it calls for. They may not even recall what a break with realistic, perspectival spectatorship this represents unless reminded of the older practices, as I was a few years ago by a conventional staging of *The Glass Menagerie*, during which I was surprised to realize that the production didn't absorb enough of my attention.

The progenitor of the idea of play as landscape was Gertrude Stein, but its proliferation may be attributed to the mid-century directors who brought back forms of choral staging, including Brecht, Grotowski, Brook, and the Living Theatre. An important epistemological role must be assigned to Beckett, who in *Godot* and then in *Endgame*, pushed to their almost parodic conclusions (implosions one might say) the two dominant dramaturgical and staging models—panoramic and concentrated—of the Western tradition.

In *Godot*, the panoramic journey of life becomes a journey in place, without origin or destination. The linear succession of scenes and times native to its structure has either frozen in place or, with the same result, entropically diluted to a timeless landscape. In *Endgame*, the intensive Aristotelian structure—one action, one setting, in compressed time—undergoes a parallel kind of white-out. In the world outside, the horizon has disappeared; in the world inside, the protagonist is paralyzed and sightless, despite his nostalgic demand to be placed "Bang! in the center" of the stage (whining, "Now I feel a little too far to the right. I feel a little too far forward").[3] Among the spectres of "endgames" the play's title raises, this ironic staging suggests an endgame for the Cartesian dramatic subject as well. The impression is reinforced in Hamm's final gesture, when he drops the bloody handkerchief—the curtain, one might say—over his own face.

The post-Beckett spectator has been trained by these two indelible images: the landscape that knows more than the figures in it, and the blank gaze of the unseeing figure in a vanished world. This spectator has grasped the groundless-ness that so discomfited the early Beckett audience: the collapse of boundaries between human and world, inside and outside, foreground and background. In this sense Beckett points the spectator to the postmodern landscape stage and the decentered figure, but he also, like Brecht, opens another frontier. If Clov sees only "Zero, zero and zero" from the upstage windows, he sees, ironically of course, "a multitude in transports of joy" when he turns his telescope toward the auditorium.[4] "Me to play" says Hamm, in occasional refrain,[5] as if in play and performing there were a way out of the awful doom of an imploding universe (including the traditional dramatic universe), a way out that is also opened across the proscenium in *Godot*.

After Beckett, experimental stage artists turn increasingly to staging theatrical worlds that no longer define themselves spatially against an unseen outside, or in a fictive temporal progression. These stage settings, sometimes representations of landscapes, as is often the case in Robert Wilson, but also imaginative hyperspaces, as in the productions of Richard Foreman, are performing worlds, elsewheres without elsewheres, imaginative spaces still shrewdly aware of their life in the theater. But given that very theatrical dimension, how seriously should one regard the term "landscape"? Is it a necessary or at least a useful term, or merely a painting term loosely and somewhat sentimentally applied to "field" arrangements of performers and decor that may have no connotations of nature?

Thornton Wilder, who knew and learned from Gertrude Stein, tried to understand her idea of play as landscape. "A myth is not a story read from left to right, from beginning to end," he reflected in his journal, seven years after her death, "but a thing held full-in-view the whole time. Perhaps this is what Gertrude Stein meant by saying that the play henceforth is a landscape."[6] Maurice Grosser, who turned Gertrude Stein's text of *Four Saints in Three Acts* into the opera scenario for Virgil Thomson, was, among other things—curious fact—a landscape painter. It was his inspiration to set the beginning of Act One

"In a garden in Avila in early Spring," Act Two "In the country out of doors,"
Act Three in the "Monastery garden with low trees . . . a bare Spanish horizon and an empty sky," and Act Four with "No scenery but the sky, tumultu-
ous clouds and a sunburst."[7] "Maurice understands my writing," Stein told
Thomson.[8]

Play as landscape: it is not perfectly clear whether Stein was talking about
the way of viewing, or the thing viewed. Reading her plays, it seems evident
that Stein uses "landscape" as a metaphor for a phenomenological spectatorship
of theater, a settled-back scanning or noting, not necessarily of a natural scene,
but of any pattern of language, gesture and design *as if* it were a natural scene.
Yet every time the term "landscape" appears in Stein's writing as a description
of her plays or of the way to approach them, it appears in the company of
natural images from actual landscapes.

As early as World War I, Stein relates in *The Autobiography of Alice B. Toklas*,
she realized that "a certain kind of landscape induces plays."[9] If she didn't write
plays from nature like a landscape painter, so to say, she wrote plays *in* them.
The idea of the landscape play, in all its ambiguity, fully took hold after the war.
In the winter of 1922–1923, when "the landscape that of all landscapes mean[t]
the most" (the valley of the Rhône), was "once more exercising its spell" over
her, Stein writes, she "meditated upon the use of grammar, poetical forms and
what might be termed landscape plays."[10]

In her 1935 American lecture tour, Stein returns to this entwining of the
Rhône landscape with theatrical form in her talk on "Plays." The interchange
between real landscape and the idea of plays as landscape continues.

> Then I began to spend my summers in Bilignin in the department of the Ain
> and there I lived in a landscape that made itself its own landscape. . . . I slowly
> came to feel that since the landscape was the thing . . . a play was a thing and
> I went on writing plays a great many plays. The landscape at Bilignin so com-
> pletely made a play that I wrote quantities of plays.[11]

The curious reference to *Hamlet* suggests what seems to have been the liberating democracy of "things" to Stein: plays were landscapes composed of things,
but landscapes were themselves things set with things. The common thingness
of landscapes and plays erased any sense of contradiction between nature and
culture, stationary features and human figures, or visual phenomena and language.

In this talk, the relationship between real landscape and play as landscape
temporarily unravels into different realms, natural and psychological: "I felt that
if a play was exactly like a landscape then there would be no difficulty about
the emotion of the person looking on at the play being behind or ahead of the
play [a problem she had earlier identified as "syncopation"] because the landscape does not have to make acquaintance . . . it is there. . . . "[12] But presently

Stein explains this "thereness" in a sentence that slides without transition from nature to literature: " . . . the landscape not moving but being always in relation, the trees to the hills the hills to the fields the trees to each other any piece of it to any sky and then any detail to any other detail, the story is only of importance if you like to tell or like to hear a story but the relation is there anyway. And of that relation I wanted to make a play and I did, a great number of plays."[13]

Stein's most extended example of a landscape play is *Four Saints in Three Acts.* In a 1927 letter describing the project to Virgil Thomson, Stein clearly had the idea of natural landscape in mind. "Make it pastoral," she wrote. "In hills and gardens."[14] As she later described the text, however, natural and conceptual landscapes become inseparable.

> I made the Saints the landscape . . . all these saints together made my landscape. These attendant saints were the landscape and it the play really is a landscape. A landscape does not move nothing really moves in a landscape but things are there, and I put into the play the things that were there.[15]

But just as we are content to understand "landscape" as shorthand for spatial and static as opposed to temporal and progressive, Stein returns to nature. "Magpies [she is speaking of the magpies in Act Three] . . . are black and white and they are in the sky of the landscape in Bilignin and in Spain, especially in St. Teresa's Avila. . . . There were magpies in my landscape and there were scarecrows."[16] (She says nothing about the pigeons on the grass, alas.)

Can it be we've been so fascinated with Stein's cubism, that we haven't seen her pastoralism? With every formal breath on play as landscape, Stein invokes an idealized view of landscape itself: like the shepherds of traditional pastoral who populated the bucolic landscape of Arcadia, landscape to Stein was wholly present to itself, simple and un-anxiety provoking to the spectator. Just as the simple rural values of traditional pastoral shine in contrast to the complex life at court or in the city, so the landscape play to Stein offers refuge from the temporally and emotionally complex theater structures that trapped her in "syncopation," made her "nervous," and at their climax drove her to seek not completion, but "relief."[17]

Let me now bring in another kind of landscape tradition in modern theater, though it is rarely associated with Stein, deriving from Maeterlinck's early one-act plays and his immensely influential essay of 1896 on "static theater," "The Tragical in Daily Life." To Maeterlinck—twelve years Stein's senior, and more than that in the theory of a static theater—the essence of tragedy was to be found not in action, as Aristotle said, but in contemplation.

> I have grown to believe that an old man, seated in his armchair, waiting patiently . . . giving unconscious ear to all the eternal laws that reign about his

house, interpreting without comprehending the silence of doors and windows and the quivering voice of the light . . . does yet live in reality a deeper, more human, more universal life than the lover who strangles his mistress, the captain who conquers in battle, or the husband who avenges his honor.[18]

Like Maeterlinck, Stein favored a static theater. A habituée of theater in the San Francisco of the 1880s, she might have been exposed to some of the same romantic plays against which he reacted. But if Maeterlinck saw in stasis the essence of tragedy, Stein's static was essentially comic. Thus her sunny, untroubled, loafing saints. "A martyr does something but a really good saint does nothing," she said, adding an appraisal of character in a static theater that could have been learned from Maeterlinck: "Generally speaking, anybody is more interesting doing nothing than doing anything."[19]

Maeterlinck didn't advance a theory of landscape as the setting for static theater, but in what was his most important play in terms of dramatic form, *The Blind* (1890), he created the first modern landscape stage, where setting goes beyond decoration and atmospherics to carry a freight of meaning exceeding that borne by the characters. If there were no dialogue uttered among the twelve blind men and women unaware that their priest sits dead among them, we would soon understand this forest setting on an island, with its rising wind, beating waves, rustling leaves, and menacing changes of light as an allegory of the human condition. There is almost no action—just waiting, mounting anxiety, and slow recognition of inevitable death. The Maeterlinckian stage of the tragic symbolic landscape persists throughout the modern period. It echoes even in Heiner Müller's *Hamletmachine*, whose opening lines ("I was Hamlet. I stood at the shore and talked with the surf, BLABLA, the ruins of Europe in back of me") conjure a destroyed physical landscape on which political and cultural ruins are prominent features.[20]

In both Stein and Maeterlinck, the spatial principle represented by landscape has virtually replaced the temporal principle. As Gurnemanz instructs Parsifal, "[H]ere time turns to space."[21] Time has expanded to a static eternal in Maeterlinck, or contracted to a series of fresh starts that Stein saw as a continuous present. Each approach—whether representational or perceptual, in the eye or in the mind—appears somehow embedded in the other. Is it possible that we could think together, as variants of a single modern tradition, these two static, spatial theaters with their concomitant resort to landscape?

This theoretical and staging history in itself might justify the use of the term "landscape," but as I contemplate the possibility of a confluent twentieth-century tradition, a new common ground seems to emerge among a number of contemporary artists and works whose connections I have sensed, but whose surface energies, materials, and visual styles are apparently quite different. What I had not previously noticed was that many works which have nonlinear spatial structures, and are concerned not with individual character or a temporal progression but with a total state or condition, also draw important moments of imagery from natural landscape, and even hint at the thematics of pastoral. The question then presents itself, whether these traits "go together," and appear not fortuitously, but as elements in a recurring configuration. Here are a number of examples.

Almost all Robert Wilson scenes take the form of a panoramic landscape view, and many have actual landscape effects, such as the village nestled in snow in Act One of the Cologne section of *the CIVIL warS*; the forest scenes from *The Forest* and the Rome section of *CIVIL warS*. *KA MOUNTAIN AND GUARDenia TERRACE* at the 1972 Shiraz Festival, with its seven-day progression up Haft Tan Mountain, was composed around a natural landscape. A bestiary of giraffes, tigers, bears, owls, and water creatures has populated Wilson's work from the beginning. His 1986 *Alcestis* of Euripides at the American Repertory Theatre in Cambridge was his most concrete and representational theatrical landscape: it presented a mountain and valley, three-dimensional and unmoving for an entire performance.

In its basis in a narrative text, the *Alcestis* was somewhat untypical Wilson, especially at that time. It was, however, typical in the extreme textual condensation and fragmentation he worked on it, and in its interpolated texts, slow-motion stage movement, and wrapped sound environment. Here a "built" mountain range extended the entire width of the stage. There were an expanse of sky above, a flowing river below with a prehistoric amphibian creeping along its banks, and scattered rocks and shrubs. Sylvan nymphs bathed in the real water of the stream. Tribal folk conducted an archaic ritual nearby. Birdsong filled the air. Mystical servants, half-man, half-beast, served at table. Nowhere to be seen was the traditional locus of Greek drama—the royal palace and its gates—that summons up the concerns of human figures challenged by the gods. Though he retained the outlines of the plot and the vestigial remains of characters—names and gestures without psychological transformation—Wilson's interest lay elsewhere, in a pastoral vision of human-blending-into-nature, and nature on a continuum with gods and magic. And yet this description of the mountain scene may be overly concrete, overly "natural," for the mountain was not only a natural, but a cultural structure, described to me by Wilson in an interview during the final rehearsal period.

> There are layers or stratified zones that are stacked from upstage to downstage. A modern highway, a highway of old stones, you have those stratified zones of reality, of time, etc. Then you also have horizontal layers, like you have in a mountain, that go through eons of time. And in that mountain you have everything. Actually that mountain range is something like the mountain range in Delphi.[22]

As a prologue to the *Alcestis*, Wilson staged Heiner Müller's prose poem, "Explosion of a Memory / Description of a Picture," itself described by the author as a "landscape beyond death." Spoken before the landscape setting was revealed, it begins, "A landscape neither quite steppe nor savannah, the sky a Prussian blue. . . . "[23] Wilson told me that owing to delays in Müller's schedule, they did not consult in advance about the content of the prologue, or about Wilson's stage design.

> If I'd ever read it I never would have designed it this way. It is the strangest thing how many parallels are in that text and how many images are in this play. . . . It is just uncanny. I would have been afraid that I was illustrating his text, which I don't like to do.

The landscape idea in both senses developed above may have formed an early basis for collaboration between Wilson and Müller. In an interview conducted in Berlin in 1984 at the time of the performance there of the Cologne section of *the CIVIL warS* (Müller's first collaboration with Wilson), Müller expressed his appreciation of Wilson's staging techniques in landscape language that could have been inspired by Gertrude Stein.

> [Wilson's] main object is to find room for all the elements in his mind or his fantasy. And that's what interests me. My texts can breathe, they have room. . . . A good text has to be like a thing, like a solid rock or stone. You can throw this stone from the mountain and maybe there's some dust flying off, but nothing else. It stays the same. Theater people in Germany always try to find something inside the text, but Wilson just takes it, like a kid playing with marbles.[24]

The "uncanny" parallel between the Müller prologue and the Wilson conception of Euripides was surely the association of landscape with death. Wilson regarded death as the subject of his production of *Alcestis*:

> Well, theater has to be about one thing first. . . . And I always have to say, O.K., it has to be about one thing, shut my eyes quick and produce it. And then it's about many things. So I had to do that for myself. I narrowed the text down to one word, and that word appears more than any other word. . . . So I reduced it that way, simply [to] . . . the basic idea that it's about death and the poetry of death.

Wilson creates landscape plays not only as spectacles set in nature, but in the double sense that Gertrude Stein unfolds. The Wilson stage is typically an entire world, encompassing humans, buildings, trains, space ships, and the creatures, rocks, water, and growing things of the natural world. But his theater, whether set in nature or not, requires from the audience the "landscape-response" appropriate to a dispersed perceptual field, a response enforced by the repetitions and slow-moving transformations of his stagings. His *Alcestis* became in both senses a landscape play.[25] The association of landscape with the theme of death, however, brings another dimension to the work, and another connection with the Müller prologue. The two comprise what might be thought of as a theatrical pastoral elegy, a meditation on death in a setting from nature that is sympathetic with the scale, the silence, and finality, of death itself.

Reza Abdoh, who died of AIDS in May, 1995, was the writer-director of an almost unremittingly frenetic, ear-splitting, and vulgar theater. His work provides the sharpest possible contrast to Wilson. His theater emerged in part from the Los Angeles club world of sex, drugs, and rock 'n roll, rather than the high art gallery world of the older, conceptual avant-garde. Yet the Iranian-born Abdoh found his way to Stein at the age of fourteen, while living and studying in England. "I think I have read eighty per cent of what she has written," he told me in a telephone interview, but accounts her more an "inspiration" than a direct influence.

In *Tight, Right, White*, created and performed in New York in the spring of 1993, performers raced from stage to stage, the audience dizzily following, playing out a crazy-quilt historical minstrel show of American racism and homophobia. The text was fragmented and only very loosely sequential as pieces of a tale of slavery and miscegenation unfolded. Until nearly the end, each bit of action or text hit with the force of a new beginning (which Stein wanted in her own work: "begin again"), same high tone, same mad energy and assaultive score, continuously punctuated by group dance numbers and offensive comedy routines.

The central element of decor was the bodies of his chorus of performers—patched with red, blue, yellow, and white paint to suggest a kind of postmodern racially marked body. The actors sometimes wore grotesque masks as well. The settings referred only occasionally to natural landscape nor were there highly-worked artificial environments. They consisted of a few painted backdrops, props, and set pieces. Still, in *Tight, Right, White* the very multiplicity of stages and the spectator's saturation with them created the perceptual demands of landscape in a total environment. The spectators, seated on cushions on the floor, pivoted to see action on four principal stages, and moved to see scenes on two peripheral stages. As performing areas opened into multiple levels, there were eventually ten stages in all.

In the final images of the performance, Abdoh slipped across the boundary from landscape as perception to landscape scene, and at the same time into the pastoral mode (forecast from the beginning, perhaps by the innocence of his field slave figure coupled with the attack on corrupt whites, traditional themes of American pastoral). Contrasting scenes appeared on the two main stages, to right and left of the spectators. On the right was a silent family camping scene, white tent, white clothing, white marshmallows, the white of purity and of privilege. On the left stood a group of trembling half-naked wretches in the contrasting white of a snowfall, a reference to the shivering Tom on the landscape of Lear's heath. In the foreground sat a figure hooked to an oxygen mask. The only sound in this otherwise silent scene was his racked coughing and a faint repeated whisper, reminiscent of Eurydice's wrenching plea for remembrance in Gluck—the orphic association itself appropriate to pastoral—"Who will be the witness?"

Abdoh productions were as raw and frantic as Wilson's are slow and controlled. Yet in both, the eye and ear function similarly: unable to absorb the entire *mise-en-scène* at once, they must scan the work on many tracks simultaneously, for visual design, sound, lights, music, arrangements of figures on the stage, and intermittent bursts of character and story fragments that then subside again into the totality of shifting configurations. This is landscape staging of the perceptual kind. Abdoh's cacophonous spatial stagings were suddenly pierced by images of natural landscape as well, often associated with the silent peace of death. Every Abdoh production I saw found its way to this place of death and landscape.

The death-infused landscape appeared in its most transparent form in Abdoh's last completed work, the harshly elegiac *Quotations from a Ruined City*, performed in 1994. The "ruins" were of bodies succumbing to AIDS, of actual cities—Beirut, Los Angeles, Sarajevo—and finally of all of history: history as ruin. But the torrent of action and images on these themes was framed by recurring representations of that supreme motif of pastoral elegy, the graveyard. The piece began in the graveyard, with gauze-wrapped cast members stilled at angles, like driftwood, against the silent scene. The graveyard continued to make its appearance in *Quotations*, at times with pathetic floral bouquets, then with birdsong and cutouts of grazing sheep, and again with headstones inscribed in Persian. It became the chief emblem of "ruin" in this long meditation on history and cruelty.

Both in Wilson and in Abdoh, landscape is at one end of a spectrum of "field" stagings (the word itself is a weak evocation of landscape), suggesting nostalgia for a lost pastoral. In their work, landscape appears as the "real" imaginary of the more abstract stage patterns, or, indeed, of the stage itself. They are not alone. Many contemporary directors—and as I use the title in this chapter it always implies a range of skills and talents that may include design, writing, choreography, musical composition, and performing—who mount performance pieces to the scale of landscape, use the imagery of landscape, and sometimes stage works in actual *plein air* landscapes. Among these are Peter Schumann of the Bread and Puppet Theatre, whose farm in Glover, Vermont, has been the annual site of large-scale festival theater, Meredith Monk, Ping Chong, Anne Bogart, Tina Landau, David Finkelstein, and on occasion JoAnne

Akalaitis and Lee Breuer. Monk provides, however, an opportunity to raise a counter-example.

Monk could be seen as the Grandma Moses of the American experimental theater, cultivating a transparent, "primitive" style to depict scenes animated by child-like emotions, such as wonder, joy, and delight. The use of sung syllables instead of language contributes significantly to the primitive effect, the non-verbal idiom preventing the performance from falling into sophisticated ambiguity or ambivalence and helping to preserve an aura of purity around the work. Monk was one of the first directors to create the landscape performance piece. This she did both in actual landscapes, and in large-scale "field" pieces in theatrical spaces, where the fluid danced/acted formations sometimes took place in landscape settings. Her *Education of the Girl Child* culminated in a grand journey against the Mexican sky and desert. *Quarry* actually incorporated film of a rock quarry, seen at different levels of magnification. In one scene of *Quarry* her entire company streamed across the stage carrying clouds mounted on poles.

The 1991 *Atlas* was in one sense the most ambitious use Monk has made of landscape settings, as its title may suggest. But the global adventure undertaken by Monk's heroine (inspired by the early twentieth century traveler and mystic Alexandra David-Neel), was a throwback to conventional narrative and scenography in several ways. It was the most solidly characterological of Monk's pieces, and it is interesting that along with (can we say because of?) that decision, a system of traditional hierarchies quite alien to the form I am describing sprang into place. Here was a leading character, surrounded by supporting leads, supported in turn by a chorus that played a number of roles. And these same characters in turn appeared before scenery of the world's climes and cultures that functioned essentially as a series of pictorial and illustrative backdrops. The reversion to a ranked character structure fed quite without irony into a hierarchical political structure as the band of adventurers traveled the globe encountering cheerful natives and contented peasants, all ready to welcome and celebrate the spiritual colonialists. Whereas Abdoh, Wilson, and others have used a landscape staging to break up and disperse the unitary character or to disturb the seamless cooperation of foreground and background, in *Atlas* landscape served to return Monk to more traditional dramaturgical assumptions.

Two directors often associated with those I have discussed are Richard Foreman and Elizabeth LeCompte, both of whose work is marked by an absence of natural imagery. Foreman is a creator of hermetic stage environments. The natural does not penetrate his rarefied world of skulls, clocks, strings, Hebrew letters, strange signs and symbols—suggestive in part of the *fin-de-siècle* occult. His prolific world of things picks up only the perceptual prong of the dual landscape tradition, and is perhaps better described as creating mindscapes than landscapes. (Yet all dictionaries note that words with "scape" as a back-formation are related to the idea of landscape and suggest a view of and from a setting limited only by the viewer's perspective.)

Foreman's debt to Gertrude Stein, and to her general idea of the landscape play with its "continuous present" is well known.[26] In a post-Beckett mode, Foreman's theater enacts a state of moment-to-moment awareness of the contents of the mind. To theatricalize this continually breaking awareness, figure, gesture, and voice may achieve a certain coherence of convenience. Unlike, say, Robert Wilson's scrupulously non-interpretive performers, Foreman's actors will be urged, under his direction, to offer definite interpretations that have no meaning. However, these figures must not be mistaken for autonomous characters with psychological interiority. They are more like characterological objects in a field crowded with things, all of which are infused with a deep, mysterious animation. Foreman himself has said that he thinks "the way a lyric poet thinks," and that his experiment is to make the lyric viable in the theater.[27] It is the lyric mode, essentially static and reflective, that is key to linking Foreman back to Stein and Maeterlinck, and horizontally to Wilson and many of his contemporaries creating landscape stagings.

LeCompte too maintains her distance from the natural. Her performing worlds are industrial and mediatized, created of metal platforms and pipes, video monitors, microphones, telephones, and a handful of signature props (the Victorian lamp and wax grapes keep returning). Unlike Wilson, Abdoh, and Foreman, all of whom stage or staged large conditions of the soul, LeCompte is more traditionally dramatic in her cultivation of conflict. Meta-dramatic is the better word, for her contraries and abrasions are not among characters but among performance modes and cultural ideas. More than any contemporary American theater artist, LeCompte has announced performance itself as the field of raw material. She forages among classic theater texts, and performance, film, television, and dance styles, for material from which to compose her own highly-worked constructions. Her pieces are arrangements in space that require the multiple, moment-to-moment shifting focus of postmodern spectatorship. In the Steinian sense they may be called landscape plays, but almost never does LeCompte appear tempted toward landscape imagery and pastoral. In her work the "natural" must run a rigorous gauntlet of testing for mere sentimentality. Real tears may perhaps be drawn by Vershinin's video departure in *Fish Story* (based on the final act of *Three Sisters*), but not before the theatrical apparatus of artificially-induced glycerine tears is exposed to view.

Yet it is striking how often LeCompte's work embraces the elegiac. Loss and mourning were at the heart of *Three Places in Rhode Island* and suffused the subsequent *Route 1 & 9*. Death was the explicit meditative object of *Frank Dell's The Temptation of Saint Antony*. Loss is again the dominant in *Brace-Up!*, her version of the first three acts of *Three Sisters*. Remarkably, LeCompte dreams, in the quotation at the beginning of the chapter, of reinventing herself as a landscape architect, as if landscape were the "other" of her stage. Where directors like Abdoh figure landscape as a refuge within the theater piece, to LeCompte it appears as the excluded ideal alternative. Particularly arresting is her edenic dream of returning the earth to the way it "might have been naturally." Such a curious fantasy from one whose work is so self-consciously mediated almost suggests that for LeCompte, artistic endeavor itself represents (both stands for and depicts) a kind of original sin, a fall from the whole of nature. In this sense LeCompte can be seen as standing at the far edge of the landscape idea I am tracing.

Landscape staging is not the exclusive domain of avant-garde stage directors. Since the late 1980s, playwright Suzan-Lori Parks has been creating a poetic American spatial dramaturgy not seen since Adrienne Kennedy's plays of the mid-1960s, or for that matter, since Gertrude Stein herself, whom Parks claims as a direct influence. Parks's *The Death of the Last Black Man in the Whole Entire World*, first produced in 1990, is part pageant play, part jazz cantata, part Greek tragedy, and always an elegy on the theme of black suffering, loss, and misrepresentation through history. Its "characters" include black biblical and historical figures; satiric exaggerations of African American stereotypes (for instance "Lots of Grease and Lots of Pork" and "Yes and Greens Blackeyed Peas Cornbread"); references to books ("Before Columbus," from the work of African American historian Ivan Van Sertima, *They Came Before Columbus*[28]); and rhetorical flourishes that summon up writing itself ("Prunes and Prisms," named from a poem in Joyce, who borrowed it from Dickens). A central emblematic couple seem more like "real" characters: Black Man With Watermelon, who inhabits—in a kind of limbo—all of black history since slavery, and his devoted wife, Black Woman With Fried Drumstick. These two might better be thought of as stereo-archetypes, archetypal in their rural simplicity and mutual attachment, and playfully stereotypical in the teasing references to chicken and watermelon. Yet the drumstick is a political pun too, for drums, like Katrin's in *Mother Courage*, alert people to danger and awaken them to resistance. Black Woman here is a kind of Courage figure.

The play's title echoes the linear intensity of Greek crisis drama—the death, the *last*—but the motif of the Black Man who is chased, beaten, lynched, hung, and electrocuted through history, keeps reappearing in an eternal arena of culture, where all times are simultaneously present, as the play's repeated refrain suggests: "Yesterday today next summer tomorrow just uh moment uhgoh in 1317 dieded thuh last black man in thuh whole entire world."[29] Black history is treated not as a chronology of events over time, but as a great space of simultaneous experience and representations of that experience, experience and representations that keep recurring, like perennials in nature. The objects on this complex landscape, whether sympathetic history, hostile distortions, fiction, popular imagery, history yet to be written, and lived lives just trying to survive, all have equal value: they are "always in relation," as Stein said, "any detail to any detail."

The landscape effect of the play arises not so much from the playwright's use of natural imagery, but from the open, spatial form of the piece, written in visual "panels," and from its imagined world as an act of mourning at a kind of funeral. There are other echoes of pastoral, in the primitive poetic diction Parks has found for the play that summons a black cultural equivalent of the speech of shepherds and shepherdesses in Shakespearean pastoral, and in the innocence of Black Man and Black Woman themselves. In production the play resonates with pastoral elegy. Director Liz Diamond set the Yale Repertory Theater production of 1992 in a brilliant green space whose floor was mined with pop-up doors, at once cemetery and planted field.

The last of Parks's five "panels," her visual term for scenes, is a garden. In a final dialogue between Black Man and Black Woman, much condensed below, tropes of human love and death, planting and renewal, become virtually indistinguishable:

BW:	Sweetheart.
BM:	SPRING-TIME.
BW:	Sweetheart.
BM:	You buried me alive with tree seeds in my pockets and time passed and spring time comes and went goes on and it rains . . .
BW:	I'll plant you.
BM:	You'll plant me . . . Re-member me.
BW:	Re-member me.[30]

As suggestive as *Last Black Man* is of landscape and its associated literary forms, the setting of Parks's subsequent play, *The America Play*, performed at the Yale Repertory Theater, Public Theater, and American Repertory Theatre in the spring of 1994, is actually set in a postmodern American landscape. The play takes place "out West," deep in the Great Hole of History, or, to be precise, in its "exact replica." But even back East, we learn, the "original Great Hole" was not a natural creation: it was a theme park. The second act becomes an archeological dig in the false earth of this false nature for clues to the grave-digging father who was also "uh greaaaaat biiiiig faker."[31] From this dubious soil the faker's son reverently retrieves the phony apparatus of his father's Abe Lincoln act.

Like the *Last Black Man* (and like the Wilson / Müller and Abdoh landscape stagings discussed above), *The America Play* echoes the pastoral elegy in its association of landscape, death, and burial, but here Parks distances the motif with withering political irony. For the black man in America, Parks implies, there is no "ground." He searches for roots, for ancestral clues, among the imitations of an already deracinated white culture, among simulations of simulations. Race is never directly mentioned in *The America Play*: it is simply the factor that turns into mordant parody all of Parks's re-inscriptions—of the high themes of American history, of the great American father-son drama (with echoes of *Hamlet*) as an expression of that history, and of the landscape play itself as a theme park of historical and dramatic shards.

Of all the postmodern landscape plays introduced here, Charles Mee's treatment of the myth of Orestes would seem the closest to a play of recognizable plot and character. Here are Electra and Orestes, Helen and Menelaus; traditional issues of revenge, responsibility, punishment, and justice would still seem central. In Mee's text of *Orestes*, however, plot and character are rhetorical surfaces in precisely the way that ethics and personhood function as emptied-out simulacra in the world of his play. They are quoted, but are not objects of exploration; even less are Mee's characters subjects in whose suffering, inner conflicts, recognition, growth, or resignation we are invited to take interest. Mee presents an entire society as a hospital ward in varying stages of breakdown, post-traumatic stress syndrome, and sanctimonious and self-forgiving "recovery." These vertiginous moral prospects are presented as objects of contemplation in a series of stand-up production numbers—monologues, occasional dialogues, and song and dance routines performed by a ghoulish chorus of hospital nurses.

Mee's true interest is the ruined moral landscape of post-Vietnam America—its violence, its greed, its warped individualism, its swagger, its impotence, its cruelty to children, its social fabric of lies and distortions, its fascination with terror, its surface of fashion, its deadly revenge on those who see and tell the truth. The spectator's object of interest in *Orestes* is not the fate of individual characters—their ruin is assumed *a priori*—but the entire dystopic environment. In this sense, the landscape setting given the play in producer Anne Hamburger's 1993 production was summoned by the text.

Hamburger may be one of the landscape visionaries of the American theater. She has worked New York from the 14th Street meat-packing district to Central Park to Harlem in site-specific productions, but no text and site have come together as definitively as did Mee's play text with the "despoiled shore" of the Hudson River. The site was the abandoned Pennsylvania Railroad yards where Donald Trump's long embattled Riverside South housing development will rise. Director Tina Landau staged the play with absolute detachment, like staging the weather, against the charred girders of burnt-out piers and the harsh neon of commercial New Jersey. Not only Heiner Müller's *Despoiled Shore*, but his *Hamletmachine* seemed a progenitor here. Beginning on the ruined shores of Europe and ending in an ice age in the heart of Africa, *Hamletmachine* is not a tragedy of character, but of culture as landscape; tragedy of character would be merely one of the losses in the general failure. The sense of a total environment of cultural failure inversely links both Müller's plays and Mee's *Orestes* to the nostalgia of the pastoral tradition, here sickened into dispastoral.

These theatrical pieces do not look or sound alike. They have very different tempi, describe different worlds, and reflect radically different artistic sensibilities. Yet when compared to a narrative theater structure where individual characters perform actions against the backdrop of particular settings, they bear a family resemblance. They seek neither the realist's psychological involvement nor Brecht's critical detachment nor Artaud's openness to the irrational. They mobilize yet another faculty. Bonnie Marranca suggests how to think about this faculty in her provocative words on Chekhov's use of space:

> Setting entraps a play in historical time; it is mere scenery, information, the dressing that frames a play in a set of gestures, speech styles and moral values. That static view of space encourages closure, preoccupation with causality, motivation; it is possessive of dramatic characters, reducing all their gestures to a specific time and environment, as if there were no world beyond the fourth wall. It separates the human being from the world, forcing the two into opposition.[32]

The key word here is "opposition." On the landscape stage there is little oppositional dynamic, just as there is none in Stein, and none really in *The Blind* of Maeterlinck. Even where thematic opposition is scored into the performance scenario, as racial conflict is in Abdoh's *Tight, White, Right*, it is presented as illustration rather than imitation. The sources of theatrical opposition—they are primarily tied to dramatic character—have been becalmed in this "static" theater: opposition between characters, as in the usual antagonistic form of realism; between spectator and character or actor and character, as there is in the dialectical theater of Brecht; and—the dimension that Marranca points to—between the foreground life of characters, and the background of visual presentation. The theatrical world of the landscape is shaded by contrast, but is not organized around the reversals of dramatic irony, sharp turnabouts in expectation or perceptual frame. We are leaving the dramatic mode behind. I don't suggest that the dancer and the dance have melted into each other in this theater, far from it. We experience distance, but without alienation, and on the other hand involvement, without identification. What then holds our attention?

How marvelously the metaphor from landscape rushes in to reply: we are interested in the entire *field*, the whole *terrain*, the total *environment* of the performance, as performance, and as imaginative construct. We are no more transported to another world than we banish all other worlds (this latter being the somewhat stultifying claim for "presence" made by some performance art theorists). I experimentally suggest that a performance genre has emerged that encourages and relies on the faculty of landscape surveyal. Its structures are arranged not on lines of conflict and resolution but on multivalent spatial relationships, "the trees to the hills the hills to the fields . . . any piece of it to any sky" as Stein said, "any detail to any other detail." Ulla Dydo recounts the story of Gertrude Stein's driving habits—she never used a map, but read road signs because she enjoyed reading. About the landscape play, Dydo concludes, "We read such a piece, as she read the road signs in the landscape, for the pleasure of reading."[33] This genre relies on the phenomenological landscape-perception that Stein pioneered, but is never far from the imagery of actual landscape, which, as we saw in Stein, asserts itself when spatiality begins to emerge over temporality as a theatrical value. The thematics of pastoral reappear surprisingly often under these conditions, as if brought along by the gravitational pull of landscape, just as landscape itself is brought along by static spatiality, by the lyric in the theater.

And so I arrive at the proposal that we have been seeing in some of the more innovative contemporary theater an extension of pastoral, or perhaps better said, a pastoral for the age of ecology, or only possible in the age of ecology. I do not, of course, make the extravagant claim that the ability to make or perceive such theater marks its creators and spectators as ideologically-committed ecologists. Indeed there is not yet an ecological movement in theater as is developing in visual and installation art.[34] Rather I would say that the new pastoral in theater draws on a perceptual faculty not unlike that developed by ecology, a systems-awareness that moves sharply away from the ethos of competitive individualism toward a vision of the whole, however defined in any given setting. In this sense we are becoming ecologists of theater. No longer fascinated by the struggles of single organisms in their habitats—which translates here into individual characters in their theatrical settings—we pull back to scan Thornton Wilder's intuited intersection of myth, Stein and landscape, where the thing-held-full-in-view-the-whole-time becomes the measure of theatrical interest.

The artist of modernity mourned the loss of forests and orchards and open spaces, but also dreamt of urban utopias—whether Chekhov's Moscow in the minds of the Prozorov sisters, or Mayakovsky's mechanized and electrified New Jerusalem, or Walter Benjamin's Paris of the arcades (literally, an urban arcadia). The postmodern artist longs for a vanishing natural world, and sometimes a vanished natural world, existing before history, before culture. Robert Wilson, particularly, creates within advanced culture a fragile memory bank of imagery from nature. In this way, and in a variety of others, postmodern theater artists hint at the possibility of a post-anthropocentric stage.

6

When Bad Girls Play Good Theaters

How can business men and women stand in a room and
discuss business without even one reference to their genitals?
I mean everybody has them. They just pretend they don't.

—Maria Irene Fornes, *Fefu and Her Friends*[1]

Foreword

The following account catches, and strives to understand, a moment in
the life of the New York alternative theater of the early and mid-1980s.[2] It
was the brief moment before obscenity on the stage became a political scandal, before Jesse Helms attacked, before the Mapplethorpe show, before the
NEA de-fundings, but these soon changed the artistic climate. One result of
the polarizing events was that the theater community—both artists and audiences—had little opportunity to examine its deeper responses to the kind of
material I describe before being enlisted in a "patriotic" defense of artistic
freedom. This was unfortunate, for just as to Helms and the right such work
was unproblematically "wrong," so to its defenders it became unproblematically right and good. Audiences confused and sometimes frightened by Karen
Finley went on shortly to greet her with knowing laughter and standing ova-
tions. Spectators ready to walk out of Annie Sprinkle's porn routine at the
Performing Garage lined up to inspect her cervix with flashlight and speculum
at The Kitchen. Everything that was "disturbational," in the resonant term
used by Arthur Danto to describe Mapplethorpe's photography, was lightened
into entertainment by audiences determined to support their artists. The most
absurd extreme of this loyalty occurred in the auditorium of the Brooklyn
Museum in June, 1992, where several obscene performances, some of embarrassing ineptitude, were all but canonized by the museum director, who had
been pressed into the fray by Martha Wilson of the Franklin Furnace. By that
time, the national furor had not only forced audiences into shallow responses,
but artists into shallow work, where attack on the NEA now became a fitting
substitute for exploring the complex of issues surrounding the breaking of
sexual taboo in an art theater setting. A further stage in the willed forgetting
of what once promised to be a debate of some depth came with the commercial exploitation of the censorship controversy by Madonna and commercial
advertisers. What follows below comes from a more molten, less certain time,

when artists like Elizabeth LeCompte were groping to understand pornography rather than simply defend it, when spectators were still willing to admit to discomfort at Annie Sprinkle's porn routines; and when Annie herself was still surprised by her own self-declared paradigm shift, from porno star to performance artist. Most important, it was a time when people could still change their minds.

I.

1987

NEARLY TWENTY-FIVE years ago the conceptual and performance artist Carolee Schneeman created a loft art environment, "Eye Body," in which she included her own body as one of the materials. Photos of "Eye Body" showing the naked, beautiful Schneeman, flowers painted on her cheeks, her breasts and body covered with slashes of paint, grease, and chalk, or lying on the floor slithered over by live snakes, speak to the shocking but also the erotic and celebratory nature of her performances. Schneeman has written of the "ritual aspect of the process" that could put her in a "trance-like state," and of her later discovery, through the study of Earth Goddess artifacts, of the sacral implications of the body images explored in that performance.[3]

In performances created by a number of women in the 1980s, Schneeman's sacred body was replaced by the obscene body—aggressive, scatological, and sometimes pornographic. The purpose of the present exploration is to gather the scattered evidence of this phenomenon, and to begin to map its location in the fraught contemporary debate over female sexuality, feminism, and pornography. What did these performances say to us about contemporary theater practice? What did it mean that women were making these performances? And how should one begin to think about these questions: with theories of the avant-garde? of modernist "transgression"? of pornography? with the feminist pornography wars? Though only one performance I write about was unequivocally pornographic (others were borderline, most were "only" obscene—the boundaries smudge instantly), I started this project by trying to find out what people who have thought about it think pornography is.

At one border of the 1980s pornography debate there was a real enjoyment and tolerance of pornography. Its defenders, such as Marxist philosopher Alan Soble, saw violent pornography as marginal. Soble makes little distinction between most pornography and erotica. He suggests a pornography without offense, gender, or marketplace.

> Pornography refers to any literature or film (or other art-technological form) that describes or depicts sexual organs, or preludes to sexual activity (or re-

lated organs and activities) in such a way as to produce sexual arousal in the user or the viewer.[4]

Many feminists defended pornography. The FACT group—Feminist Anti-Censorship Taskforce—was formed in 1984 by scholars and activists such as Anne Snitow, Carole Vance, and Ellen Willis to defend women's right to explore their own pleasure in sexuality, and to defeat the anti-pornography ordinances then being proposed in various communities. Some of the women active in FACT were responsible for the publication *Caught Looking*, a glossy book with a magazine layout in which articles defending pornography or attacking its censorship jostled a large number of nonviolent (porno)graphics.[5] Pro-porn activists included some lesbian feminists, such as the Samois group, who were creating their own S&M pornography.

At the other end of the debate were the Women Against Pornography and other anti-porn feminist activists, who supported the Andrea Dworkin–Catharine MacKinnon anti-pornography ordinance. The ordinance, which was ruled unconstitutional, defined pornography as those representations that depicted the sexual "subordination" of women. Women's crushing subordination to male sexual power was also the theme of Dworkin's book, *Pornography: Men Possessing Women*. To Dworkin, pornography is literally "the graphic depiction of women as vile whores."[6]

Reading through the literature in 1987–88, I start with less a theoretical position than an almost physical fear. I discover that I have a horror so deep of being reduced to my sexual parts by men that I can scarcely give a name to it. My lifelong avoidance of exposure to pornography begins to stir my curiosity. It is clear that pornography is not decidable on the basis of my personal aversion. Still, as I begin to write, I am unable to fix myself between the pornographies. Women Against Pornography inevitably colluded with the anti-feminist and homophobic right; FACT indirectly encouraged the pornography industry. My political sympathies are with FACT nevertheless. But there is still that fear of . . . disappearing.

Encouraged by my *TDR* editors to "state my own position," I can only state my ambivalence. This writing is a journey through that ambivalence. In it, "I" means just that: a heterosexual female spectator, a feminist groping for her own position on a divided theoretical terrain, and a critic whose formalist training did not prepare her for sexual anxiety in the theater. My starting point is my own discomfort as a spectator to the scenes described here, which took place for the most part in "alternative" New York performance spaces where the experimental theater of the late 1960s and 1970s was created. Some of this theater in its first days had encouraged its spectators to join the artists in shedding sexual inhibitions. Then followed new artists and a decade of formal sophistication. The theater I am discussing didn't reach out to unify spectator and performer in a surge of shared emotion, nor did it coolly work on the spectator's perceptual apparatus. The scenes I discuss were raw, "dirty" theater. I think they disturbed women in a particular way because they were written, directed, or performed by women before mixed audiences. Here I try to find out what that way is.

1980

My chronology begins with the decade. In the fall of 1980, Mabou Mines's production of *Dead End Kids: A History of Nuclear Power*, directed by JoAnne Akalaitis, and written by Akalaitis with the collaboration of company members, was produced at the Public Theater. The nightclub scene at the end of the second act was improvised at Akalaitis's behest by actor David Brisbin. Lenny Bruce was the model in a general sense for Brisbin's 1950s club comedian. Handling his microphone like a dildo he leeringly inveigles onto the stage a member of his fictive nightclub audience, a young grade school teacher from "Popular" Bluffs. There is a routine of insulting sexual banter. The comic uses the young woman's seductively exaggerated naiveté to degrade her. Finally, the comedian pulls a limp plucked chicken from the crotch of his trousers. He asks the teacher to manipulate the bird's neck stump ("No head? Well, give it head!") while he reads from a report, "The Effects of Radioactive Fallout on Livestock in the Event of Nuclear War."[7]

The female director's "tastelessness" was widely questioned, as in the *Philadelphia Inquirer*, which found the episode "flagrantly obscene."[8] I squirmed with discomfort throughout the scene, resisting the stereotypes. The scene felt dangerous. Why make the girl so dumb? Why make the man so menacing and vile? Even though I recognized in the scene the most unsettling version of the connection Akalaitis had been making all along between the war state and the sexist state, male nuclear fantasies and the exploitation of women, when I enthusiastically reviewed the play for the *Soho News* I didn't describe the scene, but wrote around it by describing Akalaitis's method as "coarse and slashing."[9] The work went on to be performed in many places around the country, and the shock of the scene was obscured in a halo of awards and praise. Most critics, sympathetic with the director's political intentions, finally "allowed" it on political grounds.

In an interesting sequel, the nasty nightclub routine was presented as a single excerpt at a joint anniversary celebration of the War Resisters League and Performing Artists for Nuclear Disarmament, which I attended in May of 1983. Like the nineteenth-century provincials who rushed onstage (or so the story goes) to rescue Desdemona, women in the school auditorium where we were meeting began to shout to the female character, "Don't do it honey, don't let him do it to you!" Within moments, accompanied by mounting booing and hissing, there occurred a full-scale feminist walkout led by Grace Paley. The performance was broken off, and an angry confrontation with the director followed. It is possible that an audience unaccustomed to the ironic strategies of the alternative theater lost sight of the common political ground shared with the performers, but perhaps the WRL women would not have tolerated the scene on any grounds. In any event, the episode demonstrated one problem underlying the present inquiry, the difficulty of "reading" sexually offensive material when it is taken out of its usual, politically-determined settings—that is, when it becomes unclear for whose pleasure the performance is being staged.

1981

Of all the new theatrical obscenity and pornography under discussion here, the Akalaitis is the easiest to read, in the sense that it is the most easily recognized within a right-left (and a right-wrong) political framework. The Wooster Group's *Route 1&9* was more disturbing in every way. First performed in 1981, the production created a major theatrical scandal centered on the all-white group's reconstruction of a 1965 blackface routine by the latter-day black American vaudeville entertainer, Dewey (Pigmeat) Markham. Audiences and critics were bitterly divided as to whether the piece was racist, in effect if not in intention. In the ensuing controversy over the racial issue, the group temporarily lost its funding from the New York State Council on the Arts.

In addition to the blackface routine with its wild dancing and raucous farce, *Route 1&9* included a send-up of a pedantic *Encyclopedia Britannica* teaching film on Thornton Wilder, portions of Wilder's *Our Town*, played as a dolorous all-white soap opera on a high bank of television monitors, and film footage of the despoiled New Jersey landscape actually shot on route 1&9. Toward the end of the piece, two small television sets, placed at the level of the first row of steeply-raked bleachers, began to flicker with a grainy, black-and-white, silent film scene, not noticed at first by most of the audience, in which a woman performs fellatio on her male partner in extreme closeup. The film ran for several minutes. No faces were visible. There was no sexual climax, only the concentration of the performers' bodies, and the silent intensity of the audience as spectators became aware of the film. As I watched the scene I drifted into a private, erotic world, almost relieved by the silence and physical contact of the participants after the bruising indictment of the audience as racists that had preceded it.[10] For the moment I did not ask what it meant that an entire theater audience seemed to have lost its social coherence and slipped into individual sexual reverie.

Astonishingly, in contrast to the racial furor, the scene was noted only by a single critic in passing, and was barely mentioned in the public debates that took place in the theater after some of the performances. Asked about its purpose at one of these, LeCompte defended the "porn sequence" as "erotic" and one that gave her pleasure.

How to decide whether the scene represented an erotic act between willing partners, or a pornographic image in which the female was subordinated to the male organ? I was one of those who read the blackface and the *Our Town* sequence as devastating exposures of American racism. To me, the sex scene pointed at, but still seemed to function as an antidote to, a pornography of American culture, as if to say that sex could at least be depended on to be on the side of life, unlike racism. Why then speak of pornography at all? There is more to the story.

LeCompte told me that in 1978, when working on *Nayatt School*, the company studied pornographic films and imitated their "depthless" performance style in this last work of the Rhode Island trilogy. In the summer of 1980, LeCompte and her company decided to make a sex film of their own with the distanced style and simple storyline they found in porn films. LeCompte has said in an interview with me that, as with so many other projects the group has undertaken, the suggestion to make the film originated with others in the company. In the film's rudimentary scenario, a hitchhiking couple is picked up on Route 1&9 in New Jersey, taken to an isolated house, given dinner, and enticed by their hosts into making a sex film. The film was actually shot in the LeCompte family home, representing a "middle-class space that becomes sexualized," and included a variety of sexual acts, including the scene used in *Route 1&9*.[11] The resulting 25-minute film was actually shown at the Performing Garage in a workshop season during the spring of 1981. Company readings of *Our Town* alternated with performances of the film and some of the racial material the company had begun to develop. By the fall of that year these unrelated projects had coalesced into *Route 1&9*, with a few shots of the film footage surviving in the decontextualized images of the "porn sequence."

LeCompte's theater, unlike Akalaitis's, offers the spectator few interpretative clues. This is a spectator's response theater; we write our own script out of the "pieces of culture" offered by the company. LeCompte considered her fellatio scene simply "erotic," but many feminists of the theatrical community were convinced that the actress in the film had been abused, and believed that the sequence in its full context was indeed pornographic and misogynistic. Though immersion in commercial pornography provided the background for the film, LeCompte distinguishes this project from porn. "Porn out of context is no longer porn: porn is about money."[12]

I don't agree that the exhibitionism and voyeurism entered into in this experiment necessarily constituted abuse, but it is clear that LeCompte in some sense had this sequence both ways, as porn, or simulated porn, and as not-porn. This was evident even in the context of the staging, where the erotic image, presented on small monitors placed low, was framed as a kind of peep-show.

The very unclassifiability of the sexual material, its refusal to take up a position between "bad" porn and "good" erotica, between social commentary and theatrical and even personal license, became perhaps its most uncomfortable aspect.

1984

In January 1984, the Franklin Furnace sponsored the work of a seven-woman artists' collective called Carnival Knowledge, which put on a month-long exhibit and performance series, "The Second Coming," exploring the possibility of a "new definition of pornography, one that is not demeaning to women, men, and children."[13] (Franklin Furnace and a constellation of downtown and Chelsea performance spaces such as The Kitchen, Dance Theater Workshop, and P. S. 122, serve a performance world adjacent to the alternative theater. These venues specialize in performance art, and their performers easily combine fields—theater and dance, dance and art, art and video, etc.) Eight different performance events accompanied the exhibition of art works and sale/display of adult books and sexual aids, culminating in *Deep Inside Porn Stars*, which promised "live performances by 7 top film stars from the sex industry." This performance, however, was not in itself pornographic, as it has been described to me (the Franklin Furnace event is the only one included here that I did not attend). Instead the performance became part *Chorus Line* and part consciousness-raising session about the performers' personal lives and working experience, inspired by a support group the women had organized the previous year.

1985

In the fall of 1985, two collaborations took place between female artists and male directors that were more aggressively obscene (in one case) and pornographic (in the other) than those of previous seasons. *The Birth of the Poet*, perhaps better called a coexistence than a collaboration, among director Richard Foreman, designer David Salle, composer Peter Gordon, and writer Kathy Acker, was performed in the 1985 Next Wave Festival at the Brooklyn Academy of Music, after a production the preceding year in Rotterdam.

The three apocalyptic acts of this "opera" were focused on world history at three moments of destruction and violence. In the obscene second act, the text of which was taken almost word for word from Acker's 1982 novel *Great Expectations*, the setting is Rome in 29 B.C., when poets must celebrate the newly triumphant Empire or be destroyed. Acker's central character is Cynthia, the fictional name of the Roman courtesan memorialized in the elegies of Propertius. In the second act of *The Birth of the Poet*, Cynthia has become a raucous and distraught whore.

The assault on the audience was textual: the obscene dialogue, which included stage directions, was not matched by correspondingly obscene images. Cynthia and Propertius are engaged in a struggle: each wants to satisfy sexual desire without losing power. At first Cynthia is in control, "pisses on Propertius" (a read stage direction), and thinks the best solution to the problem of men would be a "wife with a cock." He brags he wants only "split open red and black pussy" without a woman attached but begs at her "little cunt door" and weakly refuses to make decisions. She gives him an ultimatum—sex now, "I've only got five minutes," and "I want it. Flesh is it."[14]

A soliloquy of frantic fucking follows, Cynthia celebrating with such lines as, "Sex is public The streets made themselves for us to walk naked down them Take out your cock and piss over me." Propertius leaves her and she is furious. "A twelve-year-old syphilitic named Janey Smith should wrap her cunt around that prick I hate." Now in abject desire she re-approaches Propertius but he has turned against the "open cunt" and will have nothing to do with her.

Acker constructs Cynthia as an animal, first a "raging blonde leopard," then a dog. She is on the "street of dogs," even barking like one (again, a read stage direction), and whining, "I can't help myself anymore I'm just a girl." She "lies down on the street and sticks razor blades up her arms." "I am only an obsession. . . . Do you think I exist?"

In the final scene, titled "On the Nature of Art," Propertius has no more interest in the "goddamn sluts"; indeed he has become an utter pornographer. Angela Carter writes,

> [In] pornography . . . the self is reduced to its formal elements . . . the probe and the fringed hole . . . the biological symbols scrawled on the subway poster and the urinal wall.[15]

"Take the hole I slept with last night," growls this far from elegiac Propertius. "Sure she moaned hard when I stuck my dick in her. But did she have any idea that I didn't feel?" His only love now is art, gendered female. "Art, you are the black hole of vulnerability." Following the known facts of Propertius's life, Acker has his patron Maecenas make a plea for socially responsible art, but Propertius belongs to a new generation. To him, art is the "elaborating of violence" and violence is desire. "Desire violence will never stop." The birth of the (male) poet is complete.

Like Cynthia taking to the streets, Acker's language scandalously leaves the privacy of print for the publicly witnessed theater. Though I had previously read the Acker novel, hearing this language from the stage was an uncomfortable experience, but confusing as well, because the visual production took no notice of it. In an experiment in non-hierarchical stage production, the artistic principals in this undertaking proceeded in their disciplines without prior consultation, the only common ground being that all male collaborators had read the Acker text. I almost suspected a conspiracy to keep the unruly Cynthia off the streets and the playwright off the stage, shouting to be heard over the Gordon music, struggling to be seen through the abstract Foreman staging, overwhelmed by the outsize banality of the Salle designs, and finally silenced by the press, where only one critic—Erika Munk of the *Village Voice*—discussed the language and its effect: "I was *upset*. I hadn't heard a woman's voice saying these things. So much the better."[16] I shared Munk's mixed feelings. Acker made me queasy, her out-of-control, lust-ridden, ultimately pathetic Cynthia is a degrading stereotype of woman run amok. But there was also something exhilarating about the obscene force of the text, even if unrealized by the production.

The Birth of the Poet appeared to set into competition two types of theatrical experiment, one social (the testing of female authorial limits in the theater—how much offense would an obscene text by a female writer be permitted to give), the other structural or formal (the non-coordination of creative elements). Later I wondered whether the first experiment was inhibited by the second. Would a male-authored obscene text have operated on the imaginations of the male collaborators as a form of permission rather than as a signal for control? Did Acker's male collaborators in effect identify with the Propertius side of the play's "birth trauma"? In both cases, it could be argued that male poetry was "born" at the price of female repression.

In December of 1985, Richard Schechner's *Prometheus Project* was staged at the Performing Garage, the performance space he founded during the avant-garde theatrical explosion of the 1960s. Like *Dead End Kids* and *The Birth of the Poet*, the *Prometheus Project* was about apocalypse: its central image was the link between promethean fire and the destruction of Hiroshima.

The piece was assembled with the combination of quotation, improvisation, and mixed media that has become the familiar idiom of New York performance. However, its second episode put this piece in a category of its own. This episode, containing a clear example of pornography in Dworkin's sense of woman-as-whore, was given over to the "renaissance woman of porn," 42nd Street burlesque and porno film star, former prostitute, porn photographer, and porn magazine editor—Annie Sprinkle. Sprinkle had previously appeared in *Deep Inside Porn Stars* at the Franklin Furnace.

Sprinkle's show-within-a-show was framed by an onstage audience of four masturbators in trenchcoats, hands in pockets, sitting in for a burlesque house audience. In the first and most elaborated of four scenes, Sprinkle appeared in a school nurse uniform and conducted a "show and tell" sex education class, stripping as she went along. Audience members were invited to touch her nipples, then put their heads between her breasts and describe the feeling. I shared Gerald Rabkin's perception, recorded in *Performing Arts Journal*, that the rhapsodic male responses to Sprinkle's breasts were a "macho pose of knowledgeability" layered over a "general embarrassment."[17] Embarrassment deepened as Sprinkle asked any interested spectator to shine a flashlight at her genitals, examine them with a magnifying glass, and describe their texture and color. Only males volunteered.

This is a moment I won't easily forget in the theater: Sprinkle's smiling face and robust, cooing voice, her very white and soft body largely exposed, encouraging a spectator to scrutinize and describe her labia. I shrink back from the spectacle in my seat, filled with rage at Richard Schechner, who is submitting me and other women to this *assault on our bodies* via this alien medium, this . . . *who is she*? Is she a woman like me? Does she smile because she enjoys this or smile because she is encoded by pornography to convince men she "enjoys" this? The act becomes more threatening still when Sprinkle offers to "give a little demonstration of cock sucking." By now blind to objective critical judgment, whatever that might be in such a case, I feel violated and furious at my entrapment here. (The seating configuration of the Performing Garage adds an element of coercion, as it is impossible to walk out of the theater without crossing the playing area.) When there are no volunteers, Sprinkle starts to demonstrate on a dildo. Led offstage by the actor playing the MC, Sprinkle returns in a traditional burlesque costume to perform a strip act, singing "I'll Fuck Anything that Moves."

Then the slide show. One slide wittily posed the Empire State Building, 1475 feet high, next to an enormous erect prick, representing the number of feet of cock Sprinkle had sucked in her career. Following this, a pie graphic of "pornstistics" demonstrated the comparative advantages of Sprinkle's earning capacity in the sex industry ($3000 a week). The last segment showed Sprinkle masturbating on a film loop, one of the many she has made for the peep show market, with a male voiceover, added by Schechner, directing her moves. But because Sprinkle had already revealed herself as a forceful personality, this didn't quite give the impression of male exploitation (Sprinkle "spoken" by pornographic codes) that may have been intended.

A subtheme to the Prometheus-Hiroshima line in the piece developed out of the myth of Io, the priestess whom Zeus raped and turned into a cow. In the myth, Io is forced to roam the earth to avoid jealous Hera's stinging gadflies. At the end of her act, Sprinkle put on a cow mask and introduced the Io sequence, the third part of the performance. Here young women similarly masked ran back and forth, stopping to testify to their personal experiences of sexual abuse. The Io story was used to provide a link, also made by Akalaitis, between nuclear aggression and female sexual oppression.

Once during her performance, and again at the end of her sequence, Sprinkle gazed long and accusingly at the audience. Enter: the Gaze. I distantly thought then, and have subsequently confirmed, that the director was interested in the exchange of gazes this performance entailed. Ours at her, hers at us, ours at the little porn audience gazing at her, etc. To me this looked more like an effort to put a feminist "spin" on the routines than to actually explore the role of the spectator's gaze in the performance. In a telephone conversation, Schechner told me that it was Sprinkle's own sophisticated play with the gazing male in the nurse act—her distancing or "deconstruction" of pornography— noted by his performance class on their field visit to the theater on 42nd Street where Sprinkle performed—that attracted him to Sprinkle's work in the first place. In a subsequent paper describing Sprinkle's performance as the "hit of the piece," Schechner saw this toying with the spectator's view as a sophisticated distancing device: "At each increment of sexual opportunity, Sprinkle interviews the spectator—asking him [*sic*] to describe what he sees, or how he feels. This automatically distances the action from its own sexual possibilities— making it anti-porn porn, or a sendup of porn."[18]

What—or who—was being distanced? Was my spectatorship, or any female spectatorship, included in this "automatic distancing?" The "sexual possibilities" that hurt me here were not those the director had in mind, but the visual rape and sexual objectification of my body by identification. I became the Grace Paley of this performance: I refused to subsume it in a self-referential play of ironies. Any theorization of the Gaze (and the more discriminating, in a sense, the worse) seemed to me utterly anemic compared to the crush of gender, class, and performance issues brought down by this performance.

In the program, Schechner explained the Sprinkle appearance as a kind of satyr play on the Io theme. Critics (all except the writer from *Screw* magazine) fell in with this dubious classicism, and treated the Sprinkle episode with amused condescension, as a diversion from Schechner's serious theme. However, Schechner's interest in pornography and performance was expressed as early as 1966 in an essay, "Pornography and the New Expression," where he speculated that both the live body of the performer and the social nature of theater, which includes the audience's concern about the actor, makes theater much less pornographizable, to coin a term, than fiction and film.[19] Two decades later, Schechner may have been interested in testing the limits of those restrictions, introducing an abrasive "porn modernism" to make the alternative theater audience rethink theater's boundaries. Our comfortable status as theater patrons was shaken by our transformation into peep-show and burlesque hall voyeurs.

I considered making this performance a counter-example in my catalogue. The male director here controlled the theatrical experience, and male pleasure had governed Sprinkle's creation of her work in the first place. And yet. I was not prepared to take away Annie Sprinkle's voice and deny her female authorship, for this was her material. Also, I could not be blind to my own class discomfort: What was this 42nd Street venue doing invading my performance space?

Despite my turbulence, or perhaps as a deeper cause of it, I became aware again of a disturbing ambivalence, an effect also stirred in different ways by LeCompte and Acker. My problem was, if Sprinkle represented a female "other," she was also not "other" enough. This was not taking place in a barn of a burlesque hall with an elevated stage, where I might fade into the balcony (as I did once in Boston), and become an invisible or masqueraded spectator of a separate male culture with its different kind of female. In this space Sprinkle had entered my world. She was telling me she had made a pretty good bargain of it in life. She was pushing me to think her as self-respecting worker rather than as victim who could be disposed of by my condescending "pity." Porn magazines edited and published by Sprinkle were displayed at the ticket desk as one entered, evidence of Sprinkle's enterprise in extending her product to a new market. Sprinkle represented herself as independent businesswoman (the theme as well of the feminist filmmaker Lizzie Borden's feature film, *Working Girls*, released within a few weeks of the Performing Garage performance), as subject, as "I" rather than as Io, the abused woman. She made herself undismissable.

1986

My chronology ends with a number of performances in which female performers such as Karen Finley, Lydia Lunch, Johanna Went, the duo Dancenoise, and others were exploring a disturbing range of obscenity and scatological reference. I will discuss briefly only the work of Karen Finley, who had become notorious for creating a theater of disgust filled with obscene fantasies. The self of the mid-1980s Finley performance was, much like the "I" in Acker's fiction, a toxic landfill of throwaway bodies and cynical or psychotic voices. She seemed an almost emblematic figure of the "excremental culture" described by Kroker and Cook in *The Postmodern Scene*.[20]

Excrement, metaphorically speaking, was a central technique of Finley's work in the legendary club performances before late 1986, when she received her first theatrical booking at The Kitchen. For instance, in *I'm an Assman*, which I saw only on videotape, Finley poured dog food, cream, and other condiments down the open neck of her ruffled 1950s party dress. A legacy perhaps of her relationship with the Kipper Kids, whose performances degenerated into comically anarchic food fights, this gesture conveyed a surprising sense of violation. Given the deep socialization attaching to cleanliness and "good clothes," especially for women, it was shocking to witness a female performer wilfully make the clean filthy, and just for the hell of it, without the "redemptive" value of hard work or poverty usually associated with soiled clothing. In another performance, again seen only on tape, Finley initiated a scene of violation by ripping the front of a similarly "feminine" blouse, and ended up smearing diarrhea-colored canned yams on and between her naked buttocks. This was a version of the "Yams Up Granny's Ass" act documented in C. Carr's explosively controversial cover feature on Finley in the *Village Voice*.[21]

The early Finley performances were, in the exact sense of the word, sickening. I mean this quite literally. Their inner motion was to make the healthy sick and the living dead. Everything that entered her narrative stream was transformed into the dead meat of a dead world in her extreme vision. *The Constant State of Desire* at The Kitchen was less confrontational visually. Finley symbolically repeated the gesture of despoliation by breaking raw, colored Easter eggs in a plastic bag that contained a small stuffed rabbit, then used the animal as a pad to smear the raw egg mixture over her naked body. But then she covered herself with glitter and confetti, transforming herself into an icon of Easter, with its life-giving associations.

The text of *The Constant State of Desire*, however, was no less obscene than its predecessors. Like Finley's other solo performances, it took the form of discontinuous first-person narratives that might begin with her cheerful self-presentation as the girl next door, but shortly fall into strident, chaotic trances. Finley would close her eyes, enter an interior space, and erupt with fragments of stories whose themes were incest, child abuse, rape, and, frequently, the known suicide of her father. Sometimes those riffs would begin politically: for instance, "LET ME TELL YOU ABOUT PARANOIA. Sixty percent of the world's commercial fish stocks are in danger."[22] But soon such an opening would slide into excremental fantasies, than a gang rape, then mayhem.

Finley's performances create a mass of characters erupting in jerky schizoid fragments. Stories trail off in mid-sentence. There are no finished narratives, and more important, as in Acker's fiction, no finished narrators. The mutating "I" is by turn woman, man, parent, child, all finding their level in the subterranean miasma of sexual violation and numbing excess that begins virtually *in utero*. One such sequence in *The Constant State of Desire* opens, "My first sexual experience occurred at the time of my birth, passing through the vaginal canal." This evolved into two incest trances, the first in which a son sucks "my own cum juice outta my own mama's ass," and the second in which a five year-old's father puts her naked into a refrigerator and "starts working my little hole" with carrots, zucchini, etc.

Finley became the most troubling artist to deal with, and the hardest to place, because she seized upon the soul-killing essence of pornography without its interest in sexual stimulation. Nothing could be further from Carolee Schneeman's celebration of feminine sexuality a quarter-century earlier, than Finley's despoiled universe.

II.

For, if that view [from "elsewhere"] is nowhere to be seen, not given in a single text, not recognizable as a representation, it is not that we—feminists, women—have not yet succeeded in producing it. It is, rather, that what we have produced is not recognizable, precisely, as a representation.

—Teresa de Lauretis, *Technologies of Gender*[23]

There was something menacing about this aggregation of marginalia, increasingly so in the later examples, something that stirred a sort of vertigo, as if all the moral categories were beginning to slide. This experience may be Bataille's "crack in the system," the shattering of individual unity he says occurs when the erotic boils up, as in the exposure to pornography.[24] In a discussion of Bataille's theories of erotic transgression, Susan Rubin Suleiman writes that this "slipping" of the limits of the self occurs as one senses that a violation has taken place: "Indeed, it is precisely by and through its transgression that the force of a prohibition becomes fully realized."[25] Two apparently different issues can be pursued from Bataille's lead. The first relates to stage practice, the second to gender.

In her important, post-Bataille meditation on literary pornography, "The Pornographic Imagination," Susan Sontag places its effect of "psychic dislocation" within the transgressive tradition of modern art, which has measured its advance through the "dialectic of outrage."[26] Perhaps theater is making another of its periodic lunges at the limits of theatrical discourse, an extension in these performances of Ubu's "Shitr!" The "dirty" performance of 42nd Street hustles in on the "advanced art" of the experimental theater. Such a theater/class argument acknowledges that theater is still a preserve of the "slow and unsexy," as Wallace Shawn said in a 1988 interview, and that it still has the ability to protect its middle-class identity in bourgeois culture, ruling out contamination by the lower elements of burlesque and peep show.[27] Akalaitis's low-life nightclub scene is preceded by, among other elements, a scene from Part I of Goethe's *Faust*, and LeCompte's fellatio scene rubs shoulders with the "classic," very clean, very middle-class *Our Town*. Sprinkle's porn routines take their place next to Beckett and Prometheus. (The class argument would explain, for instance, why Finley toned her earlier work in the clubs down when she got to The Kitchen, a halfway house between the clubs and the theater.)

So there may be an important element of transgression against the still "legitimate" theater in these performances. It is the intrusion itself that makes us aware, following Suleiman, that theater still has firmer boundaries than film or fiction. Yet to receive these performances as merely uncomfortable exhibits of an "avant-garde" practice is itself too comfortable. Art-cultural theory can't help us to resolve the crucial issue: what *value* (besides shock value) to place upon obscenity and pornography in these theatrical contexts. One might use the theory of a Renato Poggioli or a Peter Bürger on avant-garde to "account" for these performances, yet never refer to the fact that they represent a body of women's work in the theater. Returning again to Bataille's "crack in the system," maybe the question here should be, what "system" is being cracked? Bataille may have had in mind the phallomorphic organization of male subjectivity, threatened with a loss of boundaries and self-mastery. But for the female theater directors, writers, performers, and spectators of these performances—

and for me—the "system" under stress may be not this self-same, centered subject, but its distorted "other," the riven female subject that porn constructs.

At this intersection I locate the heart of my discomfort. The ambivalence
I experience within and about this work, my sense of danger as a "good" female
spectator, results from a crack in *this* system: the systematic division of women
into opposed sexual pools, and the replication of that division in an elaborated
system of values within each female consciousness. I am helped to see this by
an article in *Enclitic*, written by Jacquelyn Zita. In a discussion of film pornography she points out that the "pornographic apparatus" constructs two female
populations, one to service the fantasies and "secret realities" of male dominion
over women, the other "ignorant" and "purified," each operating as a "necessary condition" to keep the system in place. "It is often 'good' women who do
the work of separating themselves from female sex workers and maintaining an
aura of purity and goodness for themselves."[28] Historian Gerda Lerner sees this
systematic division as the controlling condition of female socialization.

> The division of women into "respectable women," who are protected by their
> men, and "disreputable women," who are out in the street unprotected by
> men, and agree to sell their services, has been the basic class division for
> women. It has marked off the limited privileges of upper-class women against
> the economic and sexual oppression of lower-class women and has divided
> women from one another. Historically it has impeded cross-class alliances
> among women and obstructed the formation of feminist consciousness.[29]

This fundamental binary division is echoed in the feminist debate over
pornography. In an overview of books by women on feminine sexuality and
pornography in *Feminist Studies*, B. Ruby Rich writes that the discussion of
pornography "still hovers between two inadequate definitions: either a conscious degradation of women, ideologically aligned with misogyny and psycho-
logically linked to actual violence against women; or one of the few expressions
of explicit sexuality in a repressive culture."[30] The irreconcilability of the terms
of female socialization may underlie Mary Ann Doane's despair that "No true
feminist theory of pornography . . . can be constructed."[31]

I don't assume that the artists here consciously worked to break down this
division. In fact, Schechner's "Prometheus Project" functioned to sustain and
restate it by pouring Sprinkle and the young women in the show into the mold
of Io, who is cruelly punished for her sexual transgressions by the powerful,
respectably married Hera. Nevertheless, each in a different way, the performances I have been considering defy the "system" by intertwining ideologically
and iconically opposed female representations. The "good" female subjectivity
of the ordered libido and separated boundaries (the woman of autonomy, authority, authorship) slides into the "bad" woman of pornographic male fantasy
(the woman of infinite compliance, who pants with desire, who is really, secretly, a "whore").

In an apt performance, perhaps parody, of this division, Annie Sprinkle and sister porn artist Veronica Vera, billing themselves as "feminist porn activists," opened their segment of The Kitchen's February 1988 "Carnival of Sleaze" with a series of "transformation" slides, which displayed Sprinkle, Vera, and many other women not associated with the sex industry, in alternative poses, first in family or other "clean" roles, then as sex queens. Performance artist Linda Montano was shown in a flashy sex costume; Sprinkle came forward in demure dress under her given name, Ellen Steinberg. Played before a mixed, non-burlesque audience in value-free deadpan, the sequence was a kind of dare to the "good girl" female spectator, if not exactly to enter the sex trade, at least to examine her own self-division. The female spectator, who energetically defends herself against being projected into a role as the "other" of male fantasy, is shown an image of her own replication of that pattern, her cooperation in it, in her own deepest terror of being contaminated by the other side of female life. Here she is caught before men with her "other" showing (her other "other").

In an essay on *Histoire d'O*, Kaja Silverman writes that pornography is "a discourse that dramatizes with unusual clarity the disjunction between the speaking (male) subject and the spoken (female) subject."[32] If the obscene imagery and texts show the fascination of its makers with woman as constituted in male pornographic discourse, the performances in context also project a speaking female subject. This was not at first easy for me to see on the stage, for this inching together of opposed feminine categories is more a groping symptom of cultural change than an aesthetic or political program in these performances. But it is happening anyhow in these female texts, or intertexts, even when the concerns of the overall performance are not feminist. Ironically, where a conscious attempt was made to use some feminist theory in the *Prometheus Project* (Mulvey et al. on the Gaze), the masculinist assumptions of the production—the central agony of Prometheus, the unexamined implications of the Io myth, and Schechner's simple delight in Sprinkle as a "hit" performer—also made this the most questionable of my examples.

What poet, in *The Birth of the Poet*, is being born? Acker's narrative leads from Cynthia's sexual insatiability to her abasement and humiliation to the triumph of the male Word. The male poet is born out of female desire, perfected by frustrating that desire. But Acker's obscene "graffiti writing" scrawls over the tradition of Roman elegiac writing and allows Propertius's voiceless Cynthia to yell her head off.[33] No longer will the artist's model pose. The last section (titled "On the Nature of Art") of Acker's obscene second act virtually exposes the male artist's fetishization of art as a form of sexual dysfunction.

In each of the performances, this double strain can be traced. Finley's images are fished from the depths of violent and deviant pornography, but, in Jill Dolan's acute analysis, "she revises the power balance in traditional pornography . . . by claiming sexual power for herself to wield."[34] If Finley deliberately turns off male appetite by presenting all sexual exchange on a closed, interior circuit, Sprinkle enthusiastically offers herself as a sexual commodity. At the same time Sprinkle presents herself as manager, controlling her own body-as-business and enjoying her success. All three performances suggest a certain ex-hilaration, a sense of "mastery" in being on both sides of the production of obscenity, simultaneously its object and author.

The same two lines can be traced in Akalaitis and LeCompte. They over-write male texts and expose their hidden assumptions, de-idealize the male canon, ironically recycle forgotten sexist or racist performance forms as social critique. While they subvert male-speak they also try on the male gaze. Akalaitis does this through the persona of the nightclub comedian, whose scene with the young woman appears at first to cross the border between subversion and imitation. Similarly, in her more ambiguous affair with porn, LeCompte ex-periments with the male position of voyeur. But LeCompte stresses that she was not deliberately assuming an inscribed position. "I don't know what porn is, and I'm attracted to things I don't understand well. I've never been able to put my reactions to porn together with a political stance."[35]

Witnessing these performances in "my" theaters, thinking about and writ-ing this article, I have felt some ancient resistance give, perhaps not to oppres-sive pornography in Dworkin's sense, which I regard as harmful to women, but to images which, in an earlier period, I would have rejected as dangerously invading me, and leading me toward that harm. These performances exposed (Suleiman's comment on Bataille) the privileged and protected social circum-stances of most theater. The violation of theatrical norms, presumably experi-enced by all spectators, was offensive without being politically or theoretically combustive. The disturbance, the risky melting into each other, of the polar conventions of patriarchal female representation, was for me the greater viola-tion. I was forced to see the "crack" in the patriarchal system of female sociali-zation and in my own socially conditioned, deeply inscribed mental forma-tions—literally to confront this abyss in the cracks of the female body.

The two leads I took from Bataille—into theater practice and into gen-der—could be seen as a single construction. Both women's bodies and the thea-ter have traditionally been sites of prohibition and separation, subject to "pro-phylactic" separations of the clean from the dirty. Indeed, distaste for the theater has often been couched in terms of fear of the female body. In *The Anti-Theatrical Prejudice*, Jonas Barish's theatrophobes, from the Romans to Prynne, to Rousseau, to Nietzsche, all attack theatrical performance itself (whether performed by women or not) as inherently lewd and "feminine."[36] Misogyny appears always to have played a role in the periodic closing or regu-lation to which the theater has been subject. In *The Politics and Poetics of Trans-gression*, Peter Stallybrass and Allon White discuss the creation of the modern bourgeois theater in sexual terms. After the re-opening of the theaters in 1660, playwrights such as Dryden, Southerne, and Cibber conducted a campaign to socialize audiences to new standards of decorum in the theaters. By the turn of the century the space of theater was being decisively severed "from the market of sexual liaison," and converted into a "systematically scoured" and "idealized space of consciousness." The eighteenth-century theater demanded a "sublimated public body without smells, without coarse laughter, without organs."[37] That new theater is now our old theater, and today it is under pressure by these same bad manners.

Why make a fuss about manners? It is not so surprising that women would play an important role in de-socializing the theater, which has so prejudicially socialized them, but it would be a mistake to dismiss these gestures as an issue of manners. When Fornes's Emma wants to stand in a room discussing her genitals as well as business, she is contemplating not a mere breach of manners but an act of political anarchism that, if generally adopted, would lead to the collapse of business, family, and state. If, as Pierre Bourdieu points out, "the concessions of politeness always contain political concessions," then it is also true that a breakdown of accepted behavior is inescapably political.[38]

In "The Discourse of Others: Feminists and Postmodernism"—a still somewhat lonely essay given feminists' historic mistrust of postmodernism—Craig Owens utters a kind of manifesto that, theatrical metaphor and all, could almost be taken for a comment on the theater work I have described. It is at "the legislative frontier between what can be represented and what cannot," he writes, "that the postmodernist operation is being staged—not in order to transcend representation, but in order to expose that system of power that authorizes certain representations while blocking, prohibiting or invalidating others."[39] These performances showed me my own complicated positioning in the "system of power" that divides feminine representation.

In blurring the boundary between "good girl" and "bad girl," the theater of female obscenity I have been discussing is a kind of "repo theater." It is possible to sense, on contemplating its terms, the source of power the merged signs of female sexual identity would open for women, a self-repossession that would signify the most profound cultural shift. At a programmatic level, some feminists have been working to break down barriers between the two populations of women and their representations. *Caught Looking* performs the merger by making readers look at "dirty" pictures in order to read feminist texts (or encounter feminist texts in order to gaze at dirty pictures). *Good Girls/Bad Girls* documents a conference in Toronto in which an open dialogue between activist feminists and sex trade workers was attempted.[40] The performances I describe are not programmatic. However they do not need to know about "legislative frontiers" to breach them. Teresa de Lauretis characterizes the subject of feminism as the discovery of those spaces in the (male-centered) representation of gender "that representation leaves out or, more pointedly, makes unrepresentable." The semiotic merger would open up one of her "space-offs" in the representation of gender, a film term acknowledging a space already here within the terms of a particular representation, yet "not recognizable, precisely, as a representation."[41] It is still virtually impossible to think heterosexual woman without sex/class polarities, no matter how sublimated and masked such a crude division has become in an apparently liberal society. The performances I have described worked at the edges of the sexual "space-off," seeking through contradiction to find the unrepresented but present terms of a new construction.

Afterword

I want to add a few notes about Karen Finley and Annie Sprinkle, re-evaluating my own responses and recounting events occurring after this chapter was submitted for publication as an article in 1988.

Of all the artists I discuss, the one I was least able to "see" in performance was Karen Finley. I may have been one of those spectators described by Katherine Schuler in "Spectator Response and Comprehension: The Problem of Karen Finley's *Constant State of Desire*," who was so alarmed by Finley's tone that she was unable to grasp the political content of the words.[42] Finley was not only the unsocialized woman in performance that Dolan describes, but her characters were sometimes biologically uncooperative as well. For instance, in the "PARANOIA" riff in *The Constant State of Desire*, the 15-year-old girl is gang-raped "until they discover my secret of being born without a vagina. They throw me onto the train tracks with their embarrassment and the train rolls over me." That the political content of this characterization was not obvious to me now surprises me. After 1986, the recognizably political dimension of Finley's performances expanded. Finley became a more coherent feminist, a voice in the fight against AIDS, and strong critic of the National Endowment for the Arts. She became a less nihilistic and perhaps a less riveting artist. I have recently reviewed the documentation of some of her performances and the published interviews with her by Schechner and Carr.[43] For me she continues an unsettled problem, but I think not only because I "can't take the heat." She seems caught between social critique and psychic eruption, between subverting and being subverted by pornography, between a desire to outrage and a desire to be accepted and loved, and she will often name the one for the other. These conflicts get passed through to the audience, making a stable response unusually difficult. At the same time this very incoherence makes her one of the more interesting, and more symptomatic, theater artists of the 1980s.

My encounter with Annie Sprinkle came to a remarkably different resolution. I was asked to solicit some visual material from her by the journal, and as a result only then had my first telephone conversation with her. There is a short scene somewhere in Virginia Woolf that I have been unable to relocate, in which a woman—it seemed Woolf herself—is on one side of a street on the arm of a gentleman. This sexually protected woman sees on the opposite side of the street, walking unescorted, the "madam" of the local house of prostitution. The street, in the account, is an unbridgeable divide between classes of women. Placing a telephone call to Annie Sprinkle felt to me like crossing that street. My hands shook. Her voice on the answering machine announced playfully, "We've got our hands full right now, we'll call you back." They shook harder.

In our conversation, Annie told me of her project to bring to her studio suburban wives, mothers, and working women, and photograph them as "sex queens." The point of the project, she said, was to raise women's self-esteem. "When they see themselves in fishnets, great makeup, and the rest, they feel wonderful about themselves." We fell into a long discussion. Why, she wanted to know, did feminists question the positive value of looking sexy? I replied that some feminists would be highly suspicious of "buying into" male fantasy projections of female sexiness. Who owned the imagery in which she was re-creating these women? Actually thanking me, she said this was a new idea to her. Could I recommend some reading? She urged me in turn to question this feminist analysis, come to her studio, "put on fishnets" and try the experiment for myself. By the end of the conversation we were both laughing.

Regrettably, I didn't follow through on the invitation, but some time later I introduced myself at a performance at The Kitchen ("Annie Sprinkle: Post-Porn Modernist," performed in January 1990). In this piece, Sprinkle tried to show a range of female sexual experience, from exploited porn worker to ecstatic celebrant. One sequence showed the results of the "Before/After" photo sessions she had described on the telephone. The performance ended with her bringing herself to orgasm on a kind of altar, a ritual climax dedicated to those she loved who had died of AIDS. The audience response, and mine too, was hushed reverence, and something akin to love. I thanked her for her moving performance; she greeted me warmly. Ironically, perhaps because she was not funded, or de-funded, by the NEA, Sprinkle turned out to be the artist best able to bring the type of performance I am describing to a deeper level. A few years after performing her 42nd Street routine in Schechner's production, she had actually built a performance around the underlying divide it had unwittingly exposed. Sprinkle helped me to see this divide as a buried social construct in my own life, and to contemplate it without the protection of an intellectual redoubt.

7

Theater as Shopping

Shopping . . . [has] become the chief cultural activity of America.

—William Kowinski, *The Malling of America*[1]

In postmodernism . . . everyone has learned to consume
culture. . . . You are no longer aware of consuming it. Everything
is culture, the culture of the commodity . . . which accounts for
the disappearance . . . of what we used to call aesthetics. . . .

—Fredric Jameson, *Universal Abandon?*[2]

L EAVING THE Hirschhorn Museum in Washington, D.C., a friend of mine
is approached by two young women from out of town, "Excuse me," they
ask, "Do you know where we can find the Mall?" "You're on it," says my friend,
waving behind her along Constitution Avenue to the White House. "Oh!" they
chorus in disappointment, "We thought it was a *shopping* mall!"

I must be very old, for I remember, or think that I remember, an *illud
tempus*, a culture that existed before the shopping culture invaded every cell of
middle-class American life. As I grew up, shopping spread like an oil slick down
suburban roads, collected into little eddies called shopping centers, and later
congealed into huge shopping worlds: the malls. Later still came the invasion
of the shopping catalogues, and presently whole television channels were reserved for shopping. By the 1980s, no institution was too conservative to pass
up shopping. (The U.S. Postal Service opens retail stores that sell mugs and
T-shirts. A visa card from a bank makes me a member of a "shopping club.")
Few institutions were too progressive to pass up shopping. (I join a co-op dedicated to an alternative economy. Soon I receive a Christmas catalogue advertising Guatemalan shoulder bags and scores of other embarrassing third world
trinkets.)

Most important, perhaps, no institution was too "cultured" to resist shopping. The ballet, the opera, even Carnegie Hall, have succumbed to the shop.
In the 1980s, the Metropolitan Museum became a leviathan of shopping, with
more than fifteen stores across the country, six in Japan, a Bridal Registry, and
a 24-hour 800 number. In the *illud tempus*, we children knew, or thought we
knew, that culture was "culture" precisely because it was not the marketplace.

But we were wrong; the institutions we recall were not so much against the marketplace as merely pre-commodified.

Theater, for all its obvious commercial dependency, has seemed peculiarly innocent in its child-like, playful heart, of spiritual capitulation to the market. Jean-Christophe Agnew's evocation of their opposing historical images can still stir a response today:

> Market and Theater. . . . One word summons up ancient images of stalls, scales, and ledger books. . . . The other conjures up a magical world of sets, costumes, and greasepaint, of gallant heroes, scheming villains, and clowns in motley. Markets we are accustomed to think of as meeting every sort of material need. Theaters we associate with more symbolic, less tangible human longings. . . . From this perspective, the two figures appear to inhabit entirely different, if not wholly contradictory realms.[3]

Yes, theater has been slow to find its way into the vast emporium of contemporary culture. Locked in an Edwardian time warp, its notion of business opportunities remains at the level of selling Raisinets at intermission. A Swiftian might argue that instead of prostrating themselves before grant-givers, theaters could project commercials on the curtain, sell wall space for ads, rent shop concessions in the lounges, sell product placements on the stage. O Brecht! Today theater still preserves the quaint charm of the *culinary*—one man, one meal, so to speak—while the rest of the culture moves on to the circulating, interpenetrating postmodern model of the *commoditary* ("flow business not show business," as a producer who will appear later told me) with its more avid, less discriminating appetites. But theater's deep genius for representing the cultural condition always re-emerges. Thus we may be seeing a new kind of theater that mimics in its underlying structures of presentation and reception the fundamental culture of contemporary capitalism. In this theater, one could say, we are seeing the commodification of the theatrical unconscious.

The display ad for the New York production of *Tamara* read, "Fall Special—up to $40 Off! Limited Availability—Call Now!" *Tamara*, the follow-the-actor-you-choose phenomenon, which concerns the failed seduction of the Polish artist Tamara de Lempicka by the Italian writer Gabriele D'Annunzio, plus a dozen other sexual and political plot strands, emerged out of Canada in the early 1980s. With the precedent-breaking management techniques of its American producers, it ran more than nine years in Los Angeles, has played in Mexico City, Rome, Buenos Aires, Rio, Warsaw, and at the time of this writing is being produced for an interactive CD-Rom. I saw it in New York, where it played for more than two and a half years after its December 1987 opening.

In the left-hand margin, the New York *Tamara* ad provided a list of merchandise for sale: "Spies, Lying Maids, Passion, Treason, Opium, Revenge, Voyeurism, Decadence, Secret Rooms, Choice, Seduction, Aristocrats, Addiction, Steamy Sensu—" (the rest of the word is tantalizingly obliterated), plus "Lavish Buffet Presented by Le Cirque, chef: Daniel Boulud" with "Champagne and Open Bar." This last offering, as I came to discover about all the theater events discussed here, was no mere extra inducement to attend the entertainment, but its experiential and symbolic core.

At Park Avenue and 65th Street I enter the Seventh Regiment Armory under a marquee that reads TAMARA: THE LIVING MOVIE.[4] A block-wide late Victorian vastness, the Armory engages me differently from a theater. There is no mediating space between my body and the world of entitlement this environment (part real, part fiction) exudes. I am flattered into feeling not Tamara but *myself* the subject of a living movie. While chuckling at the absurdity of such a response, I see in myself and in my fellow "guests" subtle changes in voice and gait, and a heightened decorum to meet an expanded sense of privilege.

At the entrance, the *fascisto* in the black shirt has a special list on which my name appears. He hands me a passport-shaped document that is entrance ticket, program, and dinner menu. This Tamara *carta d'identità* entitles me to return five times at descending prices with a full-paying patron until I become a free "life-time member" of D'Annunzio's household. It also directs me to the after-show shop displaying the "Tamara Collection." While issuing excited warnings about my conduct at Il Vittoriale, the poet's villa for which the Armory stands in, the Blackshirt stamps the passport/program/ticket with a date in 1927. This piece of paper is clearly neither discardable nor replaceable like the usual inert "memento" of a theater program. It has become constituent in the theater experience as prop, warranting me a player in the drama that is already unfolding. Perhaps more important, it has been charged with the intensity of a certain market value, imaginatively as a "collector's item," and materially as a coupon toward future reduced-price visits.

Along the magnificent hall of flags, twenty-five feet high and wide enough for cars to pass, waitresses in starched white aprons serve "Tamara cocktails" courtesy of Seagram's. At its center, the great double mahogany staircase sweeps majestically to the landing above. To the left are rooms designed by Louis Comfort Tiffany. To the right, the maple-paneled reception room, admirably tricked out as D'Annunzio's "Oratorio," with piano, lectern, and faux-marble tomb awaiting the great writer's last remains.

The Oratorio is one of several locations on three floors among which I can thread my "personalized" journey through the welter of plot threads offered for my delectation. Although the action—exploded into simultaneous clusters, sometimes with as many as seven parallel scenes—is fully scripted and leaves no space for improvisation, the journey through it is determined by my choice of character to follow, revised every time I change from one figure to another. My choice of a servant, for instance, will bring me more frequently to the kitchen and other rooms on the lower level; my choice of D'Annunzio will bring me more frequently to the silk-draped bedroom on the floor above.

Whichever of the ten figures one elects to follow, principal features of the plot predictably emerge: D'Annunzio's dalliances with artistic women; his ambivalent role in the politics of interwar Italy; the left-wing undercover activity of his handsome new chauffeur, Mario; and finally D'Annunzio's addiction to opiates. However, some plot rivulets, such as the lesbian attraction of his head of household to a young ballerina intent on auditioning for the maestro, could easily be missed in a single journey through the play. While these gossip column secondary plot elements could be picked up on subsequent visits, it seemed to be enjoyment of the total "scene" rather than a need to master the entire narrative that inspired spectators to return.

The center of enjoyment at *Tamara* was unquestionably the food service: cocktails, buffet supper, dessert, coffee, "champagne by Perrier Jouet." Here the spectators—although the passivity connoted by the traditional term is the wrong association—fully "take in" the spectacle. We are also in turn "taken in" by it, as, armed with dinner plates and wine glasses, we invade the same baronial spaces where only moments before we had stood on the periphery as eavesdroppers. This mutual *ingestus*—audience consumes meal, setting consumes audience—points to the shift in the central organ that "shopping theater" works on in contrast to the traditional theater that Brecht presciently called "culinary." Consumption has worked its way down from eyes, ears, and emotions to the digestive organs of the theatergoer.

Just as the line of theatrical action is determined by spectator choice, albeit carefully controlled, so now choice again becomes an important element in the seduction that the *Tamara* dinner works on its guests. Before the New York admission price was dropped and the meal service streamlined, spectators were offered a buffet dinner that appeared lavish both in its range and in its details, precisely described in the "passport." "Curried chicken" may be pedestrian, but "Curried Breast of Chicken 'Le Cirque' with Creme Fraiche [*sic*], Celery, Apples, Roasted Peanut and Coconut Garnish" stirs another response entirely. The fiction was floated that all spectators were personal dinner guests of D'Annunzio at Il Vittoriale to celebrate the arrival of his guest of honor, Tamara de Lempicka. While we were not—as in some of the other entertainments I will describe presently—confronted by the game and expected to join the actors in creating the action, we collaborated with its terms as we moved about the baronial buffet board, or later settled ourselves on gold-swagged benches in the Oratorio. (To readers frustrated by my omission: the buffet dinner also included prime filet of beef, pasta primavera, green beans with hazelnuts, salad, breads, fruit, cookies, and a rich *crème brulée*, each radiant with its nimbus of description.)

In the conventional theater I am "audience" or "spectator," all ears, or all eyes, and otherwise cut off from the full response of my body. But *Tamara* wants my body. As a result, I bring a different kind of attention to this event. I must make choices, weigh my interests, and achieve them through actual physical pursuit, occasionally at a run. My attention is acute, looking for advantages—of place, storyline, and more material consumables in the form of food and drink. My zeal to possess is stimulated, extending even to other members of the audience in this East Side "silk stocking" location. It was not unusual to hear dinner talk such as "—Who's the woman in the beautiful green suede suit? She looks familiar." "—I don't know but the suit is gorgeous, wonder where she got it?" "—Let's go over and ask her." Thus even the "costumes" of the audience are not beyond range in the game of choice and acquisition fostered by *Tamara*. I am in a new relation to theater.

Tamara erased the zone between the place of action and the place of seeing. It required of me a continuous seeking out and imaginative introjection, which the act of literal consumption made explicit. It created a new theatrical space for me, an intermediate space between my personal autonomy and a fictive world whose principle was the stimulation of desire. New in theater, it nonetheless feels culturally comfortable: I've been here before. Perhaps I experienced it as a child in the violet-decorated precincts of the Bonwit Teller tearoom? Perhaps as an adult in the model rooms at Bloomingdale's? In some sense I could say that at *Tamara* I am in a theatrical department store. To make the reference more contemporary, let us say I am in a theatrical shopping mall.

In the late 1980s, *Tony 'n Tina's Wedding* spread more like a food fad than a theater piece. In New York it has played (again, at the time of this writing) for almost nine years. It has also had runs in Los Angeles, Baltimore, Atlantic City, Philadelphia, San Francisco, and elsewhere. For a while, an unlicensed, retitled, knock-off ran in Atlanta. The show bears certain resemblances to *Tamara*. Both, not unlike the nineteenth century department store announcing "Entrance Free" to draw in customers, hide their price tags under a show of aristocratic privilege or family intimacy, bypassing money and tickets at the door. Both require my immersion in their worlds, and both correspondingly enter me in the form of food and drink. Even more than *Tamara*, *Tony 'n Tina's Wedding* jumps the "no-man's" zone of a spectator's theater to be absorbed as direct experience. Since the event includes a wedding ceremony and reception, every spectator knows the script in general outline and can become a player.

When I first saw it, *Tony 'n Tina* took place in a Greenwich Village church, and, a short walk away, a seedy East Village reception hall where dinner was served and a band played for dancing. When I arrived, a crowd was gathered on the church steps, and some were already being escorted to their seats on the arms of ushers, who politely asked whether we were there for the bride (left side of the church) or the groom (the right). The edge between solemnity and send-up was deliciously observed. A large woman in a pink satin dress looms on the church steps, anxiously asking if anyone has seen her uncle, who is incontinent. But wait, this woman is a little *too* big: she is a female impersonator. Presently, Uncle Louis hobbles into sight. As the two go off to the bathroom, we "guests" regard each other, not knowing which are actors and which paying customers. This stirs a general simulation ("Whose friend are you?" "I know Tony from the club"), as no one wants to take responsibility for puncturing the bubble of the fiction. The same edge is observed in the wedding service, where guests are drawn in to sing, pray, and answer responsively. Afterwards we walk the reception line, congratulating a large extended family, who confide tiny seeds of rivalries and grievances that will escalate into a comic imbroglio, or several of them, at the nearby reception.

Like *Tamara, Tony 'n Tina* invites me to shape a "personal" theatrical experience by circulating, sampling and selecting among the sensations and encounters provided. And this I am invited to do with a much more vigorous entry into the action than was solicited at *Tamara*. The evening does not progress within the controlled periods of the dramatic text, but follows a rough and ebullient scenario, alternating between scripted ensemble scenes and continuously improvised encounters with individual spectators. At the reception following the ceremony, I can dance with the groom's father, discuss the disappointing ravioli with the bride, or commiserate with Tina's mother over Tony's father's cheap girlfriend and mob connections. I can also stay at the table to which I have been assigned and maintain a discreet distance. It is, again, my choice. At *Tony 'n Tina*, in fact, choices multiply dizzily as many "guests" enter the action and sometimes actually elaborate it by inventing fictive personalities or situations of their own. At my table, for instance, two women are staging their own improvisation, convincing their husbands that they are Tina's friends from the office. When the deception breaks down, one of the wives laughingly confesses to all of us at the table that she wanted to come because she and her husband are planning a wedding for their own daughter the following September. "See how they do the dollar dance?" she asks (at this point bills are being stuffed down the front of Tina's gown). "We do it the very same way!" By the end of the evening, they ask me and my colleague—a pair of theater writers, we in turn have confessed—for our addresses: they will send us invitations to the wedding. Sadly, the promised invitations never arrive.

I attach the name "shopping" to this proliferation of performance encounters for a number of reasons. The first, of course, is that they were set in motion by my consumer purchase: I acquired not merely a right to a seat in a theater, but in some sense directly acquired actual "goods." That I purchased a wedding, specifically, adds significantly to my sense of value received, for being a guest at a wedding continues to belong in that small class of human experiences that have not become available for purchase; weddings are mine by invitation only, and through close, personal relationships at that. But once I have acquired this wedding, my connection to it is not that of private guest so much as public shopper. It unleashes my avidity for new experience, including the experience of variations on my own personality. Here I am at the mall again, "trying on."

The makers of *Tamara* and *Tony 'n Tina* understand something about the nature of trying on, how every suit of clothing for the shopper who has choice (the shopper, that is, with disposable income) becomes a variant on self-transformation. The dream of self-transformation or self-realization could not be sustained in the shopping situation without my having the power to make a choice. My capacity for pleasurable fantasy is in fact activated by the knowledge that I have this power. This liminal, or "trying on" state, is both active, requiring a purposeful seeking, and passive, in that it encourages the sliding in and out of imaginative states. A similar psychosomatic relationship is summoned from me by both *Tamara* and *Tony 'n Tina*.

At the most material level of commodity, *Tony 'n Tina*, like *Tamara*, presents a meal as its central event, in this case a satirical wedding feast that begins with Ritz crackers, goes on to ravioli, and ends in a very white triple-story wedding cake. But just as the meals are different, so I should note that the two experiences do not correspond to the same kind of shopping—assuming the reader accepts my premise that the predictable traits of a "shopping theater" are beginning to emerge. If *Tamara* brought me imaginatively into the hushed pavilions of, say, Copley Plaza, at *Tony 'n Tina* I am raucously "slumming" in a flea market, jockeying for place, actively creating my own opportunities and searching for theatrical bargains. The flea market entertainment serves as an easy model for imitation; it can be set up anywhere out of any shabby materials, unlike the intricate *Tamara*. For instance, in 1992, an imitation entitled *Bernie's Bar Mitzvah* ran for several months at a West Side New York dinner club. There was a surfeit of food, and the most theatrical moment featured an attack on the caterer by Bernie's grandmother for serving lobster at a Jewish event. A rubber lobster was quickly whisked past confused spectators already helping themselves to herring.

As the 1990s began, and the tides of human misery released by 1980s greed began to swell, a kind of anti-shopping shopping theater emerged, a theater of degradation and ruination, to which, nonetheless, the audience was invited to bring its 1980s-sharp acquisitive instincts. Even when the theaters producing these plays used metaphors of consumption with intentional irony, the deeper structures of shopping provided a powerful means of seizing the attention of image- and commodity-saturated spectators. *Father Was a Peculiar Man*, a postmodern pastiche of *The Brothers Karamazov* written by Mira-Lani Oglesby and directed by the late Reza Abdoh, was produced in 1990 by En Garde Arts, a New York City company devoted to mounting site-specific works. Producer

Anne Hamburger works by locating unusual sites, then seeks out theatrical texts that can be adapted to those sites. It was she who first imagined the whole-sale meat district below 14th Street in Manhattan as the setting for the spec-tacular, manic talents of the 27-year-old Iranian-born Abdoh, whose theater work had only been seen in Los Angeles.

To New Yorkers, the meat district has a forbidden fascination. Congested and bloody with animal carcasses in the early morning hours and during the day, it is scarily deserted in the evening, its wide cobbled streets and wholesale meat docks now a backdrop to the transvestite street trade. There is no time of the day or night when New Yorkers can comfortably reclaim these four square blocks. For twenty-four evenings in the summer of 1990, however, spec-tator groups of two hundred or more walked, sometimes ran or loitered, about the area in another of the canny, restless, acquisitive experiences characteristic of "shopping theater."

It was an inspired idea to set *The Brothers Karamazov* in this blood-soaked, sacrificial arena, where meat hooks adorn the shuttered warehouses, and mar-quees announcing Spring Baby Lambs, Beef, and Veal gaze stolidly down onto Little West 12th Street. This imagery of the bloodiest, most elemental con-sumption and counter-consumption, worthy of a *Saint Joan of the Stockyards*, overwhelmed Dostoyevsky in Abdoh's chaotic staging, from which we gleaned horrific fragments of physical abuse, sodomy, drunkenness, rape—paused for a song or two—and concluded with martyrdom and death. Everything was per-formed in exaggerated cartoon-fashion, belted into microphones as if the entire play were a rock concert. We soon discovered that we were not so much follow-ing a story and its characters as scouting locations, both those offered by the frantic *mise-en-scène*, and others that we ourselves found in this unique setting, which, like the Park Avenue Armory and the church wedding, was surrounded by the aura of its you'll-never-be-here-againness.

The play, like so many postmodern performance texts, was in itself a little supermarket of popular cultural references, including musical production num-bers like "The Bells Are Ringing for Me and My Gal," a Nixon clown in shorts and sneakers, a transvestite costume parade, and a red Eldorado convertible carrying a waving Jack and Jackie. The central outdoor scene is, as in *Tamara* and *Tony 'n Tina*, if not an actual dinner, a vast dinner scene, with a block-long meal table set with places for perhaps one hundred members of the audience. In this scene, only water was served to spectators, an appropriate comment on the theme of consumption for the starving 1990s. Our "meal" here was of-fered in the form of actors, who used the table as a stage to perform some of the Karamazovs' more raucous and perverse obscenities. In "shopping theater" the real, material object becomes important, not so much to cling to realism as a form, as to guarantee the tangible value, the "real goods" of the spectacle. In the other plays the meal service, the part of the play we could literally consume, became the emblem of this effect. The most real substance in *Father* came as something of a shock.

The spectacle culminated in a hellish installation staged on the second floor of a warehouse building. In this cement and brick setting, spectators were free to browse on their own in three dank rooms, which were fitted out with various profane and sacred tableaux in obscene proximity. For instance, a scene of a fashion mannequin lying under a circular saw blade with blood on her neck was near a scene of hooded monks praying. In the second room, the actor playing a green-skinned Ivan lay naked, chained to his nightmare bed, tormented by clothespins pinching his flesh. At the other side of the room, naked men stood in a bathtub with shower attachment, washing themselves and each other. They kissed in gay embrace, then pissed into the water they were standing in, or the other way round, I don't recall. This urination, at the excretory end of the consumption cycle, was the realest of tangibles in *Father*. In *Tamara* and *Tony 'n Tina* the meal had invited us to close the distance between spectacle and spectator. Now, for those of us who happened to be gathered about the scene, the spectacle implicated our bodies again by the negative fascination of uncleanliness.

If spectators shopped for class in *Tamara*, and for ethnic vulgarity in *Tony 'n Tina* and *Bernie's Bar Mitzvah*, the acquisition of contaminants, the coming close to the slight but appalling chance of defilement—whether from the faint odor of bloody meat, or the bagged industrial garbage on the streets, or the transvestite streetwalkers who watched us in amusement as we watched them, or from Abdoh's extreme scenes themselves—constituted the pleasure of the chase in *Father Was a Peculiar Man*. To achieve this pleasure, we spectators were called on to engage in the characteristic hunting-gathering behaviors of consumer culture, celebrating individual initiative in quickly-learned systems of pursuit and personal choice. The fullness of the final event for each spectator depended on her appetite for "experiences," her will to acquire them by her own efforts, and even more basically on her ability to grasp the market principle that underlay the theatrical aesthetic.

An illuminating, if almost certainly unconscious, study in the contrast between the postmodern darting, grasping, nomadic, shopping aesthetic and the binary classical aesthetic—"classical" here meaning the observation of an unbridgeable distance between spectator and spectacle—briefly appeared in New York's East Village in the fall of 1992. This was a production of Heiner Müller's "synthetic fragment" text, *Despoiled Shore   Medeamaterial   Landscape with Argonauts*, whose imagery, as Müller writes, "presumes the catastrophes which mankind is working toward," catastrophes incubated in the obscene detritus of consumer culture.[5]

In 1984, I attended the much-anticipated Berlin arrival of the Matthias Langhoff and Manfried Karge Bochum Schauspielhaus production of *Despoiled*

Shore. Performed by brilliant professional actors, it was very much the rhetorical, high art, proscenium staging one had become accustomed to seeing at the annual *Theatertreffen*. The New York production was directed by Ulla Neuerburg, who began her directing career in Berlin in the 1980s, but subsequently trained at New York University's Performance Studies Department. Neuerburg approached Müller from two cultural directions, the first inspired by the postmodern values more visible in American culture, the second more classically-inspired, and Berlin-derived.

In the first half, spectators were led about the turn-of-the-century school building that now houses the community center Charas on East 9th Street. Our escort was a young actress dressed like a male valet, who wore an amusing red cap from which protruded, like feathers, a small forest of dinner forks, the emblem, one might say, of the consumer relations that lay ahead of us. Her narration offered interesting detail about the history of the site, its proud educational background, its abandonment in an earlier urban economic crisis, its invasion by drug addicts, the plundering of its vital organs of plumbing and copper flashing to be sold on the black market, and finally its inching return through determined community efforts. Knowledge that I am standing in a space itself narrowly rescued from the despoliation of Müller's theme stirs in me, and I assume in others, a strong sense of privilege, perversely analogous to walking through the never-permitted-to-decay elegance of the Park Avenue Armory.

A tour followed through the crumbling second floor of the school, in whose rooms we were shown installations and tableaux on the Medea/Jason theme as well as a Butoh performance enacted by two young actor/dancers portraying Medea's children. These dancers at one point plunged into piles of earth at either end of a long hallway, "excavating" the ruins of the contemporary marketplace—crushed cigarette packages, old plastic bags, broken egg cartons, and other garbage. All of these scenes ran simultaneously while we browsed for an allotted time that was ours to "spend" as, and in any order, we pleased. It was perhaps not accidental that on one of my two visits to the production, our guide—whose text was semi-improvised—described our opportunity here as "shopping without buying." My by now trained responses as a theater shopper made me quickly alert to the nature of this experience, the immediate ambition to see and hear as much as possible, the scanning for the best place to stand, the being confronted at every moment with the choice between lingering in a room, or hurrying on to the next. I noted that there was no food "centerpiece" in this production, but curiously, in the final room I visited, a "festival menu" of music was offered by a small orchestra as a kind of food. The musical "entrees" included brief improvisations on such themes as THANKS, SCREAM, RAGE, POWER, CREON, HEART, and NO. These pieces were performed according to requests shouted out to the musicians every minute or so by the spectators, who grew bold with the assurance that there was "no limit to the number of entrees per person."

In the second part of the performance, spectators were seated in a small black-box theater, in which the Müller text, with additions from the *Medea* plays of Euripides, Seneca, and Hans Henny Jahn, and a first-rate cabaret score by Ralph Denzer, were performed by the cast and musicians who had appeared in the installations. A reviewer in the *Voice* complained that Neuerburg had, in effect, staged the play twice, and that the second part was redundant. "Twice" was not the problem however: Beckett does *Godot* twice. The problem was that having permitted her spectators to insert their bodies into the pleasure space of a "shopping theater," having loosed our active principle of playful acquisition, Neuerburg could not quite stuff us back into a passively receptive state, position us back to "our side" of the great theatrical divide. The erasure of the divide, doubly enacted here by the unsuccessful attempt to reinstate it, links all the performances I have discussed. It is shopping theater's central gesture, and threatens not merely the "death of character," but of theatrical art itself.

In *Postmodernism, or the Cultural Logic of Late Capitalism,* Fredric Jameson searches out the aesthetic implications of Ernest Mandel's study of the third great wave of capital expansion.[6] Jameson was interested in the artist, whom he represents as market imitator in his ceaseless production of experimental novelties. I am interested in the spectator as market follower, the late capitalist consumer trained like an athlete to the hectic pace of product turnover and market strategies. I argue the creation of a new spectator, one who, like Brecht's smoker and sports enthusiast, abolishes the pedestal of the artistic event—not to gain the greater distance of dialectical inquiry, but to close the distance in what could be called *simulacrity*, to be explained presently.

In the orderly theater of the Enlightenment, whose habits still continue in traditional theater spaces (and sometimes in traditional expectations brought to non-traditional spaces), the place of theatrical seeing and the place of action are separated by an uncrossable line. Walter Benjamin sees in the orchestra pit the physical emblem of this relationship, calling it the "abyss which separates the players from the audience as it does the dead from the living."[7] Sitting in such an auditorium before the curtain rises or the lights come up, I experience a neutral expectancy without immersion. After it is raised, I extend appreciation without appropriation. Brecht called this "culinary theater," yet its "unconscious" still resided in a romantic utopia, where "art," like "home," is the refuge from rather than the imitation of the market. Functioning within these traditional theater dynamics, I may be Brecht's passive spectator conditioned to dominant social values, but my very passivity distinguishes me from the acquisitive, "shopping" spectator of the entertainments described here.

The environmental theater of the 1960s and early 1970s tried to cure the passivity of the spectator by pulling her, often to her confusion, across the abyss into the imaginative realm of the spectacle. Spectators did not understand what new behaviors were expected of them: how should they participate in a ritual enactment of Dionysian ecstasy? The problem was compounded by the fact that, for the most part, the experimental environments were still created in theaters: the actors stand their ground, but I must capitulate and cross over. The spectator, finally, refused to cross the line. These resisting spectators may have sensed that the "psychological proscenium," as Darko Suvin writes, is the "decisive factor of theater, from which all other aspects issue or depend."[8]

The "shopping" entertainment, on the other hand, has been embraced without suspicion. Tapping cannily into their spectators' contemporary social conditioning, both the frankly commercial enterprises and their poor but intellectual avant-garde cousins bridge the abyss in the other direction. Far from dragging the spectator into a transformational imaginative space, they drag the space to the spectator. They take me out of the theater and into the realm of active being, inviting not my surrender but seemingly my mastery, control, and ownership. The idea of ownership was consciously folded into the structure of reception; they gave me a meal, a menu, a "personalized" program—something tangible that turned me from mere spectator into an *incorporator*. This revision of the spectator's relationship to theater matches well with research in market studies concluding that consumers regard objects, experiences, and even places as possessions that can be claimed as part of their "extended selves."[9]

Let us suppose now that the new "shopping play" is not a wobbly term— now mocking, now serious, now superficial, now perhaps inappropriately penetrating—created by a theater critic who has not concealed her ambivalent response to what may be a new performance genre. Let us suppose instead that this new form has been struck off the forge of a daring theatrical movement that proclaims Brecht's didactic theater as its anti-model. How do its creators describe the new theatrical form? In a central inversion, they turn the "alienation effect" into a "familiarization effect." The alienation effect was an exercise in dialectics, an effort to see clearly through questioning, criticism and resistance. In familiarization it is just the opposite: the spectator is plunged bodily into the action. She is taken out of the theater (where if truth be told she always sensed herself at a distance, with or without the *V-effekt*) and invited to "make herself at home" in a strange environment whose actual historical or cultural specificity, and thus its actual distance from her life, is almost totally obscured.

Familiarization, however, does not collapse the spectator back into the old empathic relation of the "culinary" theater. Empathy implies a whole set of now banished relations: the immobilization and transfixing of the spectator in the traditional actor/spectator divide, the depth implied by that division, and the sense of temporal extension that functions as a complement to theater's traditional spatial concentration. No, empathy is not required or even possible in the new world of familiarization, where the spectator's spatial saturation essentially takes the place of his experience of characters in a drama.

The unique space now becomes the "central character" of the spectacle, the only element in it that can claim the "aura" that Walter Benjamin attributed to original and unique works of art before the age of mechanical reproduction.[10] Here actors deliberately do not exert their former claims to characterological authenticity (nor do they take the stance of Brecht's actor and claim the higher authenticity of detachment); rather, they proclaim their inauthenticity, their artificiality, exhibiting themselves as a series of ever-changing, and not necessarily connected, impressions and surfaces. The actors in effect invite me to model myself as a series of reflecting surfaces, moving in and out of the changing environment in a playful, half-immersed, half-detached state of simulacrity, an instant, ever-shifting simulation in which I "try on" the physical and imaginative conditions imposed by the surrounding space. The heavy burden of "auracity" has been lifted not only from the actors but from me as well. I am pleasantly suspended in what might be thought of as an authentic artificiality, where the true and real have been projected outward from subjectivity into the surrounding environment, with its guaranteed *verismo*.

In his theory of the *Lehrstück*, Brecht stressed the importance of taking the performance out of the traditional theater space and into workers' halls, schools, and factories. In those settings, ideally, workers themselves would become performers, learning and teaching simultaneously. Stripping away the mystifications of the theatrical apparatus would become an essential factor in making strange the familiar "normalcies" of bourgeois capitalism. In the new shopping theater, too, I abandon the theater and its mystifications, but now not to resist but to be better folded into the surrounding culture. The old-style theater puts an excessive imaginative burden on the new-style spectator. As he lightens up, empties out, his reality is now anchored and guaranteed by *real* space, *real* food, *real* clothes (not "costumes!"), even *real* piss, all operating in *real* time. Extrapolating from the new relations of spectator/spectacle in "shopping theater," we can see that the theater event is actually used to project back onto the newly de-interiorized subject a mediated, "improved" sense of her own reality. The new theater reveals thereby more about the nature of shopping than shopping does; it knows the truth of Barbara Kruger's amendment of Descartes, "I shop . . . therefore I am."[11]

As I think about the spectator as shopper, a distant figure wanders my mind: it is Walter Benjamin's flâneur, the stroller, the loiterer, the window-shopper endlessly fascinated with commodities, who frequented the great arcades of nineteenth-century European cities, but especially Paris. Susan Buck-Morss traces the fragments of Benjamin's Arcades Project, prowled by this ghost from the past. We follow the decline of this Everyman of nineteenth-century European capitalism, his potential for intellectual distance and political resistance finally reduced to the base denominator of commodity. He "takes the concept of being-for-sale itself for a walk," reads one of Benjamin's notes. "Just as the department store is his last haunt, so his last incarnation is as sandwichman," human advertisement.[12] Benjamin didn't live long enough to see his sandwichman, his consumer-connoisseur abased to consumer-product, proliferate in the millions who carry designer initial goods, or the millions more in T-shirt culture who are walking advertisements for companies, products, groups, and cultural events. The flâneur has found a new haunt in the contemporary mall, that totalizing shoppers' simulacrum of the real world.[13] He also seems finally to have arrived in the theater. Too restless and driven to be contained in a theater seat, he prowls the total entertainment, simultaneously consuming and consumed.

And what about the theater critic? What is her relation to the new aesthetic? There is a shopping confession to be made here. Toward the end of the Reagan decade, I once received 550 consumer catalogues in a single calendar year, counting museum, but not counting book catalogues. I did not count the book catalogues because unlike the goods offered in the others, I regarded the books as "goods" in the Aristotelian sense. Theory books, especially, were not commodities, but beamed straight at me the very aura that Benjamin said was destroyed with the invention of the printing press! Now in this same Reagan decade, when shopping burst all previous boundaries in middle-class America, so, by coincidence, did the critical and theoretical topics listed by the publishers of my book catalogues. Expanded truths burst upon me: hermeneutics, semiotics, reception theory, Lacanian psychoanalysis, deconstruction, post-Marxism, postmodernism, feminism, the new historicism, multiculturalism, queer theory, and ubiquitously, theories of power, violence, the body, with all kinds of attendant new vocabulary.

I was, I am, deeply interested in these subjects. In the 1980s I read unsystematically, passionately, devouring each new perspective as a true believer, trying to incorporate it into my very being. As the nineties deepened, however, a strange thing happened. The romance of partial perspectives began to wane, even though they had also made it impossible to re-attach myself, in one magnificent, empathic gesture, to some "master narrative." What to do? Despite my best resolves to keep my critical edge honed, I fell to flipping, skimming, and browsing the new theoretical production. I became, in short, a shopper of theories. Then, even my appetite for the simulacrity of theory shopping declined. Sometimes I don't read the sale catalogues until their order deadlines have expired. Further, the catalogues themselves have changed. In the nineties they have thinned, are printed on cheaper paper, and have fewer theoretical listings.

This being my confession, the question naturally arises whether the very idea of "shopping theater" is itself remaindered from the 1980s theoretical inflation; or is a parody of that inflation; or is a serious theoretical response to a theatrical phenomenon whose cusp has just begun to show itself. One never knows whether the postmodern critic is collaborative or oppositional, serious or parodic. There is a "modification in the very nature of the cultural sphere: a loss of the autonomy of culture, or a case of culture falling into the world. . . . This makes it much more difficult to speak of cultural systems and to evaluate them in isolation. . . . Thinking at once negatively and positively about it is a beginning . . . ," Fredric Jameson tells Anders Stephanson. Stephanson replies, "The old Lukácsian model of truth and false consciousness is, I suppose, one casualty in this regard." And Jameson affirms that false consciousness does indeed exist, "because it is everywhere."[14]

Having worked my way into this place of postmodern cultural dubiety, I was about to take my leave when I decided to search out Barrie Wexler, the phenomenally successful California producer of *Tamara*. "What is your chapter titled?" he asked. "I don't know if you'll like it," I answered, "it's called 'Theater as Shopping.' " "*Like it*?!," he exclaimed, "It's about time that somebody, somewhere, understood what our achievement is about!" Wexler proceeded to explain that he thinks of himself not as a "gentleman of the theater," but as a retailer. He ignores the accumulated wisdom of the theater business and has taken as his models McDonald's, the airline industry, the insurance business, and the superstores, like IKEA and Home Depot. Conventional theater, he says, "runs a show up the flagpole and sees who salutes," but Wexler, to name two of his several secrets, markets his theater seats like airplane seats (they're both "soft inventory") and, most important, he franchises rather than leases *Tamara* worldwide, replicating the product in exact and dependable detail. "It's like staying in the Hilton," he explains, "everything is exactly the same no matter where you are." Wexler doesn't even like the titles theater organizations name their officers, like "company manager." He'd rather have a "director of operations."

From his many years of experience in retailing culture, Wexler has concluded that the distance between retail and recreation is narrowing. "You will find that as the 1990s progress," he predicts, "playing environments in which you shop, and shopping environments in which you play—the line between these two will become thinner and thinner." Wexler, together with his wife and partner Lynn Wexler, is now planning not merely a lateral, but a "generational" move. They're developing a 70,000 square foot "interactive site" in Los Angeles, in which shops, restaurants, cinema, and live performers will be bound together by a unified narrative and thematic setting. This theme park raised to new altitudes will be perched precisely "at the intersection of new media technology and pop culture." Its theme will be—made for each other!—Hollywood. "The same way the still gave way to the moving picture," says Wexler, "the moving picture will give way to the experiential picture. The days of the conventional recreation experience are numbered."

Here is a vision of a grand merger—the Übermerger of theater and marketplace. Its price, undoubtedly, could be the end of theater in its classical configuration. The song for theater producers of the future will be, "How you gonna keep 'em down on the seats, once they have seen _____ ?" We can't quite fill in the blank yet, but the rough beast's paw is certainly visible around the edge of the proscenium.

8

Postmodernism and the Scene of Theater

The spectacle does not realize philosophy, it philosophizes reality.

—Guy Debord, *Society of the Spectacle*[1]

IN ITS twenty-year spasm, postmodernism has had more "moments" than Hegel's history of the spirit. Its first incarnation was celebratory and utopian, liberationist in its ideology of play, indeterminacy, and pure difference. But the question arose, was this actually "post"modernism, or a version of the old avant-gardes recycled through late modernism? The real postmodernism, we were told, especially in the popular press, was about flight from modernism: a revival of the classical, the figurative, the decorative. Postmodernism was inherently backward-looking and nostalgic.

But nostalgia, to students of the emerging field of cultural studies, was not really about the past but about its erasure by democratic mass society. Postmodernism was the great leveler of differences, horizontally across culture, vertically within history. This same identification between mass culture and postmodernism was made by neo-Marxist critics, but less tolerantly: postmodernism was the cultural "dominant" of late capitalism, commodity-driven, and fundamentally reactionary.

Perhaps this moment could or should have been its last, but through a clever graft with materialist feminism and other theories of the margin, postmodernism suddenly acquired, or re-acquired, a politics of resistance. The multiple subversions of narrative, realism, centering, and closure, earlier criticized by Anglo-American feminist critics and others as leading to a paralytic relativism, were now seen as political when used for the "right" ends in the "right" hands. And this moment was then extended into a range of multicultural and intercultural studies, some of whose devotees would like to forget the politically ambiguous postmodern route that took them there.

Like a hologram that produces three-dimensional objects through a mysterious transformation of two-dimensional images, postmodernism has been an elusive story of now-you-see-it, now-you-don't. Many of its defenders experienced quasi-religious conversions on first grasping its paradigm shifts, but to some it was always an elaborate renaming trick, a kind of intellectual magic show with smoke and mirrors. This is the postmodernism I want to take up here: not the truth claims of its moments, but the ontological ground on which they have been played out.

To introduce my own intervention in the waning discourse of postmodernism, that of the theater critic, I want first to tell two brief stories. Both are derived from the field in which postmodernism was early and most unequivocally identified, architecture.

Story one: Reading architectural critic Charles Jencks's *What is Post-Modernism?* I come across a passage that delivers a stirring contrast between the heroic modernism of Le Corbusier in 1927 and the classical "Post-Modernism" represented at the 1980 Venice Biennale of Architecture, which Jencks helped to organize around the theme, "The Presence of the Past."[2] One of Jencks's favorite entries was *Strada Novissima*, an architectural installation consisting of twenty facades designed by leading postmodern architects. These facades show renewed interest, Jencks says, in "ornament, symbolism, and other taboos," a return he describes as a "Counter-Reformation" to the "Protestant" disruption of modernism. Under the segment of the Strada that appears in color illustration 31 of this little book, Jencks inserts the legend, "The Strada illustrates the 'return to architecture,' to polychromy, ornament and above all to the notion of the street as an urban type." But two pages later Jencks lets drop the otherwise unremarked bit of information that the installation was "based on a Renaissance stage-set."[3]

On a renaissance stage-set? Jencks's central thesis is that all postmodern art proceeds by double coding, in this case the revaluing of the past and its simultaneous dislocation through the use of modernist stratagems. But here is a third element, not accounted for in Jencks's scheme: both resurgent classicism and modernist ironies are deployed not in the obvious way, through the creation and installation of a model street, but through resort to the forced perspective of a theatrical stage setting standing in for a street. The double coding is itself pre-encoded with a theatrical strategy that makes both the recouping of the classical past and the modernist commentary appear strangely weightless. The structure that is supposed to represent the recontextualization of architecture into the street and into history itself gives the impression that the street is poised in air, precisely lacking historical context. Its organizing principle is not community, history, the long tradition of architectural design: these are all seen to be subsidiary to the conventions, albeit historical conventions, of theatrical design.

Story two: At Emory University, where I taught for some years, the Atlanta hotel architect and favorite son John Portman was invited to enhance the campus by remodeling a 1927 neo-high-renaissance dining hall designed by Atlanta's then leading historicist architect, Lewis Edmund Crook. The crowning glory of the building was its entrance: a magnificent sweep of steps framed by voluted scrolls, and crowned by an elegant portico and an imposing Tuscan doorway, the whole faced in white Georgia marble. The new building was to become the university student center.

The usual architectural solution to such a problem—apart from tearing down and replacing the building—is to build adjacent to, above, or behind the original structure, attaching to the old face a new body with added height or depth. Portman did just the opposite. In one of the loopy outside-in/inside-out gestures favored by postmodern architects, he incorporated the old building, including its marble front wall, into the interior of the new edifice. Building forward from the old classical, or classicizing, structure, he left the facade of the building intact, but enclosed it within a large hemispherical atrium, through which one now enters the building. Standing inside this atrium with one's back to the old exterior wall, one faces a series of ascending, semi-circular balconies fitted out with tables and chairs to service a food concession. Reversing perspective, one gazes down from these balconies to the atrium floor below. The eye travels to the marble portico of the original Crook building as if to a stage. Indeed, one cannot escape the impression that one has become a spectator in a classically-inspired theatrical space. The old facade has become the "scaenae frons" and the atrium floor the "orchestra." The balconies complete the invocation of both an ancient amphitheater and its renaissance imitations.[4]

These two architectural "theater pieces" occupy an interesting boundary between actual theater and what we might think of as "cultural theater." Portman seems to deploy the stage as mediator, common ground, or *transition* between traditional and contemporary architectural forms. Yet beware the stability of the image "transition," for the stage in this case is not some third, intervening element between epochs, but rather a transformation of the historical into stage, the contemporary into auditorium. Their interface becomes, *eo ipso*, a theater, struck off by the force of cultural collision. Alternatively, the Strada Novissima is, I take it, *novissima* not because old and new meet at the point of the theatrical, but because the Strada subsumes or perhaps consumes old and new in the sign of the theatrical. On the Strada Novissima, nothing stands outside the theatrical. To rewrite Derrida, *Il n'y a pas de hors-théâtral.*[5]

I introduce the stagings embedded in these postmodern architectural narratives as a visual transition to the historical/cultural theatrical "spaces" that are the subject of this chapter. These spaces emerge from the theatrical metaphors that appear with surprising frequency in the poststructuralist texts—semiotic, deconstructive, neo-Marxist, feminist—that have served as both anticipation and explication of the postmodern paradigm shift. If theory and theater—from the same etymological root—were once in competition for the right to dominate the "place of seeing" (as the long anti-theatrical tradition in Western metaphysics might suggest), they seem almost to merge in this contemporary body of writing, in which trajectories of Western culture, or theories of such trajectories, have been constructed around the protean image of the theatrical.[6]

In the 1960s, the Spectacle and the Scene ubiquitously appeared as units of currency in the post-Marxist/Freudian/Saussurean discourses that laid the groundwork for the cultural and literary theory of postmodernism. The chief "spectaclist" of the 1960s was Guy Debord, filmmaker and leading theorist of the international Situationist movement, best known for his 1967 volume, *Society of the Spectacle*. Debord presents a series of 221 numbered sections, aphoristic fragments staked on the far edge of commodity aesthetics. He argues that the spectacle is "the main *production* of present-day society,"[7] the chief and entirely malign consequence of which is the dehistoricization of culture:

> The spectacle, as the present social organization of the paralysis of history and memory, of the abandonment of history built on the foundation of historical time, is the *false consciousness of time*. . . . The irreducibly biological element which remains in labor, both in the dependence on the natural cycle of waking and sleep and in the existence of irreversible time in the expenditure of an individual life, [becomes] a mere *accessory*. . . . [8]

Before industrialization, says Debord, there was natural time, measured cyclically by the operations of natural forces and human biology. Natural time was humanized and socialized into historical time. But this culturally produced time, still related to natural time, was subsequently alienated, artificially broken into dehumanized work on the one hand, and spectacularized leisure on the other. Human consciousness in societies where modern conditions of production prevail is "immobilized in the falsified center of the movement of its world." Everything "that was directly lived has moved away into a representation."[9]

Debord creates a narrative of the development of human culture in which hegemonic spectacle provides an almost apocalyptic finale. His vision of history moves from the natural, human, social, and realistic, and from the consciousness of the historical itself as a category within history, to the alienated realm of total theater. Debord can only counter this movement with a despondent late Marxism, an over-convinced call for educated cadres pursuing a "historical mission of installing truth in the world."[10]

If Debord follows Marx to arrive at the spectacle, Derrida reads Freud and attends to the "scene." "Freud and the Scene of Writing" evidences the subtle attraction that theater and its terms hold for Derrida, as do three other of the eleven essays in *Writing and Difference*, the two on Artaud and the meditation on "Structure, Sign and Play in the Discourse of the Human Sciences." In its insistence on the substitution of elusive maskings and unmaskings for unequivocal textual identities, Derrida's notion of play may be seen as inherently theatrical. His philosophical world, in which heroic figures of the metaphysical tradition, such as Rousseau, are ironically confounded by the mysterious quasi-personified force of writing, is almost Sophoclean in nature. In "The Double Session," however, Derrida moves beyond theatrical implication to connect his central notion of writing and play with actual theater. The piece owes its title (selected not by Derrida but by his 1970 *Tel Quel* editors) to two lectures offered by Derrida in early 1969 at the *Groupe d'Études théoriques*.[11] Each seminar student was given a sheet of paper on which appeared two statements, one from the *Philebus* of Plato and one from Mallarmé's *Mimique*. Through these quotations Derrida chases the problem of mimesis.

In the *Philebus*, Derrida says, the soul is compared to a book. Within the soul is the *doxa*, a natural upwelling of truth, or an attempt at truth. The *doxa* should emerge into dialogue with another, but alternatively may emerge dialogically into the book, figured as an externalization of internal speech. The book as presented by Plato, he says, is thus one face of a binary model of mimesis which splits into the image and the thing imaged. Derrida stresses the doubleness: "First there is what is, 'reality,' the thing itself, in flesh and blood as the phenomenologists say; then there is, imitating these, the painting, the portrait, the zographeme, the inscriptions or transcription of the thing itself."[12] Order consists in the discernible distinction between imitator and imitated.

Here, as in other texts, Derrida has once again made a demonstration of the binary structure of metaphysical thought, with its attendant relations of inside to outside, prior to latter, originary to alienated. But there is another model of mimesis, Derrida goes on to say, a model that consists of a non-imitative writing, behind which no originating moment hovers as a standard of truth. And where does Derrida find this radical model of a writing not preceded by, thus not separated from, speech, this destabilizing writing capable of bringing down a millennium and a half of metaphysics? He finds it in the theater.

The passage from Mallarmé recounts the poet's experience of reading a small book by the mime Paul Margueritte, based on his own stage performance, "Pierrot Murderer of his Wife." Derrida points to the seeming paradox that the mimodrama in question, in which the "text" emerges from the performer, who himself becomes the blank sheet on which it is written, exists neither in an originary present, nor as an imitation of a prior originating moment. On the one hand, "There is no imitation. The Mime imitates nothing. And to begin with, he doesn't imitate. There is nothing prior to the writing of his gestures. His movements form a figure that no speech anticipates or accompanies."[13] Yet on the other hand, the absence of an "original" of which the performance is an "imitation" or copy, does not make the performance itself the "original" of which the book by Margueritte becomes a copy. On the contrary, "*There is* mimicry. Mallarmé sets great store by it. . . . We are faced then with mimicry imitating nothing; faced, so to speak with a double that doubles no simple." This Mallarméan non-mimetic mimesis takes us into a *verkehrte Welt* in which "[T]his imitator having in the last instance no imitated . . . this sign having in the last instance no referent, their operation is no longer comprehended within the process of truth but on the contrary comprehends *it*. . . . ."[14]

I lay aside the obvious query raised by the undissolved binary "logos" of male/female embedded in the story of a Pierrot who *tickles his wife to death* (!), to join the deconstructive logic of Derrida's analysis. Among the many doublings laced through the "double session," one is clearly the structure suggested by the two texts, ancient and modern, which might be seen as representing two moments in Western culture. This pair of doubles lends itself, like many Derridean analyses, to an implied historical, or historicized, structure, a before and an after. In the "before," we accepted the logic of the logos; in the "after," the logos loses its stability and begins to dance with doubt and undecideability. In "The Double Session" a transitional term between before and after can be abstracted: it is theater.

Before theater/after theater. In the narrative suggested by this pair, Plato not only initiates but stands in for the entire tradition of Western metaphysics. Truth is still an achievable goal, the model/copy binary inherent in the Platonic view of writing functioning as its guarantee. (Plato's known suspicion of art will perhaps help to support the view that the Platonic example occurs "before theater.") But then, in this implied Derridean "history," the Platonic tradition of writing-as-truth is interrupted by a new type of writing in the form of a stage performance. Within this new writing the entire metaphysical apparatus of "truth" is subsumed, relativized, and aestheticized; instead of truth it offers "reality-effects."[15] It is not by chance that we pass into this de-ontologized world of simulacra through the medium, or—Derrida's more complex and problematical word, adopted by Mallarmé from the traditional Pierrot vocabulary—through the *hymen* of theater.[16] No better medium can be found (and here I am adding my own words to Derrida's) than theater, with its undecidable play of model and copy, presence and absence, to suggest the new post-metaphysical world that, so to speak, cries havoc and lets slip the dogs of Writing. But theater is not merely the *model* of that world, or the exemplary transition into that world. It is, with its perpetual mysterious *mise-en-scène* of emerging inscription, *in itself* that world.

Thus from two seemingly quite different ideological starting points in the 1960s, Debord and Derrida describe great historical trajectories that suppose a culture moving from stability—whether rooted in reality or in illusion universally accepted as actuality—toward and into a new instability of which theater becomes both model and agent.

This before theater/after theater model of cultural change may be found in many poststructuralist texts of the 1970s. The theatricalist move beyond metaphysics was bruited by Foucault in *The Archeology of Knowledge* (1969), where Foucault debates the status of texts in a post-logocentric world, and substitutes an Austinian standard of "performance" for the older, more stable standard of "competence."[17] Foucault doesn't merely advance the criterion of performance, but to some degree enacts it, splitting his voice in two, in the conclusion to the *Archeology*, to stage a dialogue with himself. His argument for an archeological and performative standard instead of a historical, truth-seeking standard in the evaluation of texts, itself moves toward a self-performance that recapitulates the suggestion of a before theater/after theater scheme of cultural change. Foucault makes this shift explicit in "Theatrum Philosophicum," a 1970 essay on books by Deleuze. He greets Deleuze's *Logique du sens* as a watershed in Western philosophy, ushering in an era beyond traditional metaphysics of play and the mask. Using the then current Derridean terms of the simulacrum and of mime ("repetition without a model"), Foucault concludes that Deleuze writes "philosophy not as thought, but as theater."[18]

In their 1972 *Anti-Oedipus*, Deleuze and Guattari move so decisively toward the theatrical pole of the before/after cultural binary I have been examining, that the theatrical shifts to the historical position. The book unfolds a carnivalesque social psychology, "schizoanalysis," to supersede the "classical theater" of Oedipus, Freud, and capitalism. Theater, a site for the dangerous loosing of the forces of play, sexuality, and irreality to traditional anti-theatricalists like Augustine and Rousseau, becomes itself the agent of repression in Deleuze and Guattari. Freud's procrustean primal scene has turned all psychoanalysts into "directors for a private theater": "Shit on your whole mortifying, imaginary and symbolic theater," they exclaim.[19] And this Freudian/capitalist theater is "not even an avant-garde theater, such as existed in Freud's day," they say, alluding to Wedekind's theater of open sexuality, "but the classical theater, the classical order of representation."[20]

In their trajectory of Western culture, Deleuze and Guattari place theater not in a terminal but in an intermediate position. The artificiality and false consciousness of the capitalist/Freudian theater is already being destroyed, they believe, by late capitalism itself. However, it will be succeeded by a "real" that is far from the space of stability and rootedness that Debord hankers after and that Baudrillard, as we shall see in a moment, projects back onto Western culture. Their real is a burning, Artaudian eruption of "desiring-machines"— "wild production and explosive desire"—which, pushed by the force of exchange itself, will crack through the social controls produced by nuclear family triangulation.[21]

Jean Baudrillard, the last of the male theorists in this discussion, returns us full circle to Debord's theory of the spectacle, which Baudrillard extends and sophisticates. Baudrillard's critique of Marx's theory of production is constellated around the theatrical notion of mimesis, inherent in the central image of the mirror.[22] On one side of Baudrillard's "mirror of production" is the "real" of labor and use value; mirrored back is an aestheticized economy of exchange dominated by a code of self-referential signifiers. Baudrillard sees these two worlds not merely as sides of a contemporary reality, but as stages in an implied history of culture, moving (as in Debord) from the real to the irreal, the ontologically grounded to the emptily spectacular.

By the 1980s, Baudrillard casts off the Marxist anchor of production value (last vestige of a reality-principle in his social analysis), and floats through the looking glass into the late capitalist world of "simulation." In this world the "sceno-drama" of contemporary culture does not imitate reality, but simulates it in an effort to disguise its disappearance. Even the old labor "scenario" of work and strikes is but one more instance of a "collective dramaturgy upon the empty stage of the social."[23] To express his revulsion against the spectacle of the metastatic exchange of meaning, Baudrillard reaches for extreme, trans-theatrical language. He sees a world so intensely theatrical that theater has passed over into itself:

> ... [T]he whole newsreel of "the present" gives the sinister impression of kitsch, retro and porno all at the same time. ... The reality of simulation is unendurable—more cruel than Artaud's Theatre of Cruelty, which was still an attempt at a dramaturgy of life, the last flickering of an ideal of the body. ... For us the trick has been played. All dramaturgy ... has disappeared. Simulation is master. ... [24]

Baudrillard follows, in the most extreme form yet encountered, the historico-cultural trajectory already familiar from Debord. Once there were cause and effect, he says, subject and object, ends and means. "All of Western faith and good faith was engaged in this wager on representation: that a sign ... could exchange for meaning, and that something could guarantee this exchange." But now we live "under the ecstatic sign of the technico-luminous cinematic space of total spatio-dynamic theatre."[25] Here, indeed, is the contemporary social spectacle as Wagnerian *Gesamtkunstwerk*.

In these texts, theater becomes not simply a metaphor but a structural element in a series of world-cultural narratives. Debord wishes to turn Western culture back from the spectacle to a criterion of truth. Derrida dispassionately exposes the theatrical undecidability underlying, or superseding, metaphysical truth claims. Baudrillard contemplates the movement of society from a stable real to a final and negative hyper-theater. Only Deleuze and Guattari construe theater as a form of falsely imposed order, instead of a disintegrative disorder, even though the schizoanalytic future they depict has much in common with the continuous spectacular seen by Baudrillard. Yet in all these schemas, theater, or more properly, theatricalized society, emerges as a late, and sometimes terminal and tragic, phase of Western culture.

Threaded through the writings of various feminist theorists of the 1970s, theater appears once more as a central image in a schematic history of culture. The cultural narrative theater is employed to advance, however, differs radically from those of the male writers just examined. Here theater sometimes appears as an absolute patriarchal Other to the (literally) *grounded* work of feminists, as in this statement by the Belgian feminist activist Françoise Collin, editor of *Les Cahiers du Grif*, who turns radically against all "show":

> As soon as we speak or write; as soon as we open a restaurant, a women's centre, a library; as soon as we organize a party, produce a film, a show, a book, a journal, a newspaper . . . as soon as we are seen and let ourselves be seen, we become part of this "theatrical society." . . . It is as if a revolutionary existence is only possible in absolute secrecy, underground.

To evade the ubiquitous theater of male representation, Collin concludes, women must become "ants that eat away at the earth."[26]

In her 1975 essay, "The Laugh of the Medusa," Hélène Cixous calls for the insertion of the female body into writing, and female writing into history; she envisions woman's "shattering entry into history" and the beginning of a "new history" that would emerge with that entry.[27] In Cixous's mythology, this utopian vision will mark an end to the "false theater of phallocentric representationalism." Within that theater, the Freudian/Lacanian "drama manglingly restaged" of Lack, this "oldest of farces," must finally be discarded.[28] In an encapsulated scene in the essay she actually stages this farce with characters and dialogue:

> Oh what pwetty eyes, you pwetty little girl. Here, buy my glasses and you'll see the Truth-Me-Myself tell you everything you should know. . . . You see? No? Wait, you'll have everything explained to you, and you'll know at last which sort of neurosis you're related to.[29]

As in this last passage, the new female order revealed by French feminist writing of the 1970s often uses a kind of guerrilla performance to counter what it presents as the hegemonic "classical" theater of male power/male writing. Carnivalistic scenes erupt in the texts of the Clement and Cixous collaboration, *The Newly-Born Woman*. In "The Guilty One," for instance, Clement's two protagonists, the Sorceress and the Hysteric, appear in a "Theater of the Body." and in several "scenes" of seduction.[30] But it is the Cixous-Clement "Exchange" in the final part of the book that most reveals the multi-vocal performativity embodied in their vision of a new female writing. Unlike Deleuze and Guattari, whose collaboration speaks with a single voice, Cixous and Clement open up the text to expose their own differences, and further double their dialogue by running beneath their split pages an intermittent dialogue with Brecht, Engels, Freud, and with Cixous's own text on the Dora case.[31] Thus theater occupies a double-edged position in Cixous and Clement. On the one hand, the theatrical is projected back onto history as the patriarchal mode. But on the other, this theater can only be countered by a more adroit, guerrilla theater, performing satiric skits or feats of dialogic expansion in the unexamined or forbidden spaces of the patriarchal model.

This notion of the feminine-as-performance to counter the theater of patriarchy is nowhere more systematically carried out than in Luce Irigaray's essay on Freud and female sexuality in *The Speculum of the Other Woman*. Irigaray doesn't only see scenes, she *makes* scenes. She plays all the parts: ventriloquizes Freud, then rips off the Freud mask and taunts "you men," now takes herself offstage to join an audience of superior but indulgent women ("Let us continue to listen without impatience"), and finally distances the entire performance with periodic comments about woman's relation to the stage.[32] Calling to mind Joan Riviere's brilliant female academic patient of the 1920s (not as tragedy but as farce), Irigaray masquerades the masquerade of femininity.[33]

In "Plato's *Hystera*," Irigaray deepens the theatrical structure. She constructs a world-historical narrative that could be seen as a reversal of Derrida's reading of Plato in "The Double Session." Instead of moving from the firm representationalism of the metaphysical tradition toward the modernist instability of the theatrical, Irigaray depicts a Western metaphysics deluded by theater at its inception. Deep in the cave of *The Republic*, woman both provides the stage for, and at another level is entrapped in, the male show. The cave is, after all, her *hystera*, her womb, but on the "stage" of male oblivion, she is decor for the male "stage setup," the "magic show." Men enact a false "process of mimesis" without ever knowing how the "parts [are] being cast," or what or who is behind the "dazzling *trompe l'oeil*" projected "within the symmetrical enclosure of this theater."[34]

Outside the shadowy phallic theater in the cave, Plato locates another world and this he takes, or according to Irigaray, mistakes, for unconditioned reality. But the Sun and the Good it stands for represent only another kind of show, another mind of mimesis. The "reflections" of this "spectacle above," are "guaranteed not by the cunning, the magic practices, the spells of the magicians—since these can result only in 'opinions'—but by nature."[35] To Irigaray, the great binary of Plato's parable—Illusion/Reality—is no opposition at all; in both cases, below and above, there are still only shadows, reflections, representations, the Idea. Both shows take place within something else which cannot be seen at all, "the earth, the mother, the *hystera*."[36] "*He who has never dwelled within the mother will always already have seen the light of day*," writes Irigaray.

The oblivion of incarceration in the shadow and the water of the mother's cave, room, womb, that immemorial home, the blindness shrouding the memory, blocking reminiscence, that inoperable leucoma covering the eye (of the soul)—all this the Father vows to do away with by dazzling you with an endless day. [But] . . . *Forgetting you have forgotten* requires a long and methodical initiation. Some time must elapse, some distance must be covered, some turns managed, mimes enacted. . . . Scenographies which precede and prepare the possible re-inscription of ideal forms.[37]

Irigaray indicts the metaphysical tradition at its root as an elaborate *system of theater*, a dazzling *trompe l'oeil* constructed in air and lacking a grounding that—with Heidegger—Irigaray locates precisely in and with the ground, the earth. In her epistemic narrative, there is a primary female principle outside the masculinist play of mirrors, manipulatively erased from consciousness in the male epoch of theater and spectacle. Finally, by implication, the principle of the *hystera* will be restored to consciousness in a new epistemology with the unmasking of the Platonic "show." The account of Western culture implied in Irigaray could almost be said to turn Baudrillard upside down. In Irigaray, the metaphysical tradition begins where Baudrillard's leaves off, in spectacle and simulation—his fourth and final stage of representation where the image forgets all reference to a real.[38]

The male theorists I have considered place the image of theater at a late stage in their accounts of cultural change. Some cannot envision a cultural evolution beyond theater, which they figure as a wholly degenerative symptom. Irigaray, Cixous, and Clement place theater much earlier, at the fount of the patriarchal order. They contemplate a way through the crisis in representation to new grounding in a semiotics of the body, sexuality, and writing gendered female. But it would be naive and over-essentializing to claim that the women present a simple anti-theatrical utopia in contrast to the male theatrical anti-utopia. Rather, their essays usher from a cultural moment that is full of promise precisely in its ungroundedness, a moment in which theater can also be used to explode and dismantle, and especially to experiment, through play, with new voices and subject positions in an emerging feminist discourse.[39]

Both the male and the female writers I have discussed enter the scene of theater, it seems, when grounding principles fall away; when there is—as Saroyan's philosophical Arab mutters in *The Time of Your Life*—"No foundation. All the way down the line."[40] For the generation of theorists I discuss here, this is a sobering issue. Lyotard identifies the failure of narratives of legitimation as the principal source of the postmodern paradigm shift. The male theorists mourn their passing (Debord and Baudrillard), or project the present moment of doubt both back and forward onto origins and destinations (Derrida), or adopt a rebellious stance that promises a future of even more radical delegitimation (Deleuze and Guattari). From the point of view of the feminist writers, these "meta-narratives" themselves are exposed as fundamentally flawed and illusory. In both cases, the figure of theater becomes a kind of lifeboat for those who are jumping metaphysics. In this sense, the scene of theater appears to be transitional. It arrives just after, or just before, some general quality these writers appear to regard as "virtue." To test this notion, yet half as a joke, I opened at random Alisdair MacIntyre's study of the decline of Western moral philosophy, entitled *After Virtue*, to read that "To a disturbing extent our [contemporary] morality will be disclosed as a theatre of illusions." And elsewhere, in his discussion of the importance of "characters" in modern society, I came across MacIntyre's insistence that he "intend[s] this dramatic metaphor with some seriousness."[41]

For the theater critic contemplating the spectacle of theory, yet another definition of postmodernism now presents itself: postmodernism is that moment in culture when the last ontological defenses crumble into theater. It is in that space, in that *scene*, that a poststructuralism that risks giving up politics in order to jettison metaphysical binaries coincides with a feminism throwing over the patriarchal binary in order to make a new politics. It is the intersection where once more the Sphinx and "man" confront each other.

If theater comes after Virtue, what comes after Theater? We all want to get on with it. We are bored with all these gestures. Bored with Baudrillard's fascinated horror. Bored with Deleuze's giddy release. *Bored* with Derrida's infinitely discriminating canniness. We would like, with Cixous, to see a new history, a new epistemology. But will it come? Are we already in it? How can we know? Perhaps theater itself, the actual theater of material practice, can help us here. The idea that when the metanarratives begin to slide theater appears in their place has after all been foreshadowed by the practice of modern theater itself. A theater critic could even make the not entirely far-fetched argument that the theatrically self-conscious theater of modernism, in a reverse mimesis, is the modernism that postmodernism is post.

The idea of the *theatrum mundi*, the theatrically irreal nature of the world, to which the theatricalist strain of modernist theater is indebted, can be traced to the Stoics. In the Middle Ages it became a commonplace of medieval homily. It entered theater practice in the English renaissance, but found its purest form later in the seventeenth century in Calderón's *Great Theater of the World*. There God the Author—director, spectator, and fixed guarantor of eternal values— sits on his golden globe in heaven and surveys the transitory and tragic human scene, where the human actors perform their momentary worldly roles. The idea of the *theatrum mundi* has waxed and waned on the Western stage since the renaissance. In the modern period it reappears with a vengeance, and strangely transfigured, as perhaps may be seen by compressing a complex history into one recognizable example, Pirandello's *Six Characters in Search of an Author*.

In *Six Characters*, Pirandello's obsessional figments long to be released from the purgatory of their single narrative. The actors who attempt to portray them are just the opposite; continuously in search of a text, they seem miscellaneous and under-imagined in their offstage personalities. Both require the theater for actualization, and it is only through theatrical enactment that they meet. Theater becomes a kind of security zone between non-cohering realms, the threshold between the twin problematics of the playwright's imagination and the materiality of the world.

"I have gathered it [the scene] up again into my own fantasy without removing it from the spectator's eyes," Pirandello wrote in his preface to the play. "That is, I have shown them, instead of the stage, my own fantasy in the act of creating—my own fantasy in the form of this same stage."[42] The liminal function of theater is even deeper in the play's structure than his words suggest. In *Six Characters*, theater is the "as if" space that permits actors and characters each to approach the other, to engage in ideological contestation, to assay their narratives. It is the space from which they *act*. In short—and this gesture is replicated in every modernist theatricalist play—theater itself has become the best substitute contemporary "advanced" culture can muster for the fixed point, what I call the "guarantee," once provided by God on his golden globe in Calderón's *Great Theater of the World*. In *Six Characters* it is Pirandello's version of the Real. It may have assumed this function as well for the generation of theorists I discuss here.

The day before I read an abridged form of this chapter at a conference in Montreal, this conclusion—that theater functions in much contemporary discourse as a form of "grounding principle"—was handily re-enacted at the conference itself.[43] Professor Nancy Miller, in an address to a plenary session, described the development of feminist thought from the 1960s on, both in theoretical terms and in the anecdotal terms of her own personal history. Miller explained that she had begun to write herself into the story of changes in feminist theory only in the late 1980s, when she perceived that the theoretical explosion of the past three decades of feminism was drawing to a close. From now on, she feared, feminist criticism would be submerged in simpler thought— thought so simple that it will "have a beat and you can dance to it." As Miller attached an intimate personal story to each phase of feminist theoretical awakening, it was clear that what was formerly an objective and progressive linear history had dissolved for her into a species of auto-performance. Here was a recapitulation in miniature of the first type of cultural trajectory described above: when certainty in the survival of the linear narrative ebbs for Miller, theater takes its place.

The respondent to Miller's talk, the Italian feminist Rosi Braidotti, was even more interested in performance than Miller herself. Her narrative was inseparable from theater at the outset. Braidotti did not accept Miller's sense of a decaying linearity. For her this same history, and "history" in general, needed to be rethought as multi-vocal, multi-directional, and fundamentally performative. Braidotti rendered her account of the same decades Miller addressed, the 1960s, 1970s, and 1980s, by playing tapes of songs performed by a succession of female pop stars. The performers and their lyrics constituted a feminist history in practice, seen from a radically populist perspective. Without question, Braidotti rejoined, "It has a beat and you can dance to it." Some members of the eminent academic assemblage clapped along. Braidotti gave us not history mutating into performance, but history *as* performance, and performance itself as history. Braidotti is willing to throw grounding principles to the wind—they were only an illusion anyway—and pull back the curtains to reveal that the most reliable version of reality is theatrical and performative to its core.

In 1967, in a now famous (some would say notorious) essay in *Artforum*, "Art and Objecthood," Michael Fried made the claim that "theater and theatricality are at war today, not simply with modernist painting . . . but with art as such . . . with modernist sensibility as such." His dire prophecy continued, "The success, even the survival of the arts has come increasingly to depend on their ability to defeat theater."[44] Postmodern practices have remarkably confirmed Fried's prediction of the turn toward theater, if not of the demise of art. In the decades since Fried staged this last-ditch effort, not only art but seemingly all of culture and society in late capitalism have defeated presentness, in Fried's sense, to embrace the performative. The very theoretical texts that we have read for the past twenty years to help us understand the changes that Fried sought so vehemently to stave off in art themselves construct cultural narratives to which the theatrical is central. Postmodern art and culture have not only aspired to the condition of theater, but have normalized and even celebrated the spectacle of spectacular society.

Contemporary social practice of all kinds, especially since 1980, has seemed to confirm the insight of theater as grounding principle in a period of conflicting or dissolving truths. The theatrical is where we improvise—culture, politics, ethics; it is what we have while we wait to find out, with Portman and his Emory University student center, whether theater is a phase the culture will pass through en route to new forms, or whether, with Jencks and the *Strada Novissima*, theater has become the enabling form—not only the way to the new, but the very scene itself.

Reviews and Articles 1979–1993

Reports from an Emerging Culture

1979

Des McAnuff's *Leave It to Beaver Is Dead* (*Soho News*, April 5)

DES MCANUFF'S *Leave It to Beaver Is Dead* may be one of those very few plays after which the theater is never the same. It effects a shift in what is possible in the theater as radical as the shift of consciousness attempted on its central character. At the same time the play seems a capstone on ideas of Western dramatic structure from Aristotle to Artaud. If there was ever a theatrical event in which one experiences Artaud's victim burning at the stake, signalling through the flames, this is it. Except that *Leave It to Beaver Is Dead* is post-Artaud: It is not interested in the fire or the victim, only in deciphering the signal.

Reader: If you desire a summary first, as in a normal theater review, kindly glance down the column, where you will find it indicated like this—**. But if you hang on for a while, you'll see, I hope, why I defer it.

I'll start easy, with the language. A synthetic collage speech snipped from commercials, sitcoms, news, *Time* magazine, songs. Like the play's title, the language is borrowed from, but comments on, media. *Beaver* is dead—meaning the American family, the Boy Scouts, the sunny peccadilloes of conventional morality. And not only *Beaver*, but our entire society reflected in the play is bloated with death (like the green parakeet stashed in the ice bucket stage left) and afloat in a dead linguistic sea. The marvel is that out of this murder of meaning comes a language intensely alive, as if outrageous artifice were not merely a way to reflect the end of natural life on the planet, but a strategy of some sort to reconstruct it.

McAnuff uses brilliant throw-away language but doesn't lament the garbage. When three of the four main characters suddenly change their names near the end of the second act, and a confused character questions the change, the problem is scoffingly dismissed with "that's strictly conceptual." Don't get confused and tie sense to words, he is saying. Reality is a continuum of shifting illusions. Slice through *Leave It to Beaver Is Dead* in any dimension and you find this synthetic reality.

Take the set for instance. Here is a cozy house with a couch and a TV set that shows us real shows and a john that flushes. Could be a set for *Leave It to Beaver*, right? But McAnuff is out for bigger game than parody. In the house are also a car, a fire hydrant, a park bench, a Coke machine, a merry-go-round horse. But then this house, which embraces indoors and outdoors in one airless whole, turns out to be a *set* for a show which takes place before us in the action of the play, culminating in a "real" show, a 45-minute rock concert.

"The Show," as three of the actors call what they're doing to a fourth, is terrifying as it jettisons accepted standards of human purpose and behavior, yet disarmingly abandons conventional theatrical artifice for something more natural. The stage is not controlled by unseen offstage wizards. Rather the actors turn the lights on and off, the sound up and down, and adopt a low-key playing style. These actors run "The Show" themselves (interesting in a play whose plot is about loss of control, see below) in a set which is a home, which is a set, which is a home. . . . Pirandello? Forget it. What could be drearier to this play's mind than all that reality-and-illusion obsessing? Those distinctions are "strictly conceptual" too, strictly in our heads.

For God's sake, you promised a plot! I'm getting there, but this play is in part about our notions of plot and plotlessness you see, so I run the risk. . . . *But you write for the Soho Weekly News, not some journal of philology.* All right, I have agreed to the plot.

**The Plot

Dennis J. announces to his old buddies, by home videotape, that he is on his way from Canada and medical school to take over once again the drug-abuse clinic he and his friends had set up. The straight bourgeois life up there has him half ready to commit suicide, he grins. He is behind the times. His friends Saverin and Luke junked the straight bourgeois junkies more than a year ago, and with a cool, charismatic woman (so cool she's named "Lizzard") they have a new organization which permits them to "sidestep all the Rexall paranoia crap." (Does this mean they're beyond drugs or merely beyond guilt? What kind of "coke" machine is it? Is this woman the old "Loretta" Dennis got off the stuff two years ago? We never know. Our curiosity is "strictly conceptual" anyway.) Now they're in business running "The Show," in which their customers—like the newly-arrived Dennis—become the stars and "play out their problems." Dennis's wish to reassert control of the old setup is the central problem of tonight's "Show."

With menacing feints at murder and suicide, we witness for two acts an uneven power struggle in which Dennis is stripped of his pathetic junkheap character (but no more pathetic than yours and mine) composed of shams, anxieties, denials, ideals, "values," "truths." Suddenly, in a brilliant theatrical switch Dennis converts to the new order and turns it on a guy who walks in off the street. Is this a last-ditch reassertion of control? Or a true shift in consciousness? A moment later, Dennis and two others are covered with blood. Is it real blood or the ketchup we heard about earlier? And if it is real, who drew it, and on whom? "It's all right, it's all right," the actors murmur over and over. What's all right? All this has happened in the service of—of what? Is there a new order? What's the signal coming through the flames? We don't know. These people are epistemological nihilists. Yet each step was an act of necessary compassion, for Dennis would have slit his throat in the old life.

Notice we have had, on one level, a tightly-organized plot, utterly Aristotelian in its organization and sense of crisis. Now in a breathtaking clean sweep of normal dramaturgy, McAnuff gives us a rock concert for the entire third act, which answers not a single question, but unbearably intensifies, *amplifies* them, like the sound on the electrical guitars we hear. Each song puts the issue of dead and living values before us freshly, in a series of developing variations. I was literally shaking by the time we got to:

> You can take up the slack,
> Throw the kids in the sack,
> While the train goes speeding off the track

broken by the insistent, screaming refrain, "Save the Children! Save the Children!"

And who is Des McAnuff? A human Zeitgeist? Des McAnuff is a 26- or 27-year-old American playwright, director, composer, musician, and singer— and he does all of these stunningly in *Leave It to Beaver Is Dead*—who worked in Canada until two years ago when he directed what was for me (though not for many of my critic colleagues) *the* brilliant production of that season, Stanislaw Witkiewicz's *The Crazy Locomotive*, produced by Chelsea Theater. This season he directed a fine production of Barry Keefe's *Gimme Shelter* at BAM.

The *Semiotexte* crowd better get down to the Public Theater. This play is an event in the world of signs, systems, meaning, non-meaning. Burroughs, Foucault—push any contemporary button and this play will light up just as it lights up the traditional theater structure ideas I've touched on above.

The most exact theatrical precedent I know for *Beaver* is Heathcote Williams's *AC/DC* (London, 1970; Chelsea Theater Center, 1971), but if it is more accessible, it is not because its message is less complex, but because it has swallowed the schizophrenia of *AC/DC* whole and learned to live with it as a permanent condition.

I hope *Leave It to Beaver Is Dead* can't be killed by conceptual criticism, including mine, for the play is a dazzling, frightening, thrilling experience in our theater, in and of our culture. Unfortunately, one of the leads, Mandy Patinkin (and he, along with Saul Rubinek, Brent Spiner, Dianne Wiest, Maury Chaykin and the musicians give extraordinary performances) must leave the show. I expect Joe Papp will let McAnuff re-cast and re-open the play. He should, it's not often the theater burns with excitement like this.

1979

Richard Schechner's *The Balcony* (*Soho News*, November 15)

Richard Schechner's production of Genet's *The Balcony* is a theater theoretician's dream. Its full significance does not appear openly on the stage, but in the tension between its new approach and Genet's original intentions. At that level the production is an exciting use of the theater as a forum for cultural debate, an intellectual whodunit. But this kind of interest has its price. The production, bless its abstract heart, has a Postmodern Theater manifesto for a pulmonary artery. Notwithstanding the yards of pubic hair that whisk by us in the course of the evening, the production is severe, chaste, essentially bloodless.

In Genet, a political revolution is raging outside the theatrical whorehouse of the title, where men come to play out on the bodies of women their fantasies of power. While the true bishop is having his head cut off in the real world, the imitation "bishop" is having something else cut off in the obscene cloister of illusions. The grotesque distortion of the public world of state in the private world of perversity is at the core of meaning for Genet. We must believe at least in the image (if not the fact) of an objective reality in order to be astonished when Genet brilliantly collapses the distance between worlds at the end of the play. Then, you may remember, "Queen" Irma and her kinky clients of the brothel-state create a "true image with a false spectacle" and restore order to the outer society, quashing the revolution. So much for Genet.

Enter director-teacher-theorist Richard Schechner and the Performance Group, grand masters of environmental theater (*Dionysus in '69, The Tooth of Crime, Mother Courage*, etc.). Their *Balcony* begins precisely where Genet's leaves off, at the point where false and real spectacle are no longer distinguishable. We notice strange details on the familiar landscape of the published play. In the office of Irma's brothel, a recording of machinegun fire is playing, and is broadcast at intervals to the clients in their studios. The revolutionaries are not outside: they are onstage with the whores. Their revolution is not tearing down the state. Is there a state? The "revolution" is now part of the stage show, engineered for the clients. These include the false pillars of state, false revolutionaries, and finally us, the audience (by implication equally unreal), who are incited into the action in the last scene.

The text for this interpretation is surely Schechner's "Postmodern Performance" essay, published last summer in *Performing Arts Journal.* "To see 'I' at the center of the world is a modern feeling. For the self to see itself and become involved with that reflection or doubling as if it were another is a postmodern experience," Schechner writes. Those two experiences state the distance between Genet's *Balcony* and Schechner's. Nothing can better describe the interest and difficulties of this approach than Schechner's "gender-free" casting.

Irma the Madam is now a "queen" indeed—she's a male transvestite, some of whose clients are now lesbians, women playing men playing power games. Ambiguity has proliferated to the point where it is not absolutely clear whether one actor involved in the masquerade is in fact a man or a woman. Compared to this radical subversion of conventional expectations, Genet's disorder looks positively stable in its mocking symmetries. Or put it another way: where the characters in Genet reflect images of a shattered traditional world, in Schechner they reflect a shattered traditional self.

I can imagine a dazzling production emerging from this philosophy, one with a wild emphasis on self-performance set in a constantly transforming environment, a kind of ultimate Studio 54 of the mind. Certainly the opportunity to make a strong environmental statement was lost here. Far from a mirrored brothel, the set looked more like a junk sale.

To work, Schechner's approach would also require "postmodern" actors, comfortable with a new mindspace we can only guess at but scarcely see in this production. I think Phoebe Legere, the young singer who's recently been performing her own material at the Chelsea Theater cabaret, has some of this. In her performance as Chantal, the whore of the revolution, one feels her working impassively on a number of channels at once, sexual, intellectual, political, musical.

By and large the actors look as if they were locked out of their own show. They and their mentor lead us to the border of a phantasmagoric new world, but they only point the direction. They are so busy not being classified, not being trapped in models of reality (for instance, Ron Vawter is careful to play Irma neither as a transvestite nor as a man playing a woman) that they undermine, retract, their own vision. The trap they don't avoid is that of the paralyzing intellect. It is as if a theoretical premise has been taken for a performance method, and offered as an aesthetic result. Maybe Schechner and his group should think more boldly, or at least think less.

1982

Andrei Serban's *The Marriage of Figaro* (*Village Voice*, August 10)

In Minneapolis they are calling it "the Guthrie style," but in New York we know it is ours, even when we get it freeze-dried, reconstituted, and one year later, as was the case with Richard Foreman's *Don Juan*. I certainly hope that the daft soufflé that Andrei Serban has made of Beaumarchais's *The Marriage of Figaro* finds its way east as well; the Delacorte would offer it a more congenial setting than it did Foreman's icy if farcical abstractions. But to return to the point, the "it" that is "ours" is the postmodern aesthetic that's creeping into the mainstream theater, and I'd like to share some thoughts on the subject before turning to Serban's production as a current if questionable case in point.

Foreman, Lee Breuer, JoAnne Akalaitis, Elizabeth LeCompte—these are "our" crowd, the New York experimental directors of the 70s. Most of them are no longer loft and garage operations. In the past two seasons they have moved increasingly into institutional theaters and classic texts, giving us an opportunity to see their work from the new vantage point of traditional staging expectations. (Akalaitis and LeCompte have not yet joined this trend, but note that they increasingly "deconstruct" classic texts in their own original works, from *Faust* to *Our Town*.) One by-product of this shift—in which intensely personal idioms have been domesticated by Papp, accredited by Brustein, Europeanized by Ciulei, pronounced dead in *Performing Arts Journal* by Richard Schechner, and, at the moment, popularized by Serban—is that a clearly identifiable and even imitable postmodern theatrical style has emerged.

I am using postmodern in the sense it has acquired in architecture: dissociation (or eclecticism) and sensationalism in the strict sense of the word. A broken pediment here, a Roman arch there, a bit of Art Deco here, etc.—architects are ripping the elements of structure and decoration from their proper traditions and cultures and whipping them together to create displays of frank theatricality, that is, displays that refer us back on themselves as aesthetic events rather than outwards to an objective aesthetic lineage.

Postmodernists in the theater have begun to use these same techniques with classic texts: the Guthrie productions directed by Foreman last season and Serban presently, Lee Breuer's Wedekind marathon at the A.R.T. in Cambridge, his *Tempest* in the park, and perhaps Schechner's production of *The Balcony*. A layer of "performance," sometimes composed of dissociated "bits" from diverse media and styles, alienates us from texts as they have been traditionally conceived.

Lee Breuer directed a *Lulu*—his combination of Wedekind's *Earth Spirit* and *Pandora's Box*—that became a kind of cabaret show of itself. The actors carried microphones and variously quoted or performed the text instead of creating the illusion that they were the characters they played. The cabaret itself turned into a kaleidoscope of performance styles: rock concert, film, staged reading from music stands. Breuer's *Tempest*, similarly miked, was a grand pastiche of performance quotes—rock 'n roll, Mae West, W. C. Fields, *The Wizard of Oz*, and many more.

Foreman's *Don Juan* also became a performance piece, a kind of play-within-a-play observed by a chalk-faced chorus of aristocrats invented by the director, while the principal character performed the entire role in the rigid movements peculiar to baroque opera. Inner curtains rose and fell on changing tableaux, quartz lights glared at the audience and mirrors sometimes reflected our faces, Balinese-type masks were intermittently used, wigs ritually removed and replaced. The score was a supermarket of musical conventions. In every way we were instructed that this was a performance in which we were uneasily included but of which we were to be constantly aware. Brecht was after something similar with the *Verfremdungseffekt*, but Brecht's purpose was political while these directors use alienation for the formal end of performance consciousness itself.

This eclectic style doesn't imitate reality, but imitates theatricality, as it careens from medium to medium and quote to quote, now gangster film, now soap opera, now cartoon, now opera, now ballet, now rock concert, now Noh. The overall effect is not merely pop send-up of familiar forms, but an eerie distancing which announces that coherent "reality" has collapsed, that there is nothing "out there" anymore. The postmodernist is way past regarding this perception with a modernist's despair. He has penetrated dismal reality, found that all is "show," continuously appearing and vanishing, and greets the news with outrageous glee. Which brings me at last to *The Marriage of Figaro*.

Beaumarchais's comedy, which inspired Mozart's opera, was modern enough in 1784, with its criticisms of the nobility, its feminist sallies, and its satire on the law. The resourceful Figaro who foils Count Almaviva's designs on his fiancée Suzanne has much in common with his creator Beaumarchais, a passionate literary knockabout among whose activities was gun-running to the American colonists. But Serban almost entirely lets go the play's shrewd social and political dimension. He is onto something else.

The Guthrie's assertive thrust stage has become a glistening mirrored surface. A high back wall of smooth, wheat-colored fabric cut by sliding panel doors is the only other set element. No lighting or framing device is used to lower the eye, and as a result, the Guthrie has assumed its maximal rink-like awkwardness. The panel doors open upon further depth: a mirrored corridor that catches entrances before the character is quite upon us and leaves us with his reflection after he has disappeared. Our hold on concrete reality is further loosened by the fantastic array of locomotion that propels the actors: wheelchair, bicycle, shopping cart, couch on wheels, castered chair, sliding bed, wheelbarrow, skateboard, circus swing, ballbearing platforms, and roller skates. Roller skates! Of course! The Guthrie, despair of many a realistic director, has fulfilled its destiny in this production.

Then come the quotations. Richard Peaslee's tinny silent-movie music, acting attitudes from 19th-century melodrama and *commedia*, ballet, and Spanish dancing. Bazile in his wheelchair looks like Dr. Strangelove, and Marceline and Bartholo are M-G-M Chicago gangsters in shades, or are they a quote from Ruth Maleczech's *Wrong Guys*, a quote of a quotation? Could this be a send-up

of the entire avant-garde? Here is another white-clad chorus, echoing Foreman's aristocrats from *Don Juan,* but these are stage rustics with absurd staves
and pitchforks. And somehow the trial scene (the text reduced to bare bones
with the loss of the judge Brid'oison, and the clerk Doublemain) reminds me
of André Gregory's *Alice in Wonderland,* Almaviva playing judge on a 12-foot
ladder while Figaro crouches below. Or perhaps, because as Almaviva we have
no one less than David Warrilow (the perfect postmodern, who has worked with
Breuer and Foreman, and whose very body can seem a collection of disparate
parts), I am experiencing echoes even of *The Lost Ones,* with Warrilow towering
above a black landscape dotted by tiny ladders. Maybe these connections are
more ambience than quotation, and unintended. But surely one cannot fail
to link the circus swing, on which Robert Dorfman (an ex-circus clown), as
Figaro, delivers his famous five-page soliloquy, with the swings in Peter Brook's
Midsummer Night's Dream, themselves indebted not just to circus but to an
earlier Meyerhold design.

Finally, the Ossa-on-Pelion of theatricalization comes between Acts IV and
V of the Beaumarchais text, when presumably the characters in a normal production are offstage changing clothes and donning masks for the outdoor wedding fête and fireworks. A line is inserted at this point, "Let's dress for the
masquerade," and suddenly two pipe racks of glittering 18th-century costumes
are rolled on. The overture to the last act of Mozart's *Marriage of Figaro* strikes
up *fortissimo* and the entire cast frantically strips off its modern whites down
to a veritable flea market of underwear styles (long johns, loincloths, etc.), grabs
the costumes, and rushes off. The rear wall of the set rides up, and reveals a
deeper back wall completely mirrored like the floor. A thousand dots of color—
reds, blues, golds—shimmer on this wall, as if reflecting a distant pointillist
carnival. But on closer inspection these dots are nothing other than reflections
of the multihued upholstery of the Guthrie seats! This inspired stroke by the
set designer Beni Montresor elegantly expresses the sense of the production:
there is nothing "out there," no "real world," just theater seeing itself see itself.

And yet I cannot quite resolve myself that this delightful confection has
much nutritive value, a criticism indeed that detractors of postmodern architecture vociferously level and that many New York critics hurled at Breuer and
Foreman for their offerings in Central Park. Figaro's great soliloquy, which
contains themes for more than one interpretation of the play, could have inspired Serban to take his own reading to a deeper level than he himself has
sought to find: "And who is this 'I'," muses Figaro, "that so preoccupies me?
It is but a mass of unknown parts . . . I have seen everything, done everything,
exhausted everything. Every illusion has been shattered and I am disillusioned!
Disillusioned! . . . " (I quote from Richard Nelson's new adaptation which is
terse and bright, but sometimes anachronistic and even ungrammatical. To wit,
Count Almaviva: "I doubt if it's her you are really worried about.") To keep

Figaro on a swing through all this suggests finally that Serban was out more for a romp than for meaning, even when the text gave him the opportunity to explore what one would think the postmodern subject par excellence, the emptiness of meaning. In short, this production may contain less than meets the eye, though it is brilliantly satisfying as entertainment, while the reinterpretations done by Foreman and Breuer, sometimes agonizingly unsatisfying, tantalized with hints of profundity. Still, I wish I could see this *Marriage of Figaro* again tomorrow (just to make sure).

1983

The Death of Character (*Theater Communications*, March)

POSTMODERN—the very term breeds suspicion, for it is a parasite lodged in the side of the "modern," and modern itself is subject to many and sometimes conflicting definitions. In August of 1982, I wrote an extended review in the *Village Voice* of *The Marriage of Figaro* at the Guthrie Theater, identifying Andrei Serban's directorial style and certain recurring techniques in experimental theater with the postmodern movement in architecture. Even the *Voice*, which I thought had taken the piece seriously, described David Warrilow in a photo caption as "postmoderning it up," as if to say that this newfangled theory either was, or described, passing chic rather than cultural *passage*. Nonetheless, the term alludes to an actual if amorphous phenomenon. It is in current (though not identical) use in the social sciences, art, literature, architecture, dance, and most recently theater. I believe we are stuck with it.

It comes in fits and starts, but there is plentiful evidence that we have in the theater—hence in the society as a whole, which theater reflects—entered upon an irreversible perceptual and cultural change, which the idea of "postmodernism" is getting at. This change is not merely a style or a movement, but, as Richard Palmer says, "an archeological shift in the presuppositions of our thinking."[1] Put in terms of theater art, it is a shift that promises to be as decisive as that marked by the central distinction between classicism and romanticism. There are many ways to describe what happened in that earlier transition, but one clear way to put it is that drama passed from the primacy of Plot, which Aristotle called the "soul of tragedy," to the primacy of Character, which the romantic critics—Friedrich Schlegel, Hegel—saw as the governing absorption of modern drama (modern in this case being defined broadly to mean renaissance and on).

From this shift flowed the far-reaching consequence that the energy driving dramatic structure moved from the physical realm outside the mind, and often outside the entire human order, to the psychic and spiritual realm within. Consciousness replaced action as the central fascination of the stage—it became both subject and structural principle. From *Oedipus* to *Hamlet* to *A Dream Play*: settings, characters, incidents evolve as projections of states of mind. An end point to this process is reached in *Waiting for Godot*, where voracious consciousness has laid waste the entire universe right up to the feet of an ever-retreating deity, himself a probable projection: "character" becomes merely the sum of past and present attempts to survive and evade the pain of conscious existence.

In Beckett's terminal world, the spectator is confronted with the ultimate reduction: a single mind, a gaping cosmos. "There's no lack of void," quips the agonized Gogo. This is indeed a "play of impasse," in Carol Rosen's term.[2] A new birth might do, but death appears the most likely way out, leaving only the awful question: which will expire first, consciousness or cosmos? But consider the implications of Beckett's world for the theater itself. How is theater to get out of such an impasse? Can it possibly depict an uninhabited cosmos? Or consciousness without an objective reality? Either way, the traditional dyad of human and universe, whose infinity of relations we all supposed the stage was created to witness, will have collapsed.

New work in theater after Beckett has had to reckon with this problem. Writers and directors working at the edge of theater seem to perceive that they are in a new kind of world in which there is no longer anything "out there," or anyone "in here," to imitate (in Aristotle's term) or to represent. One can no longer re-present, such artists appear to be saying. The result, seen in a decade of experimental group work, and in a number of striking new plays and adaptations of classics, has been a stage turned curiously in upon itself, blurring the old distinctions between self and world, being and thing; and doing so not through a representation of the outside world but through the development of a performance art "about" performance itself.

These characteristics—the collapse of traditional boundaries, an absorption with the theater's own artifacts and techniques and styles—are the best reason we have for calling such theater "postmodern"; the collapse of boundaries—between cultures, between sexes, between the arts, between disciplines, between genres, between criticism and art, performance and text, sign and signified, and on and on—is what postmodernism is all about. Some such perception of the inversion and breakdown of historical cultural values in the past two decades has bred the sense of "postness" that has invaded virtually every human enterprise in Western society. We are post-industrial, post-humanist, post-apocalyptic, even post-cognitive.

To return to art, we are post-literary. Under the scrutiny of the French structuralists, literary texts and even the proud certainty of authorship itself have dissolved through discovery of the myriad conventions of language. All kinds of organized behaviors, but especially written language, are being seen as systems of "signs" organized into "codes." Language used to be the clear window through which the objective world was perceived. The discovery that the pane itself is all we can know of the view "beyond" has made criticism, or writing about writing, into a new kind of literary creativity in itself.

Postmodern dance has manifested the same self-absorption with dance-as-subject. Postmodern choreographers were involved throughout the 1970s in making dance about dance, or more fundamentally, movement about movement; hence entire dances "about" skipping, walking, whirling, etc. Postmodern dancers have taken an analytic interest in movement systems formerly quite separate from dance—such as sport, play and physical labor. Some of them quote within their works from widely diverse dance styles, for instance Twyla Tharp's nose-thumbing mixture of pop, ballet, and ballroom.

Postmodern architecture, taking its cue from the linguists, has been treating the entire history of architectural design as a single language of signs, to be combined and recombined at will, independent of their culture or tradition of origin. A single building today might whip together Greek pediments, Roman arches, Art Deco, and port-holes. The architect will not thereby intend some statement about the Greeks, Romans, the 1930s, and ships—neither a serious statement nor even an ironic and critical one—but rather he will conceive his building to be composed of pure signs, "signs of signs." This is not an easy phenomenon to get hold of for it seems to have two almost conflicting faces. From one point of view, the architectural postmodernists are radical in their eclecticism, wiping away traditional cultural associations as if they were mere scratchpad doodles; and from the other, they are abandoning the stark orthodoxy of modernism for much softer and more popular touches of decoration and nostalgia.

This is postmodernism for better or worse, and once we grasp its methods we are immediately at a better vantage point from which to view what used to be called "avant garde" theater. One powerful connecting link among the diverse experimental theaters of Richard Foreman, Lee Breuer of Mabou Mines, Elizabeth LeCompte of The Wooster Group, and a scattering of new plays and classic productions I'll discuss presently is that the individual has been pushed out of the center. Or, in dramatic criticism terms, just as Character once supplanted Action, so Character in turn is being eclipsed.

Of course, character has been dying for a hundred years. In his astoundingly pre-postmodern preface to *Miss Julie*, Strindberg said his "souls" were "characterless," "patchworks of past and present stages of culture . . . pasted together from scraps of human lives, patched up from old rags that once were ball gowns. . . . " Brecht went on to scoop the actor out from under character and give her independent life on the stage, a fundamental alienation effect. It was just a step past Brecht to the fragmentation of the *actor*, that is, of the individual personality as a coherent focus of dramatic work.

From its beginning over a decade ago, Richard Foreman's Ontological-Hysteric Theater has advanced the vision that what we have taken to be human identity disintegrates on scrutiny into discrete sentences and gestures that can be perceived as objects. One might almost say that Foreman creates in his theater the post-Beckett universe in which the gaping cosmos gobbles up the flickering consciousness, leaving a Theater of Things (including Thought as Thing, Feeling as Thing, and so forth).

In 1972, Foreman wrote *Particle Theory*, one in his series of Rhoda-Max phenomenological soap operas, whose title underscores the reified world of his theater. Foreman's central, shall we say, artifact, Rhoda, was always projected *in parts* by that quintessential Foreman actor Kate Manheim—face one direction, shoulder another, eyes and mouth surgically distinguished from each other and from other features; breasts, ass, and other exposed parts on their own too. (Rhoda's clothes came off and on in mechanical repetition without sexual or emotional affect.) Her mind seemed to be separate from all of these, distinct in its stumbling inquiry in a strange zone between awareness and thingdom. Her condition as a collection of *objects*—body parts, stereotyped gestures, received ideas, hackneyed words—lugged by a searching consciousness, was summed up in the title of another Foreman work, *Rhoda in Potatoland*.

Ten years after *Particle Theory*, Foreman directed a controversial *Don Juan* of Molière at the Guthrie, later presented by Joseph Papp's New York Shakespeare Festival in Central Park. New York audiences lacked the advantage of the director's Note, included in the Minneapolis program, in which Foreman declared his debt to the French theorists, "Foucault, Derrida, Kristeva, et al., who have, I believe, profoundly rethought what it is that constitutes man." Foreman goes on to say that a play is not peopled by individual characters, but rather consists of a language system taking the form of "characters who are as a series of mirrors, reflecting and blending into each other" under the impact of the flow of language, itself a series of mirrors reflecting the "code and forms and social options available . . . in a given society."

Everything in the direction of the play told the audience to attend to argument and not to character. All the men in the play were dressed identically, and whisked white wigs on and off in unison revealing featureless bald pates. This ghoulish chalk-faced chorus of aristocrats moved and exclaimed as a single body. We were not permitted to love and hate them individually. In a sense the entire cast of characters became a set of variations on hypocrisy.

Foreman turned *Don Juan* into a performance piece of alienation effects. The chorus made the action into a play-within-a-play. Inner curtains rose and fell on changing tableaux. Musical and visual quotations from a bizarre assortment of styles reminded us that this was not life but performance. Mirrors sometimes reflected the faces of the audience, and quartz lights periodically dazzled our eyes—all there like Foreman's legendary strings across the stage to trip us into discriminating thought and to prevent the sedimentation of empathy or identification with character.

Compared to Foreman's icy displays of "thingness," the satisfying flow of the "I" in Lee Breuer's three *Animations* might seem to indicate a reassuringly human universe. But on closer inspection this more hospitable wing of experimental theater has picked up the other half of the post-Beckett universe and rescued consciousness at the expense of the objective world. These are obverse sides of a single coin, for if the "I" is everywhere, then it is nowhere.

Lee Breuer and Mabou Mines did their first theater work on short pieces of Beckett. Their postmodern insight into Beckett was that his "I's" were not so much concrete, individual characters as the great drone of the "universal bagpipe" inside everybody's head.[3] They orchestrated Beckett accordingly, and their pieces proved to be exercises in preparation for Breuer's three magnificent "animations." The central characters of these pieces were not human beings but animals, or more accurately animal *metaphors*—language collections using, as Bonnie Marranca writes, "rhetorical devices, macaronic verse, neologisms, sound rhythms . . . free associations" and outrageously embroidered puns.[4] These, in turn, were delivered in a style as patched up as the Horse, Beaver, and Dog who served as occasions for the piece, a style woven from animated cartoon, radio serials, soap operas—stereotypes edging into archetypes.

Breuer brought this same performance-about-performance method to his production of Wedekind's combined Lulu plays *Earth Spirit* and *Pandora's Box* at the American Repertory Theatre in Cambridge. This *Lulu* became a cabaret show of itself. Actors carried microphones and variously quoted or performed the text instead of creating the illusion that they were the characters they played. The cabaret in turn became a series of performance "numbers"—a rock concert, a staged reading from music stands, a Hollywood pool scene. Many A.R.T subscribers were outraged and confused, but Wedekind, himself fascinated by circus and cabaret, would probably have approved.

The accreted self of Breuer's texts, located in no particular body or mind, divided sometimes between human actors and puppets, and again between off-stage voices and onstage mimes, is not fundamentally different from the fragmented self of Foreman's stage. In both theaters, the audience is not so much following relationships between characters as relationships among places or channels—verbal, visual, musical, etc. Bits and pieces of characters take their place among all these, but character has lost its pre-eminence with its wholeness; it has dissolved into the flux of performance elements.

The work of Elizabeth LeCompte and the Wooster Group has turned postmodern theater's fragmentation of self and merging of planes of reality back onto the theater itself. Instead of taking apart individual characters or selves, LeCompte has been taking apart conventional plays of the modern canon that enshrine character. The Wooster Group has now done three major works undertaking as part of their design the "deconstruction," respectively, of *The Cocktail Party* (*Nayatt School*, 1978), *Long Day's Journey into Night* (*Point Judith*, 1980), and *Our Town* (*Route 1&9*, 1981). Most recently LeCompte opened to the public rehearsals of a fourth such work, *L.S.D.*, which incorporates long segments of Arthur Miller's *The Crucible*.[5]

Deconstruction, a critical movement that has followed in the wake of structuralism in France, entails not the destruction of a literary work but rather the exposing in that work of contradictory possibilities of interpretation. Thus in *Route 1&9*, when *Our Town* was played like soap opera in extreme close-up on television monitors and in turn juxtaposed against the blackface routine that so offended the New York State Council on the Arts, innocent nostalgia for New Hampshire small town life suddenly looked like a repelling lily-white social delusion. Whose town? The audience's own mental stereotypes about rural America cracked painfully open; our anguish was increased by a recognition of our willingness to laugh at extreme black caricature. A final stereotype was challenged when a pornographic film sequence at the end offered the evening's only real moments of human innocence. In this curiously brilliant way, theater, now consisting only of itself, of pieces of plays, old routines, and staged films—a quilt of cultural bits and wholly artificial—is able to mount a devastating social criticism. Theater has here become the wholly auto-referential place that Antonin Artaud said it should be: the space produced from within itself, and the equal of life.

LeCompte has progressively rid her "constructions," as she likes to call them, of the baggage of character and no longer even gives us the persona of the actor to hold onto. She thinks of herself as the writer of these constructions, but says that she writes "transitions" between pieces of culture. Thus even the writer here melts away into the thought and writing and performance conventions of a culture that reciprocally dissolves under postmodern theatrical scrutiny.

The postmodern in theater is not, as some might think, the exclusive province of experimental performance groups. A number of plays have appeared whose concerns revolve about the fragmentation of identity, the alienation of language, and thus the questioning of text itself. No doubt the European theatricalist tradition culminating in Pirandello prepared the way for such a school of playwriting. The major difference between the postmodern plays and Pirandello, however, is that the recent works no longer worry the question of illusion and reality. The question has disappeared with the new perception that all fixed reality is a fiction. In these plays, among which I include Heathcote Williams's *AC/DC*, Eric Overmyer's *Native Speech*, Jeff Jones's *Seventy Scenes of Halloween*, and Des McAnuff's *Leave It to Beaver Is Dead*, which follows the shift from modern to postmodern in both its title and in its very structure, all is shifting performance, and performance is the only reality.[6]

Finally, evidence of a superficial and debased postmodernism is ubiquitous on the "trendy" stage. It is now a theatrical commonplace that Javanese shadow puppets, the Kabuki orchestra, Native American ritual dances, and other "signs" from traditional cultures will be ripped from context and used for decorative purposes. Sometimes these signs recoalesce in works of "instant ritual," created by artists who hope that the theater can create a metaculture in which societal divisions will give way to the fundamentally human. This has been the ideal behind Peter Brook's experimental international company. But this cultural ransacking, especially on the commercial stage, may also be a more advanced form of the consumerism that outraged Brecht (the "culinary theater" he called it). It is a frightening thought that theater could be well on its way to becoming a vast supermarket, a Bloomingdale's of empty signs from ever more exotic sources recombined to create an artificial and dehumanized culture.

The title of Richard Schechner's book, *The End of Humanism*, seizes upon the conflicting message of postmodernism, and by extension, upon a central, painful, issue of our time. The process of cultural fission and fusion that has brought about the "death of character," and the replacement of objective reality by the autopresentational stage, is arguably a reflection of the scientific and political processes that may indeed annihilate all life on earth. But the "end of humanism" can also mean the end of post-renaissance Western arrogance— and beyond that, the end of the anthropocentrism that devastates forests, forces animals to suffer, and is making a junkyard of the moon. Seen in this light, the dissolving of character (and the idea of Man) into the warp and woof of cultural and natural forces is a humbling corrective, a dis-illusion most urgently needed by modern men and women.

This vision, grasped at some level by the postmodern—and it may be grasped as deeply and holistically in theater as anywhere—is none other than the vision of reality experienced by the Buddha, who taught that there is no such thing as a continuous self, and that all suffering arises from human grasping for permanence. All individual functions, he taught in the *Udana*, are impersonal weavings in the universal flux.[7] As restated by Heinrich Zimmer: "There is no thinker, there is only thought; no one to feel, but only feelings; no actor, but only visible actions."[8]

If we are approaching the end of character on the postmodern stage, what is replacing it? Perhaps a flux of Aristotle's six famous elements, with Character and Action no longer holding dominion over Music, Diction, Thought and Spectacle. Indeed the independence Aristotle assigned to these aspects of theater almost makes him sound like the first anticipator of the postmodern. And again, if character is "dead," then what notion of ourselves as audience is theater reflecting back to us? Perhaps we are actually coming to perceive ourselves as the fragmented, ephemeral constellations of thought, vision, and action that the Buddha saw as the truth of human nature.

1985

Peter Sellars's *The Count of Monte Cristo* (*Village Voice*, June 11)

The gratuitous contempt with which Frank Rich greeted *The Count of Monte Cristo* betrays his exhaustion by Broadway. This is Peter Sellars's debut production as director of the new American National Theater, a position to which the Kennedy Center had the temerity to appoint this brilliant practitioner of American theater experiment. What was Rich expecting, *Father Knows Best*? This production isn't funny, it isn't short, it isn't pretty, and the acting is weak, but it is monumental, and continues to haunt one afterward like a glimpse into death.

Sellars offers experience on a number of planes with this multiple-personality production—not the least of which is the social experience of attending theater at the Kennedy Center. One enters the arts complex through a corridor the height of a house and the width of a street, arrives at an intersection with a red-carpeted boulevard, and after two right turns finds oneself without transition inside the blank-faced Eisenhower Theater. Sellars gave up a jewel of theatrical intimacy and a passionately interested following in Boston to run this place. He has to create new expectations here, and the design of *The Count of Monte Cristo* is a bold beginning.

Sellars overcomes anomie by joining it, giving his audience a sensational introduction to the hidden workings of the stage, here stripped bare to the fire wall. Lights and grids are exposed, catwalks are used as playing areas, wings are unmasked, the floor traps serve as dungeon cells, and the rising and falling of the backstage elevator provides comic relief. This intimacy with show business is a perverse comfort, for Sellars's staging of one of the most popular romantic dramas—part melodrama, part revenge tragedy—ever to play the American stage is an icy-cold choreography of lost souls in a hostile universe.

The Count of Monte Cristo was the star vehicle that made the fortune of James (father of Eugene) O'Neill. O'Neill gave six thousand performances across the United States as Edmund Dantès, the innocent ship's mate wickedly imprisoned for eighteen years who emerges a rich count and an engine of vengeance. Sellars is not interested in the romantic stage values that used to draw the crowds—the enormous acting, exciting locations, and swordplay. Instead, he leaves plot and character to their own devices—the actors say the words and empathy be damned—giving us postmodern multiplicity and pastiche: swinging set panels from Meyerhold, a red-painted face from Kabuki (and Brecht) to represent rage and evil, and other visual quotations from various Soviet and American avant-garde productions. This short course in nonillusionistic staging that so enraged the uptown critic lets us know that 20th-century presentational theater has more in common with romantic melodrama's "universe of pure signs" (in Yale critic Peter Brooks's words) than we like to acknowledge.

What Sellars does want to salvage from the romantic is awe, the sickening awe that comes when cosmic ambition still exists, but can no longer find a resting place in the sacred. Sellars's staging in the cavernous space—his characters flung to its extremities—movingly depicts this uncertain, decentered universe of mysterious forces. He has introduced three fine strokes that heighten this effect. The first is an onstage string quartet that plays moments from Beethoven's F minor quartet (Op. 95) in the early part of the play, and later, just before Dantès's corruption as an avenger is revealed, plays a harrowing movement from a quartet by the contemporary Moscow composer, Alfred Schnittke. The introduction of music is an homage to the original sense of melodrama, drama with music, but the electrifying effect of this music against this text reverberating in this space is far from antiquarian.

The second is the interpolation of poems by Byron and passages from the Bible. (Since the play is a jumble of scenes and characters from the novel and various adapters' inspirations anyway, why not?) These enter at a few moments when the ear hungers for text to answer our widening sense of chiasmus in the staging. And the third is the conception of the final duel and reconciliation scene, which is played in all but stygian darkness (is this a borrowing from Lee Breuer's *Lulu?*), voices miked, flat and sorrowful, floating in the void of the empty stage. The scene concludes with David Warrilow's repetition of a passage from *Ecclesiastes*, "That which hath been is now; and that which is to be hath already been. . . . " This suggests the intersection of time and eternity so nakedly reached for by romantic drama and made visceral by this production in its naked use of the theater as a fourth dimension, out of time.

With the exceptions of the miraculous David Warrilow as Dantès's father and all-purpose wraith, Leo Leyden as a compassionate shipping magnate, Roscoe Lee Browne in a role too confusing to describe, and Isabell Monk as a compromised and villainously murdered innkeeper, the large cast—including Patti LuPone, Tony Azito, Zakes Mokae, and Richard Thomas as Dantès— trivialized what I take to be Sellars's aspirations. Nor did the three mobile black mylar armoires with their tricky doors designed by George Tsypin rise above the fussy, though James Ingalls's harsh, jumpy lighting was impressive. Not a fully "successful" production, then, but a deep one, and one that for all its three and a half hours I would see again.

1986

Robert Wilson's *Alcestis* (*Village Voice*, July 29)

Robert Wilson's beautiful *Alcestis* is the first large-scale work Wilson has created in the United States for more than a decade, and it is unlike any other production he has made. Its surprising interest in a dramatic text performed by actors, the "built" solidity of its setting, the wild eclecticism of its imagery, and its absorption with the feminine may point to a new Wilson, moving forward to a postmodern vision of culture and at the same time back perhaps towards an appreciation of older forms of theater.

The production has a vast transcultural reach, an aspect of Wilson previously known mostly from press releases about the doomed six-nation, three-continent, *CIVIL warS*. Here he puts together texts from three differing times and cultures, all of which recount a myth of death and renewal: a prologue by the contemporary East Berlin playwright Heiner Müller, the 5th-century B.C. play by Euripides, and a farce by an unknown Japanese Kyogen author, probably of the 17th century, *The Birdcatcher in Hell*. These three texts, together with a great skein of visual and aural images that are similarly both Western and Eastern, ancient and contemporary, are themselves subsumed in a larger drama enacting the erosion of nature, the fall of cultures, and the change and impermanence of all things *sub specie aeternitatis*. The nearly two-hour performance takes the form of a prologue and eight scenes.

The production opens on a harsh gray wall of stone blocks painted on a scrim, something like the opening of Wilson's 1979 *Death Destruction and Detroit* in Berlin. Images appear and vanish, Hercules with his club, Death as a startling white bird the height of the proscenium. On a small forestage is the sprawled figure of a man in seersucker pants (a recurring image of helplessness in the production). His arm rises, then drops—he may be dying. At an angle to the mainstage is a shallow third stage on which is revealed a 19-foot high Cycladic fertility figure, a kind of androgyne, under whose gaze the performance proceeds. Before its crossed arms, in the scale of infant to mother, stands a gray mummy-wrapped being, performed by the accomplished student actor Chris Moore. In an inscrutable voice, neither masculine nor feminine, this figure speaks the Müller prologue. I will return later to the hints of femininity in these ambiguous framing figures.

Against these images we grasp Carl Weber's translation of the thirteen-page, one-sentence Müller text "Description of a Picture," only in fragments, as layers of live and taped voices overlap each other. On tape, Christopher Knowles's broken reading takes language apart, Robert Brustein's melodious bass makes it whole. Still we can more or less piece together Müller's tale of a sexual encounter between a man and a woman that ends in her murder and her return as a curious spectator in her own poem. Later, sections of the prologue lap into transitions in the Euripides play like the rise and fall of a tide.

The scrim lifts to reveal a jagged mountain range, inspired by Wilson's recent visit to Delphi. Wilson has returned again and again to the landscape stage, but his landscape, always open at the horizon as in a dream, has been more of the imagination than of nature. Co-designed by Wilson and his *CIVIL warS* scenic collaborator Tom Kamm, the *Alcestis* mountain is a huge sculptural relief dominating the stage to a height of eighteen feet. Wilson has said that he didn't use masks on the actors in this production because "the entire set is a mask." What it masks perhaps is the open horizon, the "nothing" that Wilson picks up in Euripides's text and repeats live and on tape like a Zen refrain throughout the production.

Below the mountain flows a river. A prehistoric reptile moves at glacial pace along the bank. At intervals, boulders inch down the rocky wall. We are not in human but in geologic time. Near the mountain stand three cypress trees. In an eyeblink the trees turn into classical columns: we are watching not only the planetary change of nature but the rise and fall of cultures. Later in another sudden transformation, the columns become industrial smokestacks, which later still belch fire and appear to melt in an internal blaze. Yet Wilson's mountain, his monument of nature, also reveals itself a tomb of culture. The wreckage of a Viking ship, Chinese funerary heads, and other artifacts are caught in its formations. Towards the end, a glowing "city of the future" appears on a peak, looking oddly like a crèche. Moments of other cultures appear and disappear: Megalithic slabs and lintel, a Sumerian mask, the Omphala. Within the large, slow cycles of nature and culture Wilson distributes the human and superhuman events of Euripides's play.

In *Alcestis*, Death will relinquish his claim on the life of King Admetus if someone else will take his place. When friends and aged parents refuse, his faithful wife Alcestis volunteers. After she dies, the hero Heracles appears at the palace as an inebriated guest. He learns of Alcestis's fate, and rushes off to wrestle Death and win her back. The sharp turn of plot and tone mid-play makes *Alcestis* an anomaly in the classical canon and establishes strange congeniality with Wilson's own disunifying impulses. Wilson cuts the language to the bone, but adds and repeats key words, mostly on tape, for instance "death" and "nothing." Then he follows Euripides's scene order but breaks up the impression of a connected reality by taking a different visual tack in each scene.

All but gone are the surrealism and minimalism of the earlier Wilson. What we see looks more like the random specificity of postmodern pastiche. Jeremy

Geidt as Admetus's father, half-naked in a loin-cloth, his body marked with stigmata modelled after a Russian icon, wears a see-through iron lung. The royal family, son in bearskin, appears on a camping trip with pup tent and alarm clock. Thomas Derrah as tuxedoed English butler and Harry Murphy as a drunken barefoot Heracles telling bad Greek jokes ("I said to Achilles, 'For God's sake wear a boot!' ") improvise a raucous feast scene that follows the broad comedy of Euripides more closely than its critics seem to realize. The least successful of these cultural variations is the contemporary slip-and-pajama deathbed scene played between Diane D'Aquila as Alcestis and Paul Rudd as Admetus, which, through no fault of the actors, feels banal without banality being quite the point.

Alternating with these scenes are three ritual choral scenes of fertility, sacrifice and mourning. These choruses have an almost pre-Raphaelite quality, as in the opening where the women kneel at the river to wash their flowing hair and the men plant rice in rhythmic, swinging gestures. These scenes approach either the inspired or kitsch, depending on the rigor with which the Harvard student chorus keeps Wilson's iron disciplines of timing. Also, the chorus sometimes looks crowded in the available stage space.

In all of these scenes, both for principals and chorus, Wilson wants to break up the game of (his word) "ping pong" that comes from theatrical dialogue and more generally from aligning words and images. One solution is the vocabulary of formal, abstract gestures based on classical Noh dance created by Japanese dancer Suzushi Hanayagi, who worked with Wilson on the *the CIVIL warS* "Knee Plays" in Minneapolis. Another is the eclectic audio environment by the experimental German audio designer Hans Peter Kuhn (also of *CIVIL warS*), which runs a gamut of effects from the hyperrealism of chirping birds to the abstraction of Japanese flutes. And another is John Conklin's multi-cultural costumes.

But Wilson is too powerful a mythmaker to settle for mere eclecticism. I was especially struck by the abundance of feminine emblems and figures in this production. In the past Wilson's work has often been organized under the sign of male culture. Though often played by actresses, his "heroes" have been Stalin, Freud, Einstein, Edison, Rudolf Hess, Frederick the Great, Curious George; some of his subjects—death, destruction, and civil war. Feminists have been slow to lay claim to postmodern art, especially by male practitioners. Yet among its many myths of death and renewal, Wilson's *Alcestis* seems to entertain a feminist vision that is truly postmodern: the decay of patriarchy and a return of the feminine. This movement, unlike the others I have described, is not simply depicted from a galactic remove, but struggled out on the terrain of the production itself.

In the Alcestis myth male narcissism demands woman's sacrifice. Admetus loses nothing: Alcestis returns to make him "the happiest of all men," to quote a line Wilson significantly cuts. The Müller text is even more troubling. In it, sexual desire results in male violence and an uncritical compensatory invocation of the "eternal feminine" ("the perhaps daily . . . murder of the . . . perhaps daily . . . resurrected woman"). But in Wilson's staging the masculine suffers. Just as his phallic smokestacks destroy themselves, so there is no restitution for Wilson's Admetus as there is in Euripides. Indeed, the all but lifeless male on the ground in the Prologue is matched by a final Admetus whose movements suggest a near-paralytic anguish.

In an exhilarating *coup de théâtre* near the end, a green laser shoots above the heads of the audience and penetrates the mountain, slashing out a chunk of rock in the shape of an eye. A brilliant light shines through this cut in the mountain, an eye of God that restores the old Wilson open horizon: behind the seeming solidity of the world-of-matter Wilson shows us there is, precisely, "nothing." But in the last moments of Jennifer Tipton's and Wilson's heart-stopping lighting the sky turns a bloody red behind darkening mountains, and the cut looks like a mouth, and even more a wound or a vagina (words that had surfaced several times in the text).

In these final moments the production's entire male-female dialectic is again played out. And look what survives: the pre-patriarchal framing image of the Cycladic fertility figure, and the three veiled female figures—the three Alcestises or perhaps Fates—who emerge at the end from the underworld to sit motionless on rocks, like rocks, while Admetus writhes. Watching *Alcestis* I experienced a chill of mythic recognition, thinking Wilson had imagined the return of the three world-weaveresses banished by patriarchy to the underworld at the end of Aeschylus's *Oresteia*. All this is my own allegory, of course. I doubt that it is Wilson's at an intentional level, but it is all there for the finding, and permission to spin our own play is one of the enduring pleasures of Wilson's spectacles.

Alcestis ends darkly. Twenty minutes later the forestage is covered in white drops backed by a white curtain in which the same "eye" cut by the laser appears. This is the setting for *The Birdcatcher in Hell*, the Kyogen for which Mark Oshima, a Harvard graduate student, did a new translation. Through the "eye" pops the birdcatcher Kiyoyori, played by John Bottoms with the delicacy of a preternaturally alert bird. He clambers down to hell on his ladder to confront the rapacious King Yama and his minions, who are starved for the flesh of sinners. After a good deal of roughhousing to a charming if slight electronic score by Laurie Anderson (this Three Stooges staging is a genuine shocker after two decades of Wilsonian slow-motion and glacial reserve), Yama permits the wily birdcatcher a reprieve to earth. The addition of this Kyogen epilogue sets up a nice resonance with the ancient Greek satyr play, the comedy after the tragic trilogy, and also with the symbolist attempt (Yeats) to marry classical and Eastern forms of theater.

In the 1960s Andrei Serban directed the legendary *Fragments of a Greek Trilogy*, a milestone in American experimental theater. A comparison of these two "trilogies" tells a history of the past twenty years in the American theater. Serban's audience was part of an environmental stage action, following *The Trojan Women* about the theater like mourners at a rite; Wilson's audience is detached and distanced, invited to dream, space out, tune in at will. Serban gave us a savage pre-verbal language of archaic Greek sounds; Wilson gives us a sophisticated overlay of taped voices and live, modern texts and ancient. Serban gave us incantatory choruses composed by Elizabeth Swados; Wilson gives us a witty synthesizer score by Laurie Anderson. Serban gave us fire (indeed the more skittish in the audience actually feared that the LaMama Annex might go up in smoke); Wilson gives us lasers.

Think about this last one. Serban's theater imagined a primal moment, the rough emergence of culture from nature in a pre-historical past. No one who saw the work can ever forget Andromache's slow, naked descent on a slide of mud. Wilson's eclectic vision is situated at the other end of culture, certainly at a very late point in Western culture. Far from transporting us back to a primal event, his stage is pitched frankly on the bones of a score of dead civilizations. Serban's Greek Trilogy was an effort to return us to some raw essence of pre-classical Greece; for the occasion we became pre-textual, entering with gutteral chants and cries into a domain of pure myth itself. Wilson's *Alcestis* is none-theless mythic, but here we have myth not according to Fraser or Cornford but according to the Structuralists, where the motif of death and resurrection is recapitulated at a number of points on the cultural spectrum simultaneously, and no expression is presumed to carry the burden of purity or originality.

The difference between the two productions might simply be attributed to the familiar oscillation in 20th-century modernism between hot and cool, essentialist and formalist. But it could also be seen as describing the transition from modern to postmodern culture that observers in many different fields have identified.

How eerily Wilson's production embodies both the positive and the negative postmodernisms of recent cultural theory: on the one hand, a new imaging of the relativity of our own culture and a distancing from Western master narratives partly seen through a distrust of narrative itself; on the other, a representation, arguably, of the "story" of late capitalism, as evidenced in the tremendous proliferation in this production of cultural signs employed for exchange value. Their value, that is, lies not in what they suggest about their cultures of origin (other signs from other cultures might have done just as well) but in what they "purchase," an aesthetic effect, and in effect, immediately re-exchangeable.

At last year's Socialist Scholars' Conference in New York I asked Fredric Jameson, the Marxist critic and an influential shaper of the idea of postmodernism, whether he could resolve the apparent contradiction that art that could be seen as "advanced" could also be seen as imitating the market. Agreeing it was a troubling issue for which there were no ready answers, he said, "You can't ask art to utterly step out of its own time. But remember, no good art is wholly within it either."

1988

Elizabeth LeCompte and the Wooster Group's
*The Road to Immortality (Part Three): Frank Dell's
The Temptation of Saint Antony* (*Village Voice*, October 25)

"The process of making the work is the work," Elizabeth LeCompte has often said of her own impacted theater pieces. Some of them—like this one, in its fourth public incarnation but never "open" until now—take years to evolve. Traces of everything the Wooster Group has studied and experienced in this process may be tracked through their works; the longer the evolution the denser the trail. Such aesthetics require a different criticism—an avoidance of flattening judgments, an openness to process. Which I now attempt.

The full title alone of this eighth major LeCompte/group work in ten years is virtually an archeological dig.

(1) *The Road to Immortality* is the title of a dictated spirit-guide book published in 1932 by Irish author and spiritualist Geraldine Cummins. It made a powerful impression on Lenny Bruce in the months before his death, a fact discovered by the actors while working on Bruce as part of the research for *L.S.D.* (. . . *Just the High Points* . . .). That piece, a meditation on the drug counter-culture of the 1970s and its grotesque aftermath in the drug society of the '80s, now became *The Road to Immortality: Part Two*.

(2) *Frank Dell* was one of the names Bruce used for himself in his early stand-up days. In *L.S.D.*, "Frank Dell" and his shabby theater troupe appear in Miami and impersonate a dance troupe, Donna Sierra and the Del Fuegos. Bruce is one of the theatrical saint-frauds who have fascinated LeCompte since seeing Ingmar Bergman's *The Magician* nearly 20 years ago. *Saint Antony* centers on a *Magician*-like travelling theater troupe under the drugged-out leadership of this "Dell," who teeters precariously between martyr and charlatan as the group rehearses a mess of a piece that might be thought of as the "Temptation-of-Saint-Antony-According-to-Bruce-as-Mediated-by-the-Spirit-of-Bergman." There is in fact no actual Bergman text here, but a series of farce fragments by Jim Strahs sending up the world of 19th-century Boulevard theater.

(3) *The Temptation of Saint Antony* was brought to LeCompte in 1983 by Peter Sellars with an offer: would she like to work with him on Flaubert's gargantuan dramatic novel, *La Tentation de Saint Antoine*, just the way she had

earlier "deconstructed" *Our Town* in *Route 1&9*. Sellars (a bit Mr. Saint-Fraud himself) dropped out of the collaboration after staging some dances for it in the winter of 1984–85. Ron Vawter's mad death dance to Gounod's *Faust* remains from those days. LeCompte continued her valiant struggle with Flaubert, finding the text so ponderous that "for fun" she staged fragments of it to the visual accompaniment of a naked Channel J-type television talk show, taped with members of the company.

Along the way, the production picked up other components. There is Ken Kobland's film of an aging female body, and another film of underwater swimming. There are life experiences of company members. We see a poster of Willem Dafoe (who appears here only on tape) advertising his film, *The Last Temptation of Christ*. The serious illness of Ron Vawter a couple of years ago left its mark on the production.

I have watched LeCompte play restlessly with these different elements for three years, off and on. What she has finally arrived at, after earlier incarnations in which she stressed Bruce, or the "Magician" company, or Flaubert, is a strangely twirling form, part mystery play and meditation on mortality, part an in-the-theater burlesque filled with tricks, gags and numbers. And we never know which is which. When Vawter, as Bruce-Dell-Magician-Saint Antony, seems near death onstage, he is performing a "real" anguish and also rehearsing a "fake" stage routine. There are only shards left of Flaubert's enormous text, but one of them, "Appearance is the only reality," could serve as epigraph for the entire undertaking.

Lenny Bruce notwithstanding, this is by far the most European, and indeed arcane, of LeCompte's theater structures—no famous American plays to hang onto; no major social issues or legal crises to explode into controversy. It is also the most self-referentially theatrical. A theater troupe on the lam dreaming mystery plays about temptation: that's the Wooster Group.

But what a theater troupe! Have we been too busy fighting about them all these years to admire their virtuosity? Vawter, who grows more subtle and varied with each passing season, was surely always the most versatile of the group's male brilliants. Even more remarkable, the women of the company have at last emerged with fierce strength. Feminists have long complained that LeCompte never lets her women speak. In this version, *Saint Antony* belongs as much to Kate Valk and Peyton Smith playing "Frank Dell's" co-performers, as to Vawter, with Anna Kohler giving a startling performance as "the maid." The transformation of the women is layered right into the piece, for the nude videotape—shot in late 1986 and early '87—has Valk and Kohler stammering, showing their bodies but unable to complete full sentences. In the more recently completed live episodes, they take over the action. At one point—significant detail—Valk says they are "on the continent, living like men."

Jim Clayburgh's multi-level constructivist set (Wooster Group standard) has never been used with such lush theatricality. Walls rise and descend, doors with actors strapped to them fly dangerously open and slam shut. There are also trashy costumes, wigs, beards, sensational lighting, fake *mittel-Europa* accents—more nostalgia for the conventional theater than I ever recall from LeCompte and company. The music has the same sloshed together quality, with Brahms fading into Art Tatum, and a rendition of the Civil War ballad, "Just Before the Battle Mother."

For all its theatrical brilliance, the piece is unmistakably mournful, contemplating human and artistic mortality. Phyllis (Peyton Smith) keeps repeating, "Tonight is my last performance. I'm leaving the show. I'm leaving the theater." Not that the Wooster Group will fold up shop—they are at work on a new film and theater project—but this purest surviving example of our all but vanished theater avant-garde may be moving into other forms. It is as if LeCompte and her group, in their exacting struggle to realize the oddest "bits of culture" as theater, had come to the end of a certain line of thought and been pushed to consider their relation to theater itself.

1989

JoAnne Akalaitis's *Cymbeline* (*American Theatre*, December)

By the end of its run at the Public Theater, JoAnne Akalaitis's production of *Cymbeline*, the ninth in Joe Papp's ongoing Shakespeare marathon, had developed an underground following. Admirers were returning to see it for a second time. Theater professionals who have known Akalaitis's work from the beginning were saying that this was the best thing she had done for years, better than anything since *Dead End Kids* and the old *Dressed Like an Egg* days. Some were saying that a major new American Shakespeare talent had emerged, and that certainly this production was the best of the marathon, at any rate, this and Steven Berkoff's *Coriolanus*. The production also had its passionate detractors. I know someone who was congratulated on his return from Europe with, "Lucky you, you missed *Cymbeline*!"

Savagely, the critics were of this camp. Although some fringe reviewers appreciated the work (front page banner on the *New York Native*: "Hey, John Simon, We Loved *Cymbeline*!"), the major New York critics, whether daily or weekly, popular or intellectual, reacted to the production as if a sacred relic had been violated. The headline of the Barnes review read "TRAVESTY OF SHAKESPEARE," and went on to chastise Akalaitis for a reading "so ignorant as to be effectively beneath consideration." Simon condemned the production as "staggeringly, unremittingly, unconscionably absurd." Feingold called it a "horrible mess." And most reviews were sprinkled with shudders against "cheap jokes," "camp," "low humor," "vulgarity," and "farce." "This is a new Shakespearean low," wrote Simon—"at least until Papp's next venture: the one direction in which there is no limit is downward."

Even among responses such as these, the June lst *New York Times* review by Frank Rich was singular in its personal dismissiveness and absolute literalism, beginning with the don't-know-whether-to-laugh-or-cry headline, "FANTASY 'CYMBELINE' SET LONG AFTER SHAKESPEARE." So at odds was that review with Akalaitis's postmodern aesthetic that it triggered off its own special lampoon in an underground New York theater publication, the journal of the BACA/Downtown New Works Project. But the establishment critics are no laughing matter, for the case of *Cymbeline* suggests that they are literally driving innovative, daring theater out of New York.

To say that JoAnne Akalaitis's *Cymbeline* was animated by a postmodern aesthetic not acknowledged by her critics is not to say much, but it starts somewhere. Oh, postmodernism!: half the theater world thinks it's over; the other half hasn't gotten there yet. Only the New York theater critics manage to be on both sides at once. Perhaps everyone would agree that "postmodern" has become a convenient category for a Lee Breuer pastiche of pop performance quotes, a Liz LeCompte interface of seemingly unrelated texts, a Peter Sellars marriage of high art and showbiz, a Laurie Anderson nervous, silky switching among screens and voices, a Holly Hughes meltdown of female personalities and gender roles. But when the postmodern turns up in a production of Shakespeare or Molière, the director, like the Red Queen's pig child, only does it to annoy. No one seems to recognize it; it becomes merely "modish" or "arbitrary."

More important, there's the question of what is being recognized. For "postmodern" is only superficially a style. On a deeper level, it is a multiple and decentered way of understanding the world and our own subjectivity. Instead of leading the audience toward a single dominating significance or interpretation, postmodern theater, whatever its style, will be characterized by multiple tracks or channels, a demand that the audience respond to many "texts" at once. There is a wonderful sense of theatrical density, bounty, and playfulness in good postmodern work; it can be alive with not-quite-nailed-down associations, not-quite-cohered potentialities, formal, literary, political, social, sexual. Of course, critics have attacked postmodernism for just this tendency to dispersal: how can such work ever take up a political position? Yet postmodernism's very subversions of aesthetic unity, social hierarchy, and the so-called "dominant discourses" have an undoubted political potential, a fact increasingly recognized by feminist critics and theorists.

Not one of New York City's leading theater critics—all male, all conservative—*not one* appears to recognize any of this as adding up to an actual aesthetic, especially not when applied to Shakespeare. Made uncomfortable, perhaps, by the canny, off-balance relativism of a postmodern aesthetic, they scold Akalaitis for making a "horrible mess," attack her "ignorance," and leap to defend a text that won't "brook such nonsense." Yet strangely they are circling the wagons around one of the least produced plays in the Shakespeare canon, one that by their own admission nobody has ever known what to do with.

In *Cymbeline*, more than in any other Shakespeare text, the shifts of tones and materials are extreme, almost violent. This late romance rockets from Holinshed's account of the first century British king Cymbeline, whose career is lost in myth, to Boccaccio's yarn about a male wager on a wife's chastity, to fairy-tale melodrama (the wicked Queen, the poison potion, the headless corpse), to the utopian wilderness of a cave in Wales. It culminates in scenes that inhabit opposite ends of the theatrical spectrum, an historical battle scene, and a masque that includes a baroque effulgence of the god Jupiter riding in on an eagle. The play refers to, and even seems to parody, half a dozen others by Shakespeare, including *Othello, Lear, Macbeth*, and *Twelfth Night*.

Samuel Johnson and the young Shaw dismissed *Cymbeline* as inferior Shakespeare, and the New York critics teetered on agreeing with them. But contemporary critics have taken sudden interest in the play, and not less than three major productions have been mounted in England in the past decade. As Colette Brooks has written in a recent defense, the play is unique in inhabiting at once the "historical, romantic, comic, and tragic," creating its strange, lurching world through "the conscious and repeated use of incongruity." Akalaitis read the Brooks paper, and although she did not follow out Brooks's logic of the "grotesque," she clearly saw these discordances as an aesthetic to be enjoyed and even amplified rather than as a problem to be solved by imposing harmony or unity. But her production was misunderstood from its very first move.

A line in the program described the Akalaitis *Cymbeline* as taking place "In the Midst of Celtic Ruins—a Romantic Fantasy in Victorian England." This fateful line was taken by almost all reviewers literally to mean that Akalaitis had set her play in the Victorian period. Yet a read through the reviews of other Shakespeare Marathon productions suggests that if Akalaitis had in fact directed such a conventional and recognizable updating and established precisely the kind of unified ground abhorred by postmodern directors, the choice would have been shrugged off in a line, as Rich did with the "handsome late 18th-century sets" of *The Winter's Tale.*

Akalaitis directed neither the timeless ("magical," "autumnal") fantasy that critics appeared to anticipate, nor a solid event transposed to the Victorian period, but something much less stable and more sophisticated. Her idea was to add to the play's jarring layers an additional layer—screen, frame, perhaps *lens* is best—that would serve to make visible all the others. It was a kind of experiment: suppose we were to look at the incongruities of Shakespeare's text through the Victorian imagination? Fairy tale, nonsense, melodrama, gothic horror, nostalgia for a lost, green England, noble savages, sexual prurience, romantic ruins, empire, *realpolitik*, "progress"—Akalaitis culled pieces, ideas, quasi-quotations out of the Victorian "stuff," and assembled them in a variety of illuminations.

The proof, if you will, that Akalaitis's technique was one of sophisticated layering rather than the "naive" historical transposition with which Frank Rich charges her, may lie in the punctilio with which she preserved the frequently-cut theatrical excrescences of Act V, the prophetic Soothsayer, and the courtly masque with its ghostly apparitions and descent of Jupiter. We were not to lose sight of the play as a Jacobean theatrical event. That event, however, was filled with topical significance that has simply died away to a contemporary audience, such as the religious significance in James's reign of a peace between Britain and Rome. The value of the Victorian choice lay in its precise historical distance, giving it the power to revive if not the very topics that interested the Stuart court, then the live dimension of topicality itself, and in much the same way—allegorically and obliquely, through a storybook haze of nostalgia.

How did all this look and feel on the stage? Realist critics begin with the actors, whom they expect to stand for the characters in a direct, truthful relation. (Rich tests the cast for "sincere" performances and finds most wanting.) A postmodern critic is likely to start from the other end, the theatrical frame within which performances function, the setting. Many experimental theater artists have followed Gertrude Stein in composing by landscape or total environment. Some of these are mind- or mediascapes, but some, as in Robert Wilson, Ping Chong, and Laurie Anderson's new work, hunger for a lost green and animal world, showing us an emerging connection between postmodern and pastoral; sometimes, as in Heiner Müller's *Despoiled Shore   Medeamaterial Landscape with Argonauts*, we get an ironic form we might call dis-pastoral. It was not a decorative irrelevancy, then, as John Simon charged, but the corner-stone of her approach, that Akalaitis's *Cymbeline* unfolded within and against one of the most original landscape and environmental settings that has ever been created for a stage.

George Tsypin's setting, augmented by Pat Collins's lighting and Stephanie Roth's projections, was a miracle of continuous transformation involving turning architectural columns with different scenic faces, backed and enveloped by slide projections of luxuriant vegetation, creeping moss, flinty rocks. A water-filled trough dances like a brook, steams like a witch's cauldron; the rippling curtains of the bedchamber shimmer with silver light and drip with blood. The visual emphasis of this production had nothing to do with the "learn-the-lines-and-stay-out-of-the-way-of-the-scenery" school of Shakespeare production advocated by Clive Barnes in a recent review. Tsypin's setting spoke its own text: rock against water, the green world in contest with the hard, black on white world of corruption, threatened with the red of rape and war.

Mounted on these ever-moving visual tectonics was a production that might have had as its motto Robert Wilson's postmodern dictum, "Theater has to be about one big thing; after that it can be about many things." Akalaitis never intended those many things to be experienced as the unified aesthetic surface the critics were angry not to find. John Simon's complaint that periods, places, and costumes were "hopelessly scrambled" utterly misses the contrapuntal fullness, the *wit* of Akalaitis's layered method. Each character, idea, or visual effect was like a musical theme, to be developed to the limit, and to be appreciated in and for its very difference from the others. Does the Queen sound like a wicked stepmother out of Grimm? Then we'll thoroughly *do that*, without subordinating it to fit the whole. Does her son seem an oaf and a buffoon? Well let's do *that*, dress him in music hall attire, inflate the clownish side, even let him lose his pants. Is a battle thrown into the great muddle of Act V? Then make it an important battle, in fact, find a new way to do a Shakespeare battle, with surrealistic freeze-frame, long sticks for weapons, and crashing cinematic score. Add splendid costumes suggesting in 19th-century terms the fundamental conflict between dreamy imagination (the Brits in Scottish kilts) and ruthless efficiency (the Romans in modern military gray with prideful gold buttons). The theatrical fullness, the sense almost of surplus, seemed at times more novelistic than dramatic, in the picaresque vein.

Her critics took her to task for disorderly conduct, but to Akalaitis theater is neither orderly nor mannerly. It is extravagant, rude, large, risk-taking. Think of *Dead End Kids* with its scene from Goethe's *Faust* and its medieval alchemist *and* its insulting stand-up comic, and so forth. Akalaitis wants play in the system, and does best with texts that invite that play. "Play" means opening up the theater experience to much more independent signifying status for setting, lights, costumes, and music; it means making a space for actors to bring a range of attitudes to their characters (not only the "sincerity" Rich asks for); and it means—being just plain playful. Playful was the casting of the robust Joan Cusack in the leading role of the "divine" Imogen; her performance was alive with intelligence and feeling, though it periodically faded away like a distant radio signal. Cusack's feet-on-the-ground, non-Desdamonaish resistance to the Roman villain Iachimo fairly crackled as he tries with lies and flattery to worm his way into her bedroom to win his wager with the hapless Posthumus. It was playful to stage the descent of Jupiter in the first place, marvelous to make the eagle huge, glittering, knock-out-your-eye (Michael Feingold, how did this turn into a "gray papier-mâché bat"?); and to make it seem even larger, to make Jupiter very small, a boy-god in red knickers with a child's voice. No moment was more irritating to the critics (or enjoyable to the audience) than Akalaitis's most playful one, when Imogen and the faithful servant Pisanio escaped from Cymbeline's court riding a bicycle and a scooter, which silently criss-crossed the stage several times to the accompaniment of a Philip Glass interlude.

Akalaitis's cultivation of the moment rather than the unifying line gave rise to the charge that she sacrificed the play for "camp." It is true that aspects of camp as outlined a quarter-century ago in Sontag's famous essay—exaggeration, extravagance, theatricality, "bad taste"—were sometimes evident here, not as a settled approach but as part of the expanded theatrical vocabulary that Akalaitis assumes literate theatergoers can pick up and put down at will. Yet ironically, it was the critics's very resistance to the production's exuberance that led them to flatten its double levels (the moment, scene, character taken both as narratively meaningful and as pure artifice, a point Sontag made in the Camp essay) into mere gags.

Undoubtedly, some of Akalaitis's many ideas worked better than others, and some of the performers carried them out better than others. It was in keeping with her decentered approach that Cymbeline became less a tyrant than a fool, a sleepy monarch in a nightcap; but this Cymbeline was so bemused we literally could not understand the ordinarily articulate George Bartenieff. Wendell Pierce may have turned the would-be rapist Cloten into a klutz for the same reason, but I could have wished to see the threat along with the humor. The mystery of bringing Posthumus's ghostly family silently onstage in nearly every scene was rudely undercut when at last they spoke in the Act V masque. Yet the production stood or fell not on a succession of performances or bright ideas, but on a series of illuminations that situated characters in a total theatrical web, visual, aural (this was perhaps Glass's best incidental theatrical music ever), and frequently, political. The political dimension of the production went wholly unnoticed by the critics.

Iachimo's Roman house, where the wager is struck with the innocent Posthumus, became a male bath house, where in the background strange men move with decadent sensuality. In this setting, we clearly understand the performances of the male antagonists—the half-naked, sophisticated Iachimo backed by tuxedoed friends, the fustian-dressed, intimidated Posthumus with his awkward provincial manners—as framed by misogyny and male bonding.

Imogen's lost brothers—those "gentle princes" raised in a cave in Wales from childhood by the banished noble Belarius—were with breathtaking directness depicted as feathered, half-nude American Indians. Whom did Victorians think of—or whom do we imagine Victorians thinking of—Akalaitis must have asked herself, when they thought of caves, hunters, "savages"? Here the filter of Victorian imagination (after all, even Shaw named these characters "Mohicans") combined with Akalaitis's deliberate casting of a black and an Hispanic actor, brought a social edge to a sub-plot that in a less venturesome production would have been set in some gracefully tangled Arcadia. With this staging, Imogen's exclamation,

> Gods, what lies I have heard!
> Our courtiers say all's savage but at court.
> Experience, O, thou disprov'st report!

lit up the problem of prejudice against the Other in a succession of worlds: ours, Victoria's, the Stuart court. Imogen's "heart-sickness" two lines later seemed in this reading a direct result of social injustice.

Akalaitis cast in the role of Philharmonus, Soothsayer to the Roman general, the Indian dancer Rajika Puri. Akalaitis introduced this sari-wrapped figure early. Trailing silently behind Caius Lucius she seemed just one more eccentricity in an already eclectic tapestry. When she spoke in the final scene, prophesying the success of the union between Rome and Britain, "which shines here in the west," we realized that Akalaitis had deftly framed the imperial "deal" of the play in the ironic perspective of British colonialism. It was a brilliant stroke of self-conscious "orientalism," an extra turn of the political knife, to confound prophet and colonized, and to gender the colonial subject both exotic and female.

For all her playfulness, or perhaps *with* it, Akalaitis created a serious moral space in *Cymbeline*. Nowhere was this more evident than where she was most shockingly misunderstood, in her use of multi-racial casting. It beggars belief that critics would protest the casting of a white mother and a black son, or the mistaking of a black corpse for a white one, as excessively taxing the imagination of the audience in a play they call a "fantasy"; or that a production using four actors of color in major and sensitive roles could be accused of "arbitrary tokenism." Akalaitis's cast reflects in racial terms the same boldly multiple and decentered approach that her critics could read only as a lack, an incompetence in achieving "coherence." Akalaitis's commitment to postmodern "difference" in theater aesthetics cannot be separated from her profound acceptance of American and world culture as inextricable intertwinings of many races and cultural traditions. Surely this was the most American of the Papp series, and a justification of his own bitterly-criticized "incoherence" in planning the Marathon.

And so—this apparently small squabble among critics, over a production that reasonable persons could dispute in many of its details, finally comes down to this: a very real ideological divide. The Aristotelian demand for consistency does not represent, though the critics may think so, some sort of natural or divinely-ordained aesthetics; it is a formal choice like any other, and carries along with it an ideological price tag, as their racial discomfort enormously demonstrates. All the big cultural battles these days, from reforming the canon in the English curriculum at Stanford to the Mapplethorpe show in Washington, organize themselves around these two poles: on one side a cry for "standards," "taste," "high culture"; and on the other, a move by hitherto invisible perspectives—racial, sexual, multi-cultural—to invade the dominant culture. Akalaitis wouldn't be, or cause, a problem if she would stay away from the canonic Shakespeare and reserve her techniques for Mabou Mines collage theater in its safe avant-garde cove.

This is not an argument over differing tastes. Between Akalaitis and the New York establishment critics lies a cultural gulf so wide that the same words can be used to stake out wholly different aesthetic positions. When Frank Rich rejects the Akalaitis production as one that "straitjackets" the work with a "narrow . . . idée fixe," and calls for a *Cymbeline* that "rides Shakespeare's every dexterous change of mood and style as demonstrated by James Lapine in his magical recent *Winter's Tale*," he sounds like the very model of a multiplex postmodernist. Yet his review of Akalaitis is coded with the language of not even a modernist but a realist aesthetic value system, praising "credibility," "coherence," the "consistent," the "dignified," the "sincere." Indeed, when you go back to his *Winter's Tale* review, you find Rich admiring James Lapine not for his skill in changing mood and style as such, but for his "ability to knit Shakespeare's many moods into elegant unity." Akalaitis's breach of this critical code, by which the highest value is a transcendent consistency, earned her production Rich's special condemnation as the "most reckless" of the Marathon.

New York's critical establishment seems ever more deeply establishmentarian. Its view of theatrical aesthetics, based on the long tradition of Western idealism as it has infused the dominant American theater practice, is conservative and hierarchical. It appears unaware of, or unwilling to acknowledge, the obvious erosion of the humanistic certainties associated with that tradition. This corrosive but ineluctable century-long process has profoundly altered the way those who have absorbed it view the world and read literary texts, and should alter the way we perceive theatrical experience. Reading today has become an elusive activity of intertextuality, discerning veils through veils. We may still read "for the story," but we read through Freud, through Marx, Saussure, Darwin, Einstein and Relativity, Heisenberg and the Uncertainty Principle, through Foucault, Derrida, Lacan and other poststructuralists; and through a host of feminist interpreters who have in turn achieved their own dislocations on those of Lacan, Derrida, etc. We don't read or re-read only the classics in this way, but history, anthropology, and the contemporary "text" of society and culture: all are subject to continuous re-examination through the shifting lenses, each of which offers a partial view within the decentered cultural milieu. Akalaitis may not have rushed out to bone up on Foucault and cultural archeology, or Derrida and the substitution of "play," for the transcendental signifier, but her mind has for years moved in the same postmodern currents that these authors both reflect and created. The postmodern perception that unity, coherence, and closure are false ideals that erase contending elements in culture generally, is reflected in Akalaitis with an aesthetic that values multiple expressivity. This mode of understanding shapes the look, sound, movement, casting, choice of material, and results in a knowable aesthetic that is not realist, not essentially modernist, but treats all styles as parts of an available vocabulary. A handful of theater artists, the largest concentration based in New York, create theater that expresses this paradigm shift, but the New York theater press, after twenty years of evolving exposure to this work, continues fundamentally uncurious about it.

The lack of curiosity, the disrespect, the *indifference*—the indifference, that's the word: New York critics don't seem to know whom to cultivate. As Robert Brustein wrote in his mixed defense of this production, its "uniformly savage" New York reception could not distinguish those who bring fresh eyes to Shakespeare from those who trash him. Even in its own venues where they have devoted followings, the avant-garde, experimental, or progressive wing as some now call it, of the New York theater world continues to be attacked by the press with a vigor one would have thought familiarity would have dulled by now. But familiarity with their innovations seems to breed contempt. For instance, Gordon Rogoff announced in the *Village Voice* a few years ago that he had walked out of Elizabeth LeCompte's masterwork *L.S.D. (. . . Just the High Points . . .)* at intermission, but nonetheless ripped the work in the most contemptuous terms. Far from scornful, the traditionalist critics should be grateful to this wing of the theater; for twenty years it has been the most vital repository of the classic repertoire in America. Think of Serban's *Fragments of a Greek Trilogy*, Sellar's *Ajax*, Wilson's *Alcestis*, Foreman's *Don Juan*, Breuer's *Gospel at Colonus*, the incomparable Ludlam's *Camille*.

Akalaitis gave us not just a reading of a text, not a conventional interpretation. She is in some sense "against interpretation," so much so that her refusal to grind out advance publicity for *Cymbeline* with explanatory interviews may have damaged her cause with the press. Yet her dense exercise in reading through, reading alongside, reading against the text created an entire theatrical world just thick with imagination. That this creativity was made *as nothing* by every major critic in America's still most prominent theater city—why it takes the breath away. In July, Andrzej Wajda brought his Stary Theatre *Hamlet* to the PepsiCo Summerfare festival. He set it in the theatrical dressing room of the actor playing Hamlet, who happened to be a woman. The audience sat on backstage bleachers, and gazed through this dressing room to the stage of the theater, and to the empty house beyond. Can you imagine what would have happened to the *Hamlet* of an American director in New York, if she had crazily attempted to do that?

1993

On the AIDS Quilt: *The Performance of Mourning* (*American Theatre*, January)

In the five and a half years since Cleve Jones, a San Francisco AIDS activist, decided to stitch a 6' x 3' grave-shaped "quilt" in memory of his lover, the AIDS Memorial Quilt has become the chief focus of mourning for hundreds of thousands bereaved by AIDS, as well as a canny organizing tool in the global battle against the disease. Ironically, in its present immensity—filling eight 48-foot tractor trailers, weighing twenty-six tons, covering the equivalent of twelve football fields when displayed on the grounds of the Washington Monument in October, and growing by another football field and a half just that weekend from new panels streaming in—the Quilt is perhaps nearing its effective social and political limits. This may have been the last display of the Quilt in its entirety, say its coordinators, who are beginning to find themselves the stewards of a sacred leviathan of mourning, difficult both to preserve and to show, and subject to much debate now as to its future course.

Yet as a great community artwork and symbol of postmodern culture, even as postmodern performance, the quilt's measure has hardly been taken. It is startling to visit the Quilt, for instance, and realize that its plan is inspired by the modern cemetery. This walking along the nine miles of black plastic walkways, this searching the eleven different color fields on the Quilt map to find which of the 22,000 "plots" is dedicated to, say, Charles Ludlam, suddenly feels familiar: this is what we do at Woodlawn, Mount Auburn, and Laurel Hill. And indeed I did feel that I had come to a site radiating the specificity of what Walter Benjamin called an "aura," that Charles Ludlam was in some sense actually "here." Perhaps it is the acute sense of hereness about each person remembered in the Quilt, impossible not to experience, that leads on to the thought—Wait now! This is *not* Woodlawn, but its symbolic double, its parody even, or better still, its *performance*. And a road show at that. The AIDS Quilt as travelling graveyard.

How do you "perform" a graveyard? First you need performers. There are the live ones, like the white-clad volunteers, fully 1000 of them in Washington, who have developed a balletic ritual of laying out the Quilt. There are the readers—some five hundred were scheduled over the weekend—who make the showing of the Quilt a performance by tolling off the sad litany of names and names and names: thirty-two for each speaker at the podium, eight hours a day, for three full days. There are also the visitors, who are invited to leave their own names and messages on the signature squares set aside for that purpose.

But in truth it is the *brio* of the dead performers that captures our attention. There are moments when the entire vast field of the Quilt, riotous with the iconography of show business, takes on the aspect of a players' cemetery. The top hats, tap shoes, gleaming black and white keyboards with flying notes, or actual staves of music stitched in; the cut-work doublets, smiling and frowning masks, the programs and ticket stubs carefully sealed in plastic, the feathers, ribbons, junk jewels, a whole black slinky drag costume, the painting of Charles as Camille with all the ring curls—these brilliant traces of vanished talent not only tell a tale of devastation to "our crowd," but lead to reflections on the deeper structures of performance here.

Real cemeteries, of course, specialize in "permanence." Granite and marble are their natural materials. They seek to foster a "sense of perpetual home," as one 19th-century enthusiast put it, and will offer, for a prepaid fee, "perpetual care" for your gravesite, though the idea lacks somewhat in historical probability. Despite the fact that a tangential cult of stitchers and gluers called "Handmaidens of the Quilt" has sprung up to repair panels already aging, the Quilt, like painted flats of scenery representing rocks or pyramids, is clearly *not* for all time. Its fragile materials will decay long before a tombstone, and must always be protected from the weather. October's showing of the Quilt, in fact, was marred by rain for the first time in four Washington displays. Volunteers gloomily waited out the rain for half of the three-day weekend, then had to leap into a one-minute rain-fold when the weather on the final day posed another serious threat.

Still, one must not understand words like "serious" too seriously around the Quilt. With all the suffering it represents, the Quilt playfully sends up the solemnity, the *rigidity*, of mourning, including "permanence." Imagine a cemetery putting all its attendants in white jeans and sneakers. Then imagine rows and rows of marble headstones etched with teddy bears, Hawaiian shirts, and Mickey Mouse. Imagine jumbling Jews, Catholics, Muslims, and New Age Buddhists in the same subdivision of the "everlasting abode." *Imagine* finding a sublime design of mountains, bordered with "Comfort, oh comfort my people" in Hebrew right next to a splash of sequins celebrating "Boogie," and directly below a grinning depiction of Bugs Bunny. The Quilt is cemetery as All Fool's Day, a carnival of the sacred, the homely, the joyous, and the downright tacky, resisting, even *in extremis*, the solemnity of mourning. There's room for everything here: a joke, a prayer, a flower, a measuring spoon, a Harvard flag, a beer can, even (I saw it) an air-conditioner vent.

Washington abounds with official versions of solemnity-aesthetics. In October, the Quilt was laid out beneath the Washington Monument, that mighty Egyptian obelisk once used to celebrate gods and commemorate the lives of rulers, swollen to the size of America's aspiring imperial ego. In 1988 and 1989, the Quilt was spread on the Ellipse, a few yards from the First Division Memorial, an eighty-foot marble pillar designed by Daniel Chester French, festooned with wreathed swords, and topped by a statue of triumphant Victory. Compare that memorial's bronze tablets naming the first division of soldiers to fall in America's three major 20th-century wars, with the 58,000 names in order of reported death on the Vietnam Memorial's sunken granite wall a few blocks away, with the Quilt names so fiercely collected by the NAMES Project, and you follow a historical trajectory from modern imperial politics, through chastening transition, to the postmodern breakdown of the "master narratives"— these being not only the stories we tell ourselves about how our world is organized, but the cognitive devices that organize the stories.

The organization of the Quilt, for instance, relies on none of the ways cultures have traditionally classified their dead. We do not make a fuss here about religion or family or even complete names. There are twenty-eight quilts naming only "Dennis," fifty-three for "Joe." These may or may not be different Dennises and Joes, but Michel Foucault, the *same* Michel Foucault, appears on three different panels in widely separated locations. (Imagine a cemetery providing three gravesites for the same man, and you have the stuff of farce.) As the Quilt grows, each new panel assumes a permanent place in an eight-quilt unit, but this so-called "12 x 12" circulates in different company depending on whether its appearance is local, regional, national as in the Washington displays, international as in the showings in Moscow, Israel, New Zealand, Botswana, Helsinki—the list is long—or in a special "gig," like last summer's showing on daytime television's *One Life to Live.*

The very idea of the Quilt, combining monumentality with patchwork, expresses at once the scale of the leaping world AIDS crisis and its assault on humanist faith in order and social continuity. Pastiche and defiant disunity are by now familiar hallmarks of the postmodernist artwork, but here they are returned to a humanism which insists that this exuberant life not be forgotten. In the way it remembers, the Quilt is more relaxed, more inclusive, more sensual, more human, more *theatrical* than anything previously imagined in the protocols of mourning. It rolls into town on its three-day bus and truck tour, throws down its brilliant rags and rugs like the players before Claudius, and with chilling clarity performs its play of mourning in the very face of remote and fearful authority. Each Washington appearance has been a calculation to catch the conscience of the king.

Cleve Jones is reported to have said, when he first envisioned the Quilt and the gathering of the names, that he wanted to make something he could take his grandmother to. Who can miss the shrewd conflating of tradition and subversion in the gay community's reaching back to a 19th-century collaborative women's craft form for inspiration? Women have long understood how to "give the needle" to dominant social forms while perfectly fulfilling them. Thus the Quilt, without an ounce of apparent confrontation in its soft and comforting body, is a hugely visual riposte to official culture's fervent wish that AIDS would just disappear from view, like some distant famine. By now the Quilt includes many panels dedicated to women, children, I.V. drug users, and hemophiliacs. But its association of gay sexuality with Reaganite cultural mythology—the celebration of the rural American, family American, homemade American, nostalgic American, in effect forcing its spectators to embrace in a single image what to many is an impossible contradiction—this is no doubt the Quilt's most brilliant and far-reaching element of ironic masquerade.

Without losing its healing associations, the Quilt is far more than "comforter." It is an inspired multiplex of grieving, art and social activism. Shaped by thousands of hands, it is, one might almost say, a seismic social art eruption, in so deep a region of the mind does it originate. It plays out a terrible connection between death and the erotic, thinks past mourning's ancient links to church, family, class, and state, yet re-imagines a connection between politics and the sacred. The Quilt is a new cultural form, a unique symbolic representation emerging in response to an unprecedented crisis, but it is renewing tragic themes that have always been the province of ritual performance.

Notes

Introduction

1. Karl Marx and Friedrich Engels, *The Communist Manifesto* (New York: International, 1948), p. 12.

2. Charles Jencks, *What Is Post-Modernism?* (New York: St. Martin's, 1986), p. 19.

3. Premiere, February 8, 1973, the Joffrey Ballet, Chicago. See Twyla Tharp, *Push Comes to Shove* (New York: Bantam, 1992), pp. 184–85.

4. Kathleen Hulley, "Transgressing Genre: Kathy Acker's Intertext," Robert Con Davis and Patrick O'Donnell, eds., *Intertextuality and Contemporary American Fiction* (Baltimore: Johns Hopkins University Press, 1988), pp. 171–90, 177–78.

5. Guy Debord, *Society of the Spectacle* (Detroit: Black & Red, 1983), #9.

6. Jean Baudrillard, *The Mirror of Production*, trans. and intro. Mark Poster (St. Louis: Telos, 1975), pp. 122, 126, 128. See also Steven Best and Douglas Kellner, *Postmodern Theory: Critical Interrogations* (New York: Guilford, 1991), p. 53.

7. Fredric Jameson, *Postmodernism, or the Cultural Logic of Late Capitalism* (Durham: Duke University Press, 1991). See esp. pp. 410–15.

8. Roland Barthes, *Roland Barthes*, trans. Richard Howard (New York: Hill and Wang, 1977), p. 168.

9. Craig Owens, "The Discourse of Others: Feminists and Postmodernism" (Port Townsend, Washington: Bay, 1983), pp. 57–82.

10. *Les immatériaux*, Éditions du Centre Georges Pompidou, Paris, 1985.

11. As I write, Peter Sellars has worked a similar change on *The Merchant of Venice*. David Richards's *New York Times* review of October 18, 1994 (p. C18), states that this production "dismantle(s) characters' psyches and spread(s) out all the pieces for us to examine. . . . Rather than address each other, the characters often talk into the microphones that stand at either side of the stage and sit on the various tables."

12. See "Reviews and Articles," pp. 161–64.

13. Des McAnuff, *Leave It to Beaver Is Dead*, in Mac Wellman, ed., *Theatre of Wonders* (Los Angeles: Sun and Moon, 1985), p. 135. The reader should be cautioned that the play appears here without the lyrics of the songs that constituted a third act of the play, and without any indication that the dramatic action was followed by a concert.

14. Ibid., pp. 135 and 219.

15. Unpublished ms. provided by the author.

16. *Beaver*, pp. 180 and 206.

17. *New York Times*, April 4, 1979, p. C20.

18. Bruce Wilshire, *Role Playing and Identity: The Limits of Theatre as Metaphor* (Bloomington: Indiana University Press, 1982), pp. 42–43.

19. See "Reviews and Articles," pp. 169–76.

20. This quotation from Toynbee has proved as elusive as it is well known. Akizuki Ryomin (*New Mahayana: Buddhism for a Postmodern World*," trans. James Heisig and Paul Swanson [Berkeley: Asian Humanities Press, 1990]) renders it as follows: "When historians a thousand years hence look back on the 20th century and ask what was most distinctive about it,

they will not remember it for the great face-off between liberalism and communism, but as the century in which the encounter between Buddhism and Christianity began" (p. 41).

21. Anton Chekhov, *The Seagull*, in *Seeds of Modern Drama*, ed. Norris Houghton (New York: Applause, 1986), p. 357.

22. Thornton Wilder, *The Journals of Thornton Wilder, 1939–1961*, ed. Donald Gallup (New Haven: Yale University Press, 1985), entry of August 6, 1953, p. 316.

23. For a useful chronology of the prolonged political battle over the NEA up to 1990, see Richard Bolton, ed., *Culture Wars* (New York: New Press, 1992), pp. 331–63.

24. Walter Benjamin, "What is Epic Theater?", *Illuminations*, ed. and intro. Hannah Arendt, trans. Harry Zohn (New York: Schocken, 1969), p. 154.

25. Bonnie Marranca, ed. and intro., *The Theatre of Images* (New York: Drama Book Specialists, 1977).

26. From DeMusset, *Lettres de Dupuis et Cotonet*, in Lilian R. Furst, ed., *European Romanticism: Self-Definition* (New York: Methuen, 1980), pp. 46–48.

27. Tony Kushner, *Angels in America: A Gay Fantasia on National Themes, Part Two: Perestroika* (New York: Theatre Communications Group, 1994), pp. 13–14.

28. Hélène Cixous, "The Character of 'Character,' " trans. Keith Cohen, *New Literary History*, vol. 5, no. 2 (Winter 1974), pp. 383–402, 387.

29. Robert Jay Lifton, *The Protean Self: Human Resilience in an Age of Fragmentation* (New York: Basic, 1993).

1. The Rise and Fall of the Character Named Character

1. Tadeusz Rozewicz, *The Card Index*, in *The Card Index and Other Plays*, trans. Adam Czerniawski (New York: Grove, 1970), p. 68. All subsequent quotations are from this translation.

2. Francis Fergusson, ed., *Aristotle's Poetics*, trans. S. H. Butcher (New York: Hill and Wang, 1961), pp. 62–63.

3. G. M. A. Grube, trans. and ed., *Aristotle on Poetry and Style* (Indianapolis: Bobbs-Merrill, 1958), p. 14.

4. Aristotle, *Poetics*, Gerald F. Else, trans. and ed. (Ann Arbor: University of Michigan Press, 1970), p. 27.

5. John Jones, *On Aristotle and Greek Tragedy* (London: Chatto & Windus, 1967), p. 30.

6. Ibid., p. 31.

7. Ibid., pp. 36–38.

8. Elizabeth S. Belfiore, *Tragic Pleasures: Aristotle on Plot and Emotion* (Princeton: Princeton University Press, 1992), p. 91.

9. See Francis Barker, *The Tremulous Private Body: Essays on Subjection* (New York: Methuen, 1984), pp. 25–41, and Jonathan Goldberg, "Shakespearian characters: the generation of Silvia," *Voice Terminal Echo: Postmodernism and English Renaissance Texts* (New York: Methuen, 1986), pp. 68–100.

10. Luigi Riccaboni's 1738 treatise on acting, *Pensées sur la déclamation*, held up a naturalistic ideal for actors, requiring that they actually experience the emotions expressed in their dialogue (see Marvin Carlson, *Theories of the Theatre* [Ithaca: Cornell University Press, 1984], p. 159). In his entry on Tragedy in Diderot's *Encyclopedia*, appearing in 1765, Marmontel drew a distinction between ancient characters, the causes of whose tragedies lay outside them, and modern characters, whose tragedies arose inwardly from quality of soul without reference to "the station, name, birth of the unfortunate person. . . . " See Bernard F. Dukore, *Dramatic Theory and Criticism* (New York: Holt, Rinehart and Winston, 1974), pp. 290–91.

11. G. E. Lessing, *Hamburg Dramaturgy*, intro. Victor Lange (New York: Dover, 1962), pp. 178–211 (nos. 75–78).

12. Horace Leland Friess, trans. and ed., *Schleiermacher's Soliloquies* (Chicago: Open Court, 1926), "Reflection," p. 22.

13. August Wilhelm Schlegel, "A Course of Lectures on Dramatic Art and Literature," trans. John Black (New York: AMS, 1973), p. 25.

14. Ibid., p. 363.

15. Ibid., p. 362.

16. Herder is generally credited as the first to make this link, after which Schelling almost mystically connected romantic art with Christian inspiration. In the later period of his criticism Friedrich Schlegel picked up and extended Schelling's ideas, while personally converting to Catholicism. August Wilhelm Schlegel, influenced not only by his brother but by Herder, made the connection between Christian spirit and romantic form explicit in the 1808 lecture cycle.

17. G. W. F. Hegel, *Aesthetics: Lectures on Fine Art*, trans. T. M. Knox (Oxford: Clarendon, 1975), vol. I, pp. 504–505, 521.

18. Ibid., p. 236.

19. Ibid., vol. II, p. 1178.

20. Ibid., vol. II, p. 1070.

21. Ibid., vol. I, p. 579.

22. Ibid., vol. II, p. 1229. While Hegel does not mention Kleist in this passage, he nonetheless appears to have in mind *The Prince of Homburg*, criticism of whose central character for "duality, disruption and inner dissonance" appears on p. 589 of vol. I. And yet Kleist imagines that he is a "disciple of Shakespeare!" Hegel concludes, with a rhetorical flourish.

23. Ibid., vol. I, p. 243.

24. Friedrich Nietzsche, *The Birth of Tragedy*, in *The Birth of Tragedy and the Case of Wagner*, trans. Walter Kaufmann (New York: Random, 1967), pp. 31–32.

25. Ibid., p. 74.

26. Ibid., pp. 73–74.

27. Ibid., p. 114.

28. Ibid., pp. 91 and 108.

29. The term "dramaturgy" is used by Peter Sloterdijk in *Thinker on Stage: Nietzsche's Materialism*, trans. Jamie Owen Daniel, foreword Jochen Schulte-Sasse (Minneapolis: University of Minnesota Press, 1989), p. 27 and throughout.

30. Michel Foucault, *The Archeology of Knowledge*, trans. A. M. Sheridan Smith (New York: Pantheon, 1972).

31. *The Birth of Tragedy*, section 18. But Nietzsche also makes a somewhat different division in asserting that "there is either an Alexandrian or a Hellenic or a Buddhistic culture," p. 110.

32. Michel Foucault, "Nietzsche, Genealogy, History," in *Language, Counter-Memory, Practice*, ed. and intro. Donald F. Bouchard, trans. Donald F. Bouchard and Sherry Simon (Ithaca: Cornell University Press, 1977), pp. 139–64. See also Alan Sheridan, *Michel Foucault: The Will to Truth* (New York: Tavistock, 1980), p. 92, and John Rajchman, *Michel Foucault: The Freedom of Philosophy* (New York: Columbia University Press, 1985), p. 50ff. Rajchman uses the term "nominalist" to describe Foucault's anti-realist understanding of history.

33. Michel Foucault, *The Order of Things: An Archaeology of the Human Sciences* (New York: Random, 1973), pp. 344–87.

34. See, among others, Fred R. Dallmayr, *The Twilight of Subjectivity: Contributions to a Post-Individualist Theory of Politics* (Amherst: University of Massachusetts Press, 1981); Timothy J. Reiss, *The Discourse of Modernism* (Ithaca: Cornell University Press, 1982), and

Elizabeth D. Ermarth, *Realism and Consensus in the English Novel* (Princeton: Princeton University Press, 1986). Working in different fields, and isolating different cultural periods, each of these authors identifies a historical break in the organization of subjectivity. Dallmayr focuses on the modern/postmodern divide in the political subject; Reiss on the transition from "patterned" to "analytico-referential" (the last of medieval, the first of modern scientific) discourse in the seventeenth century; and Ermarth on the shift from a simultaneous, spatial organization to a temporal, perspectival organization of vision and thought in the Renaissance. All three studies are influenced by Foucault's theory of epistemic shift.

35. Robert L. Delevoy, *Symbolists and Symbolism* (New York: Rizzoli, 1982), p. 71.

36. Ibid., p. 74.

37. Jacques Robichez, *Le symbolisme au théâtre: Lugné-Poë et les débuts de l'oeuvre* (Paris: Editions de l'Arche, 1957), pp. 49–50. Translation mine.

38. Maurice Maeterlinck, "The Tragical in Daily Life," in *The Treasure of the Humble*, trans. Alfred Sutro (New York: Dodd, Mead, 1913), pp. 98–99.

39. Bettina Knapp, *Maeterlinck* (Boston: Twayne, 1975), p. 77.

40. Evert Sprinchorn, "The Transition from Naturalism to Symbolism in the Theater from 1880 to 1900," *Art Journal* (Summer 1985), p. 115. Sprinchorn cites an article in the *Contemporary Review*, 86 (November 1904) by S. C. de Soissons, who in turn cites as his source *La Jeune belgique*, 1890, no. 9.

41. William Butler Yeats, *Uncollected Prose*, ed. John P. Frayne (New York: Columbia University Press, 1970–1976), pp. 270–71.

42. Anton Chekhov, *The Seagull*, in Norris Houghton, ed., *Seeds of Modern Drama* (New York: Applause, 1986), p. 357.

43. Bradford Cook, trans. and intro., "Hamlet," in *Mallarmé: Selected Prose Poems, Essays, and Letters* (Baltimore: Johns Hopkins University Press, 1956), pp. 56–60, see esp. p. 59 as well as note pp. 139–40, quoting Mallarmé as saying that *Hamlet* approaches the "Monologue," the drama of the future.

44. John A. Henderson, *The First Avant-Garde, 1887–1894* (London: Harrap, 1971).

45. I use the term "allegorical" without intending to suggest that the works I refer to are, as Frye says, a "disguised form of discursive writing." This is still the popular (mis)conception of allegory despite two generations of subtle rethinking of the mode. (See chapter 2, n. 20 for bibliography in this genre.) Rather, I intend something akin to what Benjamin finds in the baroque *Trauerspiel*, that the hieroglyphic-like abstraction of allegory "established itself most permanently where transitoriness and eternity confronted each other most closely." (*The Origin of German Tragic Drama*, trans. John Osborne, intro. George Steiner [London: New Left Books, 1977], see pp. 175, 224, 234.)

46. Bertolt Brecht, *The Messingkauf Dialogues*, trans. John Willett (London: Eyre Methuen, 1965), p. 76.

47. *Brecht on Theatre*, trans. John Willett (New York: Hill and Wang, 1964), p. 124. Also see John Fuegi's discussion of Brecht and Aristotle in *The Essential Brecht* (Los Angeles: Hennessey & Ingalls, 1972), p. 61.

48. The term "metatheater" has been used by Lionel Abel and others to describe plays in this mode going back to the renaissance. The term "theatricalism," which I prefer as consistent with other stylistic inflections that have acquired "isms," has been used cogently by Harold B. Segel in *Twentieth Century Russian Drama: From Gorky to the Present* (New York: Columbia University Press, 1979), pp. 56–57. See also his discussion of theatricalism from Blok to Mayakovsky, pp. 123–46.

49. John Willett, *The Theatre of Bertolt Brecht: A Study from Eight Aspects* (London: Methuen, 1959), pp. 111–12.

50. *Six Characters in Search of an Author*, in *Naked Masks: Five Plays by Luigi Pirandello*, ed. Eric Bentley (New York: Dutton, 1952), p. 265.

51. The peculiarly modern explosion of theorizing about the actor's craft and function may suggest that in the modern period the human image on the stage had ceased to be an unquestioned given, but had become a problem to be solved.

52. Michael Goldman, *Acting and Action in Shakespearean Tragedy* (Princeton: Princeton University Press, 1985), p. 163.

2. Pattern over Character

1. August Strindberg, "Jacob Wrestles," *Inferno, Alone and Other Writings*, trans. and intro. Evert Sprinchorn (Garden City, New York: Doubleday, 1968), pp. 305–306.

2. Maurice Bouchor's *Tobie* (1889), based on *Tobit* of the Apochrypha, as well as *Noël, ou le mystère de la Nativité* (1890), and his *La Légende de Sainte Cécile* (1892) were published as *Trois mystères* (Paris: Ernest Kolb, n.d.). See also John A. Henderson, *The First Avant-Garde* (London: Harrap, 1971), pp. 115–16 and 126.

3. Bettina Knapp, *The Reign of the Theatrical Director: French Theatre 1887–1924* (Troy, New York: Whitston, 1988), p. 102.

4. Quote attributed to 1901 commentator R. de Souza by Francine-Clair LeGrand, *Le Symbolisme en Belgique* (Brussels: Laconti, 1971), p. 48 (translation mine).

5. It is often forgotten that the profane and scatalogical King Ubu takes the part of the Antichrist in Jarry's opaque heraldic mystery play, *Caesar Antichrist* (trans. James H. Bierman [Tucson: Omen, 1971]).

6. Michael Hamburger, *Hofmannsthal: Three Essays* (Princeton: Princeton University Press, 1972), p. 22. Hofmannsthal's attraction to medieval theater was evident as early as 1893 with his one-act mystical morality play, "Death and the Fool."

7. Gunnar Brandell, *Strindberg in Inferno*, trans. Barry Jacobs (Cambridge: Harvard University Press, 1974), p. 110. In the early 1980s interest began to grow in the relationship of the occult to *fin-de-siècle* theater. See Daniel Gerould and Jadwiga Kosicka, "The Drama of the Unseen—Turn-of-the-Century Paradigms for Occult Drama," and Haskell M. Block, "Symbolist Drama: Villiers de L'Isle-Adam, Strindberg, and Yeats," in *The Occult in Language and Literature*, ed. Hermine Riffaterre (New York: New York Literary Forum, 1980), pp. 3–42 and 43–50. See also Daniel Gerould, ed. and intro., *Doubles, Demons, and Dreamers: An International Collection of Symbolist Drama* (New York: Performing Arts Journal Publications, 1985), pp. 7–34.

8. Haskell M. Block, *Mallarmé and the Symbolist Drama* (Detroit: Wayne State University Press, 1963), p. 85.

9. In that year Strindberg was also moved to publish for the first time "Coram Populo!" the miniature mock-mystery he had written twenty years earlier as an epilogue to a revision of *Master Olof*, but then not used.

10. For a succinct discussion that distinguishes the "neo-mystery" from the neo-romantic play, see Harold B. Segel, *Twentieth-Century Russian Drama: From Gorky to the Present* (New York: Columbia University Press, 1979), pp. 50–55.

11. Edward Braun, ed., *Meyerhold on Theatre* (New York: Hill and Wang, 1969), pp. 53–54 and 60–61.

12. Vyacheslav Ivanov, "The Theatre of the Future," trans. Stephen Graham, *English Review*, vol. 10, March 1912. The 1907 article came out in Ivanov's collection *By the Stars* in 1909. It was his first essay to be published in English.

13. Maurice Tuchman, "Hidden Meanings in Abstract Art," in *The Spiritual in Art: Abstract Painting 1890–1985*, ed. Edward Weisberger (New York: Abbeville, 1986), p. 18.

14. John Gassner, *The Theatre in Our Times* (New York: Crown, 1954), p. 175, and Richard Gilman, *The Making of Modern Drama* (New York: Farrar, Straus & Giroux, 1974), pp. 105–106.

15. Martin Lamm, Strindberg's biographer, quotes a 1901 Strindberg letter to his German translator Emil Schering stating that Maeterlinck's *Le Trésor des humbles* was "the greatest book I have ever read" (*August Strindberg*, trans. and ed. Harry G. Carlson [New York: Benjamin Blom, 1971] p. 381). In addition to many similar letter references to Péladan, marked copies of *Le Prince de Byzance* and other Péladan *wagnéries* are to be found in Strindberg's Stockholm library.

16. Robert Pincus-Witten, *Occult Symbolism in France* (New York: Garland, 1976), pp. 32–34.

17. Maurice Maeterlinck, "The Tragical in Daily Life," in *The Treasure of the Humble*, pp. 102 and 98–99.

18. Maeterlinck, "The Awakening of the Soul," p. 37.

19. See note 37, chapter 1. Mockel continues, "The illusion and in consequence the only true reality will be negated if the work does not carry inside itself its own distinctive mystery."

20. The romantic embrace of the symbol and rejection of allegory may have obscured for succeeding generations of critics this actual *fin-de-siècle* turn, or re-turn, toward allegory. A more charitable view of allegory began to emerge only much later, with Northrop Frye's distinction between continuous and *freistimmige* allegories (*Anatomy of Criticism* [Princeton: Princeton University Press, 1957], pp. 89–92). Since the 1960s, a major critical reconsideration of allegory has taken place, including the pathbreaking work of Fletcher, then Tuve, Quilligan, Bloomfield, MacQueen, Kantrowitz, and others. For excellent bibliographies on allegory, see Carolynn Van Dyke, *The Fiction of Truth: Structures of Meaning in Narrative and Dramatic Allegory* (Ithaca: Cornell University Press, 1985), and Joanne Spencer Kantrowitz, *Lindsay's Ane Satyre of the Thrie Estaitis* (Lincoln: University of Nebraska Press, 1975). My own view of allegory here must be seen as filtered through this revaluation, which grants the form independent, and not always parallel, life at the level of both sign and signified. Yet even as late as 1975, a commentator on Beckett could acknowledge the "embarrassment of allegory" (Dougald McMillan, "The Embarrassment of Allegory," in Ruby Cohn, ed., *Samuel Beckett: A Collection of Criticism* [New York: McGraw-Hill, 1975]).

21. Rosamund Tuve, *Allegorical Imagery* (Princeton: Princeton University Press, 1966), p. 55, and Frye, *Anatomy of Criticism*, p. 90. Contemporary theories of allegory have gone so far to reject this view of allegory that Stephen J. Greenblatt (*Allegory and Representation* [Baltimore: Johns Hopkins University Press, 1981], pp. vii–viii) can assert the deconstructionist claim that traditional allegory only pretends to "the recovery of the pure visibility of the truth, undisguised by the local and accidental" but "inevitably reveals the impossibility of this project."

22. For the past quarter-century, allegorical theory has rejected the distinction made by C. S. Lewis and Auerbach between allegory and typology (or figura). See, for instance, A. D. Nuttall, *Two Concepts of Allegory* (New York: Barnes and Noble, 1967), pp. 15–48.

23. Walter Benjamin, *The Origin of German Tragic Drama*, trans. John Osborne, intro. George Steiner (London: New Left, 1977), p. 229.

24. Tuve, *Allegorical Imagery*, p. 18.

25. Egil Tornqvist, *Strindbergian Drama, Themes and Structures* (Atlantic Highlands, New Jersey: Humanities, 1982), p. 95. See also Carl Dahlstrom, "Situation and Character in *Till Damaskus*," *Publications of the Modern Language Association of America*, September 1938, vol. LIII, no. 3, p. 888.

26. Orjan Lindberger, "Some Notes on Strindberg and Péladan," *Structures of Influence: A Comparative Approach to August Strindberg* (Chapel Hill: University of North Carolina Press, 1981), p. 247. Also see Pincus-Witten, *Occult Symbolism in France*, p. 31.

27. On the progress as the dominant narrative form of medieval allegory, see John MacQueen, *Allegory*, Critical Idiom series, John D. Jump, ed. (London: Methuen, 1970), p. 63.

28. Par Lagerkvist was the first to point out the parallels between the medieval passion play and Strindberg's passion motif in the pilgrimage plays ("Strindberg and the Theater of Tomorrow," in *Strindberg: A Collection of Critical Essays*, ed. Otto Reinert [Englewood Cliffs: Prentice-Hall, 1971]).

29. August Strindberg, *To Damascus III*, trans. Arvid Paulson, *Eight Expressionist Plays* (New York: New York University Press, 1972), p. 329.

30. Paul Piehler, *The Visionary Landscape: A Study in Medieval Allegory* (Montreal: McGill-Queen's University Press, 1971), p. 4.

31. One mysterium writer who does place herself as a writer in the center of her plays is Liliane Atlan. See *The Messiahs* and *The Carriage of Flames and Voices* in *Theatre Pieces: An Anthology*, trans. Marguerite Feitlowitz (Greenwood, Florida: Penkevill, 1984).

32. *To Damascus*, Part I, trans. Evert Sprinchorn, in *The Genius of the Scandinavian Theater*, ed. Evert Sprinchorn (New York: New American Library, 1964), p. 360. All subsequent quotations are from this translation.

33. See Piehler, *The Visionary Landscape*, "The Psychology of Landscape: Wilderness and City," pp. 72–78.

34. J. M. Ritchie, ed., *Georg Kaiser: Plays, Volume One* (New York: Riverrun, 1985), p. 7. All subsequent quotations will be taken from this edition.

35. MacQueen, *Allegory*, p. 44.

36. Antonin Artaud, *The Spurt of Blood*, in Susan Sontag, ed. and intro., *Antonin Artaud, Selected Writings* (New York: Farrar, Straus & Giroux, 1976), pp. 72–73. All subsequent quotations are from this translation.

37. The Knight and the Wet Nurse might seem at first to resist being drawn into the allegorizing tendencies of the mysterium. Yet, as Angus Fletcher writes (*Allegory: The Theory of a Symbolic Mode* [New York: Cornell University Press, 1964] p. 198), it scarcely matters whether the allegorical character is a "real, human semi-abstraction" or an "unreal, nonhuman abstraction" as long as he or she participates in "forms that are ritualized or symmetrically ordered."

38. See Kenneth A. Strand, *Interpreting the Book of Revelation* (Worthington, Ohio: Ann Arbor, 1976), p. 47.

39. M. H. Abrams, "Apocalypse: Theme and Variations," *The Apocalypse in English Renaissance Thought and Literature*, C. A. Patrides and Joseph Wittreich, eds. (Manchester: Manchester University Press, 1984), p. 346.

40. I give the title of the play as it appears in the translation by Lee Baxandall in Erika Munk, ed., *Brecht* (New York: Bantam, 1972). The title might be literally rendered, *The Baden-Baden Learning Play of Agreement*. All quotations from the play are from the Baxandall translation.

41. The radio learning play was *The Ocean Flight*, originally entitled *Lindbergh's Flight*. Charles Lindbergh's name was dropped because of his support for the Nazi party.

42. O. B. Hardison, *Christian Rite and Christian Drama in the Middle Ages* (Baltimore: Johns Hopkins University Press, 1965), p. 288.

43. "Allegory . . . must always fail in the hands of a poet," quoted in Vivian Mercier, *Beckett/Beckett* (New York: Oxford University Press, 1977), p. 173.

44. Robert S. Knapp, "Samuel Beckett's Allegory of the Uncreating Word," *Mosaic*, VI/2 (Winter 1973), p. 73.

45. Samuel Beckett, *Waiting for Godot* (New York: Grove, 1954), p. 51a. All subsequent quotations are from this edition.

46. Per Nykrog, "In the Ruins of the Past: Reading Beckett Intertextually," *Comparative Literature*, vol. 36, no. 3 (Fall 1984), pp. 289–311, p. 292.

47. Maurice Valency has said that Beckett represents the "terminal aspect" of nine-

teenth-century symbolism (*The End of the World* [New York: Oxford University Press, 1980], p. 389); Katherine Worth reminds us that *Waiting for Godot* echoes both Maeterlinck's *The Blind* and Yeat's *The Cat and the Moon* (*The Irish Drama of Europe from Yeats to Beckett* [London: Athlone, 1978], pp. 242–46); and Anthony Swerling details formidable (if speculative) debts owed by *Godot* to Strindberg's pilgrimage plays (*Strindberg's Impact in France, 1920–1960* [Cambridge: Trinity Lane, 1971] pp. 111–25).

48. David Cole's *The Moments of the Wandering Jew* is unpublished. Part III, "The Hochhimmelfahrt Passion Play," was produced at New York's Theatre of the Open Eye, directed by Bevya Rosten, in 1979. Another American playwright whose early plays are related to the mysterium tradition is Adrienne Kennedy. See my article, "Adrienne Kennedy and the First Avant-Garde," in Paul K. Bryant-Jackson and Lois More Overbeck, eds., *Intersecting Boundaries: The Theatre of Adrienne Kennedy* (Minneapolis: University of Minnesota Press, 1992), pps. 76–84.

49. Edwin Honig, *Dark Conceit* (New York: Oxford University Press, 1966), p. 180.

50. See, for instance, Sixten Ringbom, "Art in the 'Epoch of the Great Spiritual': Occult Elements in the Early Theory of Abstract Painting," *Journal of the Warburg and Courtauld Institutes*, 29, 1966.

51. Alan Bowness, "An Alternative Tradition?" in *French Symbolist Painters* (London: Arts Council of Great Britain, 1972), p. 14.

52. See Tuchman, *The Spiritual in Art*, pp. 17–62, esp. p. 18.

3. Counter-Stagings

1. Lou-Andreas Salomé, *Ibsen's Heroines*, ed. and trans. Siegfried Mandel (Redding Ridge, Connecticut: Black Swan, 1985) pp. 101–22, and Henry James, "Henrik Ibsen," *Essays in London and Elsewhere*, rpt. (Freeport, New York: Books for Libraries, 1972), p. 238.

2. Brian Johnston, "The Turning Point in *The Lady from the Sea*," *Text and Supertext in Ibsen's Drama* (University Park: Pennsylvania State University Press, 1989), pp. 193–294.

3. Ibid., p. 205. Johnston's spelling of proper names differs from that used below, which follows the Fjelde translation (see note 8).

4. Ibid., p. 223.

5. Johnston defines a dramatic "supertext" as "the store of cultural reference a poet or thinker can draw upon and from which is derived his or her own identity," ibid., p. 77.

6. Teresa de Lauretis, "The Technology of Gender," *Technologies of Gender* (Bloomington: Indiana University Press, 1987), p. 24.

7. Ibid., p. 32.

8. All quotations from *The Lady from the Sea* are taken from Rolf Fjelde trans. and intro., *Ibsen: The Complete Major Prose Plays* (New York: Farrar, Straus & Giroux, 1978).

9. Francis Fergusson, "The Lady from the Sea," *Contemporary Approaches to Ibsen*, vol. 8, 1965–1966 (Oslo: Universitetsforlaget, 1966), p. 54.

10. Ibid.

11. Johnston, "The Turning Point," p. 225.

12. Fergusson, "The Lady from the Sea," pp. 54–55.

13. Orley I. Holtan, *Mythic Patterns in Ibsen's Last Plays* (Minneapolis: University of Minnesota Press, 1970), p. 77.

14. Sandra E. Saari, " 'Hun, som ikke selv har noe riktig livskall. . . . ': Women and the Role of the 'Ideal Woman' in Ibsen's Munich Trilogy," *Contemporary Approaches to Ibsen*, vol. V (Oslo: Universitetsforlaget, 1985).

15. Holtan, *Mythic Patterns*, p. 66.

16. Hélène Cixous, "Sorties," in Hélène Cixous and Catherine Clément, *The Newly Born Woman*, trans. Betsy Wing (Minneapolis: University of Minnesota Press, 1986), pp. 64–65.

17. We read in Naomi Schor's *Reading in Detail: Aesthetics and the Feminine* (New York: Methuen, 1987), p. 26, that to valorize the detail is to "aid in the dismantling of Idealist metaphysics."

18. Charles Lyons, *Henrik Ibsen: The Divided Consciousness* (Carbondale: Southern Illinois University Press, 1972), p. xi.

19. In "The Mermaid's End, or the Domestication of the Species," a paper given at the Ibsen Sesquicentennial Celebration at Pratt Institute in 1978, Sandra Saari also argued that the ending of *The Lady from the Sea* is a "human tragedy" in which Ellida chooses the "bourgeois view of life as opposed to the artistic view of life" (unpub., p. 13).

20. Salomé's essay on Ellida Wangel affirmed Ellida's development away from the Stranger and characterized as "vague and substanceless" Ellida's fantasies of boundless freedom. She remarkably lacks the nostalgia for the freedom of the sea that tugs at modern critics (*Ibsen's Heroines*, p. 121). See also Yvonne Schafer in "The Liberated Woman in Ibsen's *The Lady from the Sea*," *Theatre Annual*, no. 40, 1985. Schafer sees the play as a positive version of *A Doll's House*, one in which "Ibsen presents a view of women and of marriage far in advance of his time."

21. M. C. Bradbrook, *Ibsen the Norwegian: A Revaluation* (London: Chatto and Windus, 1966), pp. 108–109. The book was first published in 1946.

22. Evert Sprinchorn, *Ibsen: Letters and Speeches* (New York: Hill and Wang, 1964), p. 297.

23. Edvard Beyer, *Ibsen: The Man and His Work* (London: Souvenir Press [E & A], 1978), p. 157.

24. Charles R. Lyons, *Henrik Ibsen: The Divided Consciousness*, p. xiv.

25. Holtan, *Mythic Patterns*, p. 81.

26. Errol Durbach, "The Apotheosis of Hedda Gabler," *Scandinavian Studies*, XLIII, 1971, pp. 143–59.

27. Elinor Fuchs, "Mythic Structure in *Hedda Gabler*: The Mask Beneath the Face," *Comparative Drama* (Fall 1985), pp. 209–21.

28. Walter McFarlane, *The Oxford Ibsen*, vol. 7 (London: Oxford University Press, 1966), p. 488.

29. Sandra Saari's "Hedda Gabler: The Valkyrie Manqué," a paper delivered at the annual meeting of the Scandinavian Studies Association, 1976 (unpub.) is one such source; also see Nina da Vinci Nichols, "Racine's *Phaedra* and Ibsen's *Hedda*: Transformations of Ariadne," *American Imago*, vol. 40, no. 3 (Fall 1983), pp. 237–56.

30. "Ibsen's Ironic Muse," Nina da Vinci Nichols (unpub.), p. 2.

31. Nichols, "Racine's *Phaedra*," p. 253.

32. Ibid. p. 237. By "myth" and "form" I assume Nichols is pointing to manifest and symbolic or hidden levels of the play. The play's coherence is to be found in their correspondence, just as it is in Johnston's reading of "text and supertext."

33. Philip E. Larson, "French Farce Conventions and the Mythic Story Pattern in *Hedda Gabler*: A Performance Criticism," (Oslo: Universitetsforlaget, 1985), pp. 202–28, 202–203.

34. For high comic readings of the play, see also Jens Kruuse, "The Function of Humour in the Later Plays of Ibsen," *Contemporary Approaches to Ibsen* (Oslo: Universitetsforlaget, 1971), pp. 42–59; and Rick Davis, " 'Buried Truths to Light': Mel Shapiro on *Hedda Gabler*, Charles Ludlam and Other Classics," *The Repertory Reader*, vol. 1, no. 3 (Spring 1984), pp. 2–3.

35. Larson, "French Farce Conventions," p. 220.

36. Ibid., pp. 213 and 215.

37. Salomé's sensitive, if masculinist, character study of Hedda (*Ibsen's Heroines*, pp. 123–45) sternly takes her to task for her cowardice and conventionality, and her terrible confusion of freedom and titillation.

38. A connection between the two works has been pointed out by many and discussed by a few, principally by Brian Johnston and in my own earlier article on *Hedda Gabler*, both cited above. Larson suggests that *The Birth of Tragedy* "may have influenced the conceptual design" of the play (p. 219), but doesn't say how. Brian Johnston writes that "the argument of *Hedda Gabler* is that of *Emperor and Galilean* and of Nietzsche's *The Birth of Tragedy*," and in a perhaps overly-lucid reading, conceives of the play as a battle between pagan and Christian "armies" (pp. 144–53).

39. Evert Sprinchorn, "Ibsen and the Immoralists," *Comparative Literature Studies*, vol. IX, no. 1 (March 1972), pp. 58–79.

40. George [*sic*] Brandes, *Friedrich Nietzsche* (New York: Haskell, 1972), pp. 21–22.

41. Henrik Ibsen, *Hedda Gabler*, in Fjelde, pp. 751 and 777. All subsequent quotations will be taken from this edition.

42. Friedrich Nietzsche, *The Birth of Tragedy and the Case of Wagner*, trans. and ed. Walter Kaufmann (New York: Random, 1967), p. 109.

43. Ibid., p. 114.

44. "Greek tragedy met an end different from that of her older sister-arts: she died by suicide, in consequence of an irreconcilable conflict; she died tragically, while all the others passed away calmly and beautifully at a ripe old age . . . (and) when Greek tragedy died, there arose everywhere the deep sense of an immense void." Ibid., p. 76.

45. Ibid., pp. 91 and 74.

46. Among the "classic" moderns, only Chekhov has been radically re-examined in theatrical production. Strindberg's plays, like Ibsen's, can also be approached in dual or multiple focus. I would urge the reader and potential producer of *To Damascus* not to be overly swayed by my own "totalizing" reading of the play as a modern mysterium in the previous chapter, even though that form itself embraces contradictions. See my counter-reading of *To Damascus*, Part I, in Göran Stockenström, *Strindberg's Dramaturgy* (Minneapolis: University of Minnesota Press, 1988), pp. 75–86.

4. Signaling through the Signs

1. Michel de Certeau, *The Practice of Everyday Life*, trans. Steven Rendall (Berkeley: University of California Press, 1984), p. 134.

2. Richard Foreman, *The Mind King*, in *My Head Was a Sledgehammer and Other Plays* (Woodstock, New York: Overlook, 1995), p. 137.

3. Antonin Artaud, *The Theater and Its Double*, trans. Mary Caroline Richards (New York: Grove, 1958), p. 13.

4. Ibid., p. 10.

5. Joseph Chaikin, *The Presence of the Actor* (New York: Atheneum, 1972), p. 62.

6. Thomas R. Whitaker, *Fields of Play in Modern Drama* (Princeton: Princeton University Press, 1977), p. 16.

7. Ibid., pp. 129–30.

8. Julian Beck, *The Life of the Theatre* (San Francisco: City Lights, 1972), no. 10.

9. Michael Goldman, *The Actor's Freedom* (New York: Viking, 1975), pp. 160–61.

10. Beck, *Life of the Theater*, no. 84.

11. "Come and Go," *The Collected Shorter Plays of Samuel Beckett* (New York: Grove, 1984), notes, p. 196.

12. In his January 1, 1970 review in the *Village Voice* of Wilson's *The Life and Times of Sigmund Freud*, reprinted in Stefan Brecht, *The Theatre of Visions: Robert Wilson* (Frankfurt am Main: Suhrkamp, 1978), p. 426, Richard Foreman remarked that Wilson's actors did not project the "pre-determined energies and meanings" associated with professional actors. Foreman here points to an inherent contradiction in the idea of stage presence.

13. Keir Elam, *The Semiotics of Theatre and Drama* (New York: Methuen, 1980), p. 139.

14. Walter Benjamin, "The Work of Art in the Age of Mechanical Reproduction," in *Illuminations*, ed. Hannah Arendt (New York: Schocken, 1969), p. 221.

15. Thornton Wilder, "Some Thoughts on Playwriting," quoted in Bernard Dukore, *Dramatic Theory and Criticism* (New York: Holt, Rinehart and Winston, 1974), p. 892.

16. Jacques Derrida, "Freud and the Scene of Writing," *Writing and Difference*, trans. Alan Bass (Chicago: University of Chicago Press, 1978), p. 212.

17. Gayatri Spivak, intro. to Derrida, *Of Grammatology* (Baltimore: Johns Hopkins University Press, 1976), p. lxix.

18. Richard Rorty, *Contingency, Irony, and Solidarity* (New York: Cambridge University Press, 1989), p. 74.

19. Christopher Norris, *Deconstruction: Theory and Practice* (London: Methuen, 1982), p. 28.

20. Ibid., p. 29.

21. From *Conversations with Eckermann and Soret*, in Barrett H. Clark, ed., *European Theories of the Drama* (New York: Crown, 1965), p. 283.

22. Brecht used the term "literarization" to theorize his use of scene titles in *The Threepenny Opera*. ("The Literarization of the Theater," *Brecht on Theatre*, ed. John Willett [New York: Hill and Wang, 1964], pp. 43–44.) He implies that the act of reading itself (he had the idea that perhaps written footnotes could be appended to live performance) would help to break up the malign identification between spectator and dramatic narrative created by the dramatic text fashioned on principles of empathy. I use the term "literalization" or, alternatively, "textualization," for a type of drama that makes literal the process of writing and reading that lies behind the enacted performance.

23. Richard Foreman, *Reverberation Machines: The Later Plays and Essays* (Barrytown, NY: Station Hill, 1985), p. 219.

24. Samuel Beckett, *Krapp's Last Tape and Other Dramatic Pieces* (New York: Grove Weidenfeld, 1960), p. 21.

25. In the provocative "Shakespearian characters: the generation of Silvia," in *Voice, Terminal, Echo*, Jonathan Goldberg suggests that for Shakespeare dramatic character was caught up with the idea of inscription. He cites the definition in the nearly contemporaneous Overbury's "What a Character Is" (1615) "to ingrave, or make a deepe Impression" (p. 87).

26. I am of course well aware that Derrida's sighing cadence was intended as an antidote for the nostalgia for a lost origin.

27. Peter Handke, *Kaspar and Other Plays*, trans. Michael Roloff (New York: Hill and Wang, 1969).

28. "Prompter" in English may suggest more of the book than Handke's word for these offstage voices, *Einsager*, literally, sayer-in. It is close to one of the German words for stage prompter, *Vorsager*, or sayer-for.

29. "Were they as prime as goats, as hot as monkeys," *Othello*, III, iii.

30. Adrienne Kennedy, *A Movie Star Has to Star in Black and White*, in *Adrienne Kennedy in One Act* (Minneapolis: University of Minnesota Press, 1988).

31. Harold Rosenberg, *Act and the Actor* (New York: World, 1970). Rosenberg remarks that "anti-drama" is the modernist form since Joyce and Pirandello that has created the "formula . . . : no act, no actor. . . . " (p. 12).

32. Annette Michelson, "Film and the Radical Aspiration," *Film Culture*, no. 42 (Fall 1966), pp. 34–42 and 136. The quotation appears on pp. 38–39.

33. Daryl Chin, *Act and the Actor* (unpub.) pp. 1 and 3.

34. See, for instance, Gayle Austin, "*The Doll House Show*: A Feminist Theory Play," *Journal of Dramatic Theory and Criticism*, vol. 7, no. 2 (Spring 1993), pp. 203–207. Also see my review of the Schechner *Don Juan*, "Reviews and Articles," pp. 164–65.

35. Joan Schenkar, *The Universal Wolf, Kenyon Review*, vol. 13, no. 2 (Spring 1991).

36. This term is also used by Michael Vanden Heuvel in *Performing Drama / Dramatizing Performance* (Ann Arbor: University of Michigan Press, 1991). I am not aware of its use elsewhere.

37. See in this connection Elinor Fuchs, "Performance Notes: *North Atlantic* and *L.S.D.*," *Performing Arts Journal* #23, vol. VIII, no. 2. (1984), pp. 51–55.

38. Richard Foreman, "Ontological-Hysteric: Manifesto I," *Richard Foreman: Plays and Manifestos*, ed. and intro. Kate Davy (New York: New York University Press, 1976), p. 73.

39. In an interview I conducted on November 25, 1993, Foreman cites the French occultist Eliphas Levi as one of his links to Kaballah. In 1894, Levi re-presented the *Zohar* as *Le Livre des splendeurs*. Foreman notes that the plural form of the title was suggested to him by Levi's use of the plural. See Fuchs, "Today I am a Fountain Pen: An Interview with Richard Foreman" in *Theater* Vol. 25, No. 2 (Spring 1994), pp. 82–86, 84.

40. Jonathan Culler, *On Deconstruction* (Ithaca: Cornell University Press, 1982), p. 99.

41. Richard Foreman, *Lava*, in *Unbalancing Acts*, ed. Ken Jordan (New York: Pantheon, 1992), p. 310.

42. Ibid., pp. 356–57.

43. Ibid., pp. 319–20, and 348.

44. Ibid., pp. 327, 328, and 351.

45. Ibid., p. 319. Foreman disparages the significance of this staging decision (interview of November 15, 1993). The young woman, a member of the crew, was put in as a last-minute decision; she happened to be wearing red; as for the writing *before*, which the published text explicitly directs, he remembers instructing the actor to write down whatever she heard.

46. Author's unpublished interview with Richard Foreman, June 25, 1983.

47. Richard Foreman, *Book of Splendors/ II*, in *Reverberation Machines*, p. 42.

48. Interview with Richard Foreman, November 15, 1993.

49. Foreman, *Lava*, p. 314.

50. Foreman, *Reverberation Machines*, p. 216.

51. Foreman, *Lava*, p. 315.

52. Ibid., pp. 322–23.

53. Gertrude Stein, "Plays," *Lectures in America*. (London: Virago, 1988), p. 93.

54. Ibid., pp. 95 and 122.

55. Ibid., p. 131.

56. Ibid., p. 125.

57. Geraldine Cummins, *The Road to Immortality: Being a Description of the Life Hereafter, with Evidence of the Survival of Human Personality* (New York: Psychic, 1947).

58. Michel Foucault, "Fantasia of the Library," *Language, Counter-Memory, Practice*, ed. and intro. Donald F. Bouchard, trans. Donald F. Bouchard and Sherry Simon (Ithaca: Cornell University Press, 1977), pp. 87–107.

59. Ibid., pp. 89–91.

60. Ibid., p. 91.

61. Beck, *Life of the Theatre*, no. 35.

62. The following discussion condenses the argument in Certeau, *The Practice of Everyday*

Life, on "The Scriptural Economy," pp. 131–54, that Certeau makes under the general heading "Uses of Language." All quotations are taken from pp. 133–37.

63. Roberta Smith, "Art in Review," *New York Times*, October 22, 1993, p. C24.

64. See Julian Dibbell's marvelous account, "Rape in Cyberspace: A Tale of Crime and Punishment On-line," *Village Voice*, December 21, 1993.

5. Another Version of Pastoral

1. Richard Foreman and Elizabeth LeCompte, "Messing Around: Off-Broadway's Most Inventive Directors Talk about Their Art," *Village Voice*, August 19, 1994, p. 34.

2. Heiner Müller, "A Letter to Robert Wilson," *Explosion of a Memory*, ed. and trans. Carl Weber (New York: PAJ, 1989), p. 154.

3. Samuel Beckett, *Endgame* (New York: Grove, 1958), p. 27.

4. Ibid., p. 29.

5. For instance, ibid., p. 68.

6. Thornton Wilder, *The Journals of Thornton Wilder, 1939–1961*, ed. Donald Gallup (New Haven: Yale University Press, 1985), entry of August 6, 1953, p. 316.

7. Gertrude Stein and Maurice Grosser, *Four Saints in Three Acts*, unpub. libretto distributed at performances by Opera Ensemble of New York, November 12–30, 1986.

8. Virgil Thomson, *Virgil Thomson* (New York: Da Capo, 1977), p. 195.

9. Gertrude Stein, *The Autobiography of Alice B. Toklas* (New York: Harcourt, Brace, 1933), p. 202.

10. Ibid., pp. 228 and 256.

11. Gertrude Stein, "Plays," in *Lectures in America* (London: Virago, 1988), p. 122.

12. Ibid., p. 122.

13. Ibid., p. 125.

14. Thomson, *Virgil Thomson*, p. 91.

15. Stein, "Plays," pp. 128–29.

16. Ibid., p. 129.

17. The only reference I have so far seen to Stein and pastoral appears in Empson, who in a single provocative mention ties her to the Lewis Carroll "child-cult" variation of pastoral he assigns to the nineteenth century. See William Empson, *Some Versions of Pastoral* (London: Chatto & Windus, 1950), p. 15.

18. Maurice Maeterlinck, "The Tragical in Daily Life," in *The Treasure of the Humble*, pp. 105–106.

19. Quoted in Gertrude Stein, *Last Operas and Plays*, ed. and intro. Carl Van Vechten (New York: Rinehart, 1949), p. x.

20. Heiner Müller, *Hamletmachine and Other Texts for the Stage*, ed. and trans. Carl Weber (New York: PAJ, 1984), p. 53.

21. Richard Wagner, *Parsifal*, English libretto version Stewart Robb (New York: Schirmer, 1962), p. 7.

22. Author's interview with Robert Wilson in February 1986, unpublished. Fragments of the interview appear in "The PAJ Casebook: *Alcestis*," *Performing Arts Journal* 28, vol. X, no. 1, 1986, pp. 80–115.

23. Heiner Müller, "Explosion of a Memory/Description of a Picture," *Explosion of a Memory* (New York: PAJ, 1989), p. 97.

24. Elinor Fuchs and James Leverett, "Life on the Wall," *Art and Cinema*, vol. 1, no. 1 (Summer 1986), p. 5, and Elinor Fuchs and James Leverett, "Back to the Wall: Heiner Müller in Berlin," *Village Voice*, December 16, 1984, p. 67.

25. In "Images in the Interstice: The Phenomenal Theater of Robert Wilson," *Modern Drama*, vol. XXXI, no. 4 (December 1988), pp. 571–87, Gordon S. Armstrong asserts Wilson failed in *Alcestis* to create his usual mythic "dreamscape" because he "began with the language." His images could not "untangle themselves from the weight of their origin in rational discourse" (pp. 584–85). To the extent I permitted myself as spectator to shed the text (and much was already shed and fractured by Wilson), I received a far more visual and holistic impression.

26. Richard Foreman, *Plays and Manifestos*, ed. and intro. Kate Davy (New York: New York University Press, 1976), pp. x–xiv.

27. Elinor Fuchs, "Today I Am a Fountain Pen: An Interview with Richard Foreman," p. 85.

28. I am indebted to Harry J. Elam and Alice Rayner for pointing this out in "Unfinished Business: Reconfiguring History in Suzan-Lori Parks's *The Death of the Last Black Man in the Whole Entire World*," *Theatre Journal*, vol. 46, no. 4 (December 1994), pp. 447–61, 454.

29. Suzan-Lori Parks, *The Death of the Last Black Man in the Whole Entire World*, *Theater*, vol. XXI, no. 3 (Summer–Fall 1990), p. 82.

30. Ibid., pp. 92–93.

31. Suzan-Lori Parks, *The America Play*, *American Theatre* (March 1994), pp. 32–33.

32. Bonnie Marranca, *Theatrewritings* (New York: PAJ, 1984), p. 197.

33. Ulla Dydo, "Landscape Is Not Grammar: Gertrude Stein in 1928," *Raritan*, vol. 7, no. 1 (Summer 1987), pp. 97–113, 106.

34. For a description of some of these projects, see the "Art and Ecology" issue of *Art Journal*, vol. 51, no. 2 (Summer, 1992). Of particular interest is Timothy W. Luke, "Art and the Environmental Crisis: From Commodity Aesthetics to Ecology Aesthetics," pp. 72–76.

6. When Bad Girls Play Good Theaters

1. Maria Irene Fornes, *Fefu and Her Friends, Wordplays: An Anthology of New American Drama* (New York: PAJ, 1980), p. 19.

2. This chapter, without Foreword and Afterword, was published in substantially the same form as "Staging the Obscene Body," in *TDR*, vol. 33, no. 1 (Spring 1989), pp. 33–58. I have edited the article slightly, and have adjusted tenses to accommodate this later publication.

3. Carolee Schneeman, *More than Meat Joy* (New York: Documentext, 1979), p. 52.

4. Alan Soble, *Pornography: Marxism, Feminism and the Future of Sexuality* (New Haven: Yale University Press, 1986), pp. 8–9.

5. Hannah Alderfer, Kate Ellis, etc., eds., *Caught Looking* (Seattle: Real Comet Press, 1988).

6. Andrea Dworkin, *Pornography: Men Possessing Women* (New York: Putnam, 1981), p. 200.

7. The text of *Dead End Kids* appears in *Theater* magazine, Summer–Fall 1982. The nightclub scene is positioned in the text, but not reproduced.

8. William B. Collins, "This Protest of Nuclear Policy is neither Art nor Propaganda," *Philadelphia Inquirer*, February 25, 1983, p. C4.

9. Elinor Fuchs, "Too Late for Kidding," *Soho News*, November 19, 1980.

10. When the scene was first presented in 1981, it played entirely in silence. When the piece was revived in December 1986, LeCompte had added a sparse, intermittent sound track which repeated some of the language spoken earlier by the male actors in the blackface scene.

11. Interview with Elizabeth LeCompte, September 28, 1988, unpublished.

12. Ibid.

13. Advertising copy for "The Second Coming," quoted by Arlene Raven, "Star-Studded," *High Performance*, 28 (1984), p. 26.

14. All quotations are taken from Kathy Acker's published text, which appears in *Word-Plays 5*, ed. Bonnie Marranca and Gautam DasGupta (New York: PAJ, 1987).

15. Angela Carter, *The Sadeian Woman and the Ideology of Pornography* (New York: Pantheon, 1978), p. 4.

16. Erika Munk, "Cross Left," *Village Voice* (December 17, 1985), p. 120.

17. "The Controversial 1985–86 Theatre Season: A Politics of Reception," *Performing Arts Journal* #28, vol. X., no.1, p. 24.

18. Richard Schechner, "Uprooting the Garden," unpub., p. 18. A shorter version of this article, "Uprooting the Garden: Thoughts around the 'Prometheus Project,' " appeared in *New Theatre Quarterly* vol. 2, no.5 (1986), pp. 3–11.

19. Richard Schechner, "Pornography and the New Expression," in Irving Buchen, ed., *The Perverse Imagination* (New York: New York University Press, 1970), pp. 110–11. The article was first published in *Atlantic Monthly* in 1966.

20. Arthur Kroker and David Cook, *The Postmodern Scene: Excremental Culture and Hyper-Aesthetics* (New York: St. Martin's, 1986).

21. C. Carr, "Unspeakable Practices, Unnatural Acts: The Taboo Art of Karen Finley," *Village Voice* (June 24, 1986), p. 17.

22. From *The Constant State of Desire*, *Drama Review*, vol. 32, no. 1 (Spring 1988), pp. 139–51.

23. Teresa de Lauretis, "The Technology of Gender," *Technologies of Gender: Essays on Theory, Film and Fiction* (Bloomington: Indiana University Press, 1987), pp. 1–30, 25.

24. Georges Bataille, "Sexual Plethora and Death," in *Eroticism* (San Francisco: City Lights, 1986), p. 105.

25. Susan Rubin Suleiman, "Pornography and the Avant-Garde," in *The Poetics of Gender* (New York: Columbia University Press, 1986), p. 120.

26. Susan Sontag, "The Pornographic Imagination," in *Styles of Radical Will* (New York: Delta, 1981), p. 45.

27. David Savran, *In Their Own Words: Contemporary American Playwrights* (New York: Theatre Communications Group, 1988), p. 220.

28. Jacquelyn N. Zita, "Pornography and the Male Imaginary," in *Enclitic*, vol. 9, nos. 1–2, p. 39.

29. Gerda Lerner, *The Creation of Patriarchy* (New York: Oxford University Press, 1986), p. 139.

30. B. Ruby Rich, "Feminism and Sexuality in the 1980s," *Feminist Studies* vol. 12, no. 3 (Fall 1986), pp. 540–41.

31. Mary Ann Doane, "Excerpts from a Forum on Pornography," in *subjects/objects* (Spring 1984), p. 53.

32. Kaja Silverman, "*Histoire d'O*, Construction of a Female Subject," in Carole S. Vance, *Pleasure and Danger: Exploring Female Sexuality* (Boston: Routledge & Kegan Paul, 1985), p. 327.

33. Kathleen Hulley, "Transgressing Genre: Kathy Acker's Intertext," *Intertextuality and Contemporary American Fiction* (see n. 4, p. 199). Discussing other works by Acker, Hulley develops the idea that a special brand of Acker obscenity consists in scrawling "graffiti" across canonic texts.

34. Jill Dolan, *The Feminist Spectator as Critic* (Ann Arbor: U.M.I. Research Press, 1988), p. 67.

35. LeCompte, interview, 1988.

36. Jonas Barish, *The Anti-Theatrical Prejudice* (Berkeley: University of California Press, 1981), pp. 42–44, 85, 227, 237, 271, 303, and 409.

37. Peter Stallybrass and Allon White, *The Politics and Poetics of Transgression* (Ithaca: Cornell University Press, 1986), pp. 92–93.

38. Pierre Bourdieu, *Outline of a Theory of Practice*, trans. Richard Nice (Cambridge: Cambridge University Press, 1977), p. 95. Though it is beyond the scope of the present article, it would be interesting to explore what links might be sustained between the transgressive female of carnival and the transgressive females of the contemporary obscene theater. In an article modeling such an attempt, "Female Grotesques: Carnival and Theory," which appears in de Lauretis's *Feminist Studies/Critical Studies*, Mary Russo draws out from Bakhtin what is only implicit in *Rabelais and His World*, the figure of the female carnivalesque transgressor as a destabilizing force in culture. Russo acknowledges that the Unruly Woman of carnival occupied a "complicitous place in dominant culture," yet also played at least an emblematic role—and here she quotes the work of Natalie Zemon Davis on women and seventeenth-century European carnival—in the "efforts to change the basic distribution of power within society."

39. Craig Owens, "The Discourse of Others: Feminists and Postmodernism," in Hal Foster, ed., *The Anti-Aesthetic* (Port Townsend, Washington: Bay, 1983), p. 59.

40. Laurie Bell, ed., *Good Girls/Bad Girls* (Seattle: Seal, 1987).

41. de Lauretis, "The Technology of Gender," pp. 25–26.

42. Katherine Schuler, "Spectator Response and Comprehension: The Problem of Karen Finley's *Constant State of Desire*," *TDR*, vol. 34, no. 1 (Spring 1990), pp. 131–45.

43. Richard Schechner, "Karen Finley: A Constant State of Becoming," *TDR*, vol. 32, No.1 (Spring 1988), pp. 152–58, and C. Carr, "Telling the Awfullest Truth": An Interview with Karen Finley, in *Acting Out: Feminist Performances* (Ann Arbor: University of Michigan Press, 1993), pp. 153–60.

7. Theater as Shopping

1. William Kowinski, *The Malling of America* (New York: Morrow, 1985), p. 24.

2. Anders Stephanson, "Regarding Postmodernism—A Conversation with Fredric Jameson," in *Universal Abandon? The Politics of Postmodernism*, ed. Andrew Ross (Minneapolis: University of Minnesota Press, 1988), pp. 3–30, 26.

3. Jean-Christophe Agnew, *Worlds Apart: The Market and the Theater in Anglo-American Thought, 1550–1750* (New York: Cambridge University Press, 1986), p. ix.

4. The fluid, multi-dimensional nature of *Tamara* is well-represented in the printed version. See John Krizanc, *Tamara* (London: Methuen Drama, 1989).

5. Heiner Müller, *Hamletmachine and Other Texts for the Stage*, ed. and trans. Carl Weber (New York: PAJ, 1984), p. 126.

6. Fredric Jameson, *Postmodernism, or the Cultural Logic of Late Capitalism* (Durham: Duke University Press, 1991). See especially the first essay, "The Cultural Logic of Late Capitalism" (pp. 1–54), the seminal essay first published in *New Left Review* in 1984. See also Ernest Mandel, *Late Capitalism* (London: NLB/Verso, 1975).

7. Walter Benjamin, "What is Epic Theater?" in *Illuminations*, ed. and intro. Hannah Arendt, trans. Harry Zohn (New York: Schocken, 1969), p. 154.

8. Darko Suvin, "Approach to Topoanalysis and to the Paradigmatics of Dramaturgic Space," in *Poetics Today*, vol. 8, no. 2 (1987), pp. 311–34, 324.

9. Russell W. Belk, "Possessions and the Extended Self," *Journal of Consumer Research*,

vol. 15 (September 1988), pp. 139–68, 141. A less Adlerian, more archetypal view, however, is advanced by Colin Campbell in *The Romantic Ethic and the Spirit of Modern Consumerism* (London: Basil Blackwell, 1987), which argues that shoppers shop romantically to actualize an ever-regenerating daydream of anticipated pleasure and fulfillment, a dream of a lost golden age projected forward onto commodities.

10. Walter Benjamin, "The Work of Art in the Age of Mechanical Reproduction," *Illuminations*, pp. 217–52.

11. Quoted in the *New York Times*, August 5, 1990.

12. Susan Buck-Morss, *The Dialectics of Seeing: Walter Benjamin and the Arcades Project* (Cambridge: MIT Press, 1989), p. 306.

13. See Michael Sorkin, ed., *Variations on a Theme Park: The New American City and the End of Public Space* (New York: Noonday, 1992), in which it is argued that contemporary culture destroys the idea of the democratic polis but creates in the shopping mall its simulacrum based exclusively on market principles.

14. Stephanson, "Regarding Postmodernism," pp. 13–14.

8. Postmodernism and the Scene of Theater

1. Guy Debord, *Society of the Spectacle* (Detroit: Black & Red, 1983), #19.

2. Charles Jencks, *What Is Post-Modernism?* (New York: St. Martin's, 1986). Note that Jencks renders the term postmodernism with a hyphen and initial caps, as "Post-Modernism." For consistency, however, following this acknowledgment, I revert to my own standard usage.

3. Ibid., pp. 45 and 47.

4. The late Thomas Lyman, Emory's eminent Romanesque art historian, told me that in conversation Portman acknowledged a debt to an actual theater: the late sixteenth-century Palladio-designed Teatro Olimpico in Vicenza, the most important renaissance attempt to build an archeologically correct Roman theater.

5. Derrida's famous line is, *Il n'y a pas de hors-texte.* See *Of Grammatology*, trans. Gayatri Chakaravorty Spivak (Baltimore: Johns Hopkins University Press, 1976), p. 158.

6. I will take references to theater, spectacle, performance, the "scene," and "*mise-en-scène*," to be aspects of a single, multi-faceted theatrical metaphor. I will not for these purposes distinguish metaphors of traditional theater from those of the contemporary form, "performance." This distinction is in any event less viable today than it was when it was first floated in the 1970s.

7. Guy Debord, *Society of the Spectacle*, #15.

8. Ibid., #158 and #160.

9. Ibid., #160 and #1.

10. Ibid., #221.

11. Jacques Derrida, "The Double Session," in *Dissemination*, trans. and intro. Barbara Johnson (Chicago: University of Chicago Press, 1981). See editor's note, p. 173.

12. Ibid., p. 191.

13. Ibid., p. 195.

14. Ibid., p. 206.

15. Ibid.

16. Ibid., p. 215, and n.27.

17. Michel Foucault, *The Archeology of Knowledge*, trans. A. M. Sheridan Smith (New York: Pantheon, 1972), p. 207. Fredric Jameson says in his introduction to Jean-François Lyotard's *The Postmodern Condition: A Report on Knowledge* (Minneapolis: University of Minnesota Press, 1984), "The admission to France of such Anglo-American linguistic notions as that of

Austin's 'performative' is now largely an accomplished fact (although a rather unexpected development)." While this key concept in philosophy of language is not unrelated to the concerns I pursue in this essay, "performativity" itself is not a sufficiently imagined eruption of theatrical space into discourse to warrant my including such examples in the present discussion. For a discussion of the criterion of performance in Lyotard, see Bill Readings, *Introducing Lyotard* (New York: Routledge, 1991), pp. 77, 80–85, and 93–97. See also Lyotard's "The Unconscious as Mise-en-scène," in Michel Benamou and Charles Caramello, *Performance in Postmodern Culture* (Madison: Coda, 1977), pp. 87–98.

18. Michel Foucault, "Theatrum Philosophicum," in *Language, Counter-Memory, Practice*, ed. and intro. Donald F. Bouchard, trans. Donald F. Bouchard and Sherry Simon (Ithaca: Cornell University Press, 1977), pp. 179 and 196.

19. Gilles Deleuze and Felix Guattari, *Anti-Oedipus* (Minneapolis: University of Minnesota Press, 1983), p. 334.

20. Ibid., p. 55.

21. Ibid., p. 54.

22. See Introduction, n.6.

23. Jean Baudrillard, *Simulations*, trans. Paul Foss, Paul Patton, and Philip Beitchman (New York: Semiotext(e), 1983), p. 48.

24. Ibid., p. 72.

25. Ibid., pp. 55 and 139.

26. Françoise Collin, "Reflections on the Women's Liberation Movement," in *French Connections*, ed. and trans. Claire Duchen (Amherst: University of Massachusetts Press, 1987), p. 142.

27. Hélène Cixous, "The Laugh of the Medusa," Elaine Marks and Isabelle de Courtivron, eds. and intro., *New French Feminisms* (New York: Schocken, 1981), pp. 250 and 252.

28. Ibid., pp. 254–55.

29. Ibid., pp. 262–63.

30. Hélène Cixous and Catherine Clement, *The Newly Born Woman* (Minneapolis: University of Minnesota Press, 1986). See "The Guilty One," pp. 10–13 and 40–59.

31. Ibid., "The Untenable," pp. 147–60.

32. Luce Irigaray, *Speculum of the Other Woman* (Ithaca: Cornell University Press, 1985). These theatrical gambits are all drawn from the opening pages of "The Blind Spot of an Old Dream of Symmetry," pp. 13–22.

33. Joan Riviere, "Womanliness as Masquerade," in *Formations of Fantasy*, Victor Burgin, James Donald, and Cora Kaplan, eds. (London: Methuen, 1986), pp. 35–44.

34. Luce Irigaray, "Plato's *Hystera*," *Speculum of the Other Woman*, pp. 250–52.

35. Ibid., pp. 289–90.

36. Ibid., p. 277.

37. Ibid., pp. 295–96.

38. Baudrillard, *Simulations*, p. 11.

39. It is striking that Susan Rubin Suleiman and Alice Jardine, two leading feminist literary critic/theorists, have adopted theatrical forms to make theoretical statements. See Suleiman, "Metapolylogue: On Playing and Modernity," in her *Subversive Intent: Gender, Politics and the Avant-Garde* (Cambridge: Harvard University Press, 1990), pp. 5–10; and Jardine, "in the name of the modern: feminist questions *d'après gynesis*," in Susan Sheridan, *Grafts: Feminists Cultural Criticism* (New York: Verso, 1988), pp. 157–92.

40. William Saroyan, *The Time of Your Life*, in *The Critics' Prize Plays*, George Jean Nathan, intro. (New York: World, 1945), p. 219.

41. Alisdair MacIntyre, *After Virtue* (Notre Dame: University of Notre Dame Press, 1981), pp. 77 and 27.

42. Luigi Pirandello, "Preface to *Six Characters in Search of an Author*," in *Naked Masks*, ed. Eric Bentley (New York: Dutton, 1952), pp. 372–73.

43. The annual conference of the International Association for Philosophy and Literature, Montreal, May 16–18, 1991.

44. Michael Fried, "Art and Objecthood," reprinted in *Minimal Art: A Critical Anthology*, ed. Gregory Battcock (New York: Dutton, 1968), p. 139.

Reviews and Articles

1. Richard Palmer, "Toward a Postmodern Hermeneutics of Performance," *Performance in Postmodern Culture*, Michel Benamou and Charles Caramello, eds. (Madison: Coda, 1977), p. 21.

2. Carol Rosen, *Plays of Impasse* (Princeton: Princeton University Press, 1983).

3. Heathcote Williams, introduction to *AC/DC and the Local Stigmatic* (New York: Viking, 1973), p. vii.

4. Lee Breuer, *Animations: A Trilogy for Mabou Mines*, Bonnie Marranca and Gautam Dasgupta, eds. and Bonnie Marranca, intro. (New York: PAJ, 1979), p. 9.

5. The first public rehearsals of *The Crucible* sections of *L.S.D.* took place in January 1983. However, Arthur Miller refused to grant the group rights to use his play in any form, and eventually *L.S.D. (. . . Just the High Points . . .)* was re-worked without it.

6. I have omitted brief discussions on McAnuff and Serban, as this material is covered in the introduction and reviews.

7. "In the seen there will be just the seen, in the heard, just the heard. . . . " *Udana: Verses of Uplift; and Itivuttaka: As it Was Said*, trans. Frank Lee Woodward, intro. Mrs. Rhys Davids (London: Oxford University Press, 1935), ch. 1, v. 10. See also Bhadantacariya Buddhaghosa, *Path of Purification* (Berkeley: Shambhala, 1976), pp. 587 and 700.

8. Heinrich Zimmer, *Philosophies of India*, ed. Joseph Campbell (Princeton: Princeton University Press, 1969), p. 514.

Index

Elinor Fuchs is a New York theater critic noted for her writing on contemporary experimental theater. She is on the faculty of the School of the Arts of Columbia University and is Lecturer at the Yale School of Drama. She has also taught at Harvard University and Emory. Her essays and criticism have appeared in numerous anthologies, as well as in such publications as the *Village Voice, American Theatre, TDR, Modern Drama, Performing Arts Journal,* and *Theater,* to which she is a Contributing Editor. She is the editor of *Plays of the Holocaust: An International Anthology,* and author, with Joyce Antler, of the documentary play *Year One of the Empire,* published by Houghton-Mifflin and produced in Los Angeles, where it won the *Drama-Logue* Best Play award for 1980. She holds a Ph.D. in theatre from the Graduate Center of the City University of New York and has been the recipient of Rockefeller and Bunting fellowships.